Monographs on soil survey

General Editors
P. H. T. BECKETT
V. C. ROBERTSON
R. WEBSTER

Quantitative and numerical methods in soil classification and survey

R. WEBSTER

CLARENDON PRESS · OXFORD
1977

Oxford University Press, Walton Street, Oxford OX2 6DP

OXFORD LONDON GLASGOW NEW YORK
TORONTO MELBOURNE WELLINGTON CAPE TOWN
IBADAN NAIROBI DAR ES SALAAM LUSAKA ADDIS ABABA
KUALA LUMPUR SINGAPORE JAKARTA HONG KONG TOKYO
DELHI BOMBAY CALCUTTA MADRAS KARACHI

British Library Cataloguing in Publication Data

Webster, R
    Quantitative and numerical methods in soil
    classification and survey. — (Monographs on
    soil survey).
    1. Soil-surveys — Statistical methods
    2. Soils — Classification — Statistical methods
    I. Title II. Series
    631.4′7   S591

    ISBN 0-19-854512-6

Typeset at the Alden Press Oxford London and Northampton
Printed in Great Britain
by J.W. Arrowsmith Ltd., Bristol

Foreword

Robin Clarke's classic *A study of soil in the field* still has much to say to field pedologists and soil surveyors after forty years.

Even so, no science remains static. As our understanding of the soil in the field has increased, the aims of soil survey and land evaluation have broadened and new techniques have been developed to achieve them.

Forty years ago even qualitative methods of describing and comparing soils were themselves matters of research, and of course there were no computers to tackle lengthy or complex calculations. Soil scientists wishing to make their work quantitative have for the most part had to adapt the results of statistical theory to their particular circumstances, often with little guidance. Dr. Webster has often found himself in this position, and here he records that part of his experience relevant to other pedologists. This is a textbook on quantitative procedures for soil scientists, written by a soil scientist.

It is the second of a series of new handbooks of which some are intended for reference in the field and some, like this one, are intended to inform the field scientist and guide him in the application of sound modern technique.

Handbooks on remote sensing and air photography, soil description and field records, soil classification, soil survey contracts, and land evaluation are also in preparation. The editors will appreciate any suggestions for further titles.

P.H.T. BECKETT
V.C. ROBERTSON

Preface

This book is addressed to those scientists — pedologists, agronomists, engineers and ecologists — who study the soil by what are broadly speaking survey methods as distinct from experiments. It is written for those who observe, record and analyse information about the soil with its ever-present spatial variation over which they have no experimental control. It describes methods for making survey quantitative, stressing the need for measurement, sensible estimation, and proper planning. It discusses the role of classification, indicating those situations in which it can be helpful. It explains why data should be obtained in particular ways, why certain forms of statistical analysis are appropriate, and illustrates the methods with examples. It aims always to help the reader to choose suitable techniques for tackling his problem.

Some of the examples drawn from my work in the Soil Survey have not previously been published, and I am most grateful to Mr. K.E. Clare for allowing me to use the material here and for his encouragement. I thank Dr. T.R. Harrod, Messrs. S.J. Staines, D.V. Hogan, W.M. Corbett, and Dr. S. Nortcliff whose data I have mapped in Chapter 12, and Mr. M.G. Jarvis who provided the measurements from which Fig. 3.3 was obtained. I also thank Dr. P.A. Burrough for the data used to illustrate regional classification (Chapter 9), analysis of dispersion (Chapter 10), and optimization (Chapter 11).

Over the years several people have discussed the application of statistics and computers to soil survey with me and given me a deeper insight of the subject. I am especially grateful to Dr. F.H.C. Marriott, not only for much helpful advice but also for reading and criticizing the whole of this text. I thank Mrs. B.M. Hersom, Dr. D. Rhind, and Dr. S.W. Bie for suggesting improvements to Chapters 2 and 12, Dr. P.H.T. Beckett for his long and stimulating interest in the subject and for editing my script, and Mrs. M. Cox for typing it. I also thank the authors and publishers for permission to reproduce the following figures and tables: Blackwells, Fig. 3.1; Dr. A.W. Moore and Messrs. Angus and Robertson, Fig. 7.9; Elsevier Scientific Publications, Figs 12.1 to 12.4; John Wiley and Sons, Table 4.1; and Dr. K. Kyuma and the Society of the Science of Soils and Manures of Japan, Tables 8.3 and 8.4.

Oxford   R.W.
October 1976

Contents

1. Introduction

A sensible philosophy controlled by a relevant set of
concepts saves so much research time that it can
nearly act as a substitute for genius.

N.W. PIRIE
Concepts out of context

Classification and measurement

For centuries peasant husbandmen have lived in close harmony with
the soil they till. They have learned how the soil responds to their
treatment of it and to classify it according to its appearance and
behaviour. They have also recognized where the soil changes from one
kind to another in the landscape, and divided their land into parcels to
be managed more or less differently. Classification is a practical tool
by which man traditionally deals with his environment and with the soil
in particular. It is also the means by which he communicates information about soil to his neighbours and descendants, matches soil in
different places, and predicts behaviour where experience is lacking.

The first soil scientists adopted this approach, both for practical
purposes and for more fundamental understanding. There were big
differences to be seen and placed on record. The layman's classes and
descriptive terms were meaningful and convenient. But once the more
obvious distinctions had been made, pedologists turned their attention
to finer differences. And in the practical sphere agronomists and
engineers needed to describe the soil with which they worked more
exactly and consistently, and to predict behaviour more precisely.
In both cases the desired consistency and precision could be achieved
only by measurement, and so, as in many other branches of science,
observation became quantitative. Thus, to describe the soil at some
place as 'acid' (classification) was no longer adequate; scientists wanted
to say how acid, and they devised methods of measuring its acidity
in terms of pH. There is now a large body of literature concerned with
individual properties of the soil and how to measure them.

However, there is more to measurement than this. The soil is a more
or less continuous mantle. The scientist cannot record what it is like
everywhere: he can at best measure properties, whether directly in the
field or on material taken into the laboratory, of small portions of the

mantle – that is, from a *sample*. Soil also varies from place to place, often very considerably, so measurements of the soil at one sampling site cannot be used to describe all the soil. In practice, information is usually wanted for areas, and surveys are made in many parts of the world to obtain such information. Fully quantitative information can be obtained by measuring the soil at several, perhaps many, sites.

There is another kind of data that may properly be regarded as quantitative. Surveys are often carried out to determine how much land is of a particular kind (say, suitable for growing rice) or what proportion possesses some attribute (say, waterlogged soil). We might attempt to delimit such land and measure its area by geometry. Alternatively and more economically we could inspect the soil at a number of suitably chosen places and *count* those where the soil possessed the attribute in question. Individual observations would be qualitative, but in total they would assume a quantitative character.

But the matter does not rest here, for we need to know to which of all the soil a particular measurement or set of measurements apply. To what extent may the value obtained at one site be extrapolated? And is it sensible to take an average of several measurements, especially when there are large regional differences? It is often more meaningful to use averages to describe the soil of each region separately; and, of course, the recognition of regions means classification – dividing the area into classes. Similarly prediction can be more secure if it is restricted to individual regions and classes of soil. Further, when measurement is expensive or time consuming it can pay to classify the soil on easily observed characters and sample each class separately for those that are costly to observe. By doing so, unnecessary measurement in large reasonably homogeneous areas can be avoided while at the same time adequate attention is given to smaller but different areas. When a large body of data is collected in the course of an investigation it often needs simplifying to be intelligible: we must be able to see the wood rather than the trees. This can often be achieved by classifying the data. Similarly, when a survey is carried out for planning land-use the sampling sites, though initially described quantitatively, usually need to be grouped. The farmer cannot vary his management continuously in response to continuous variation in the survey records. He has to treat finite tracts of land in a uniform manner as though they were homogeneous. Likewise the engineer cannot easily change his design for every minor fluctuation in soil character.

So although we replace classification by measurements for consistent description and communicating precise information about soil at particular sites, classification can have an important complementary role in increasing the utility of soil data and enabling us to economize on sampling. Just how important this role is or can be has been a matter of debate, and in recent years classification itself has been the subject of quantitative study. Questions like: how much does my classification improve prediction; how might this population be classified to provide a simple but useful picture; which classification is best for that purpose; to which class should the new individual I be allocated; and if classification seems unprofitable is there an alternative, can all be answered quantitatively. Questions such as these are discussed at length later in this book.

Statistical methods

Quantitative description of the soil of different areas and its behaviour involves analysis of more or less large bodies of data. Simple statements about the soil must be seen against the background of ever-present variation, which must be taken into account in the analysis. This is the province of statistics, and most of the techniques described in this book are in some sense statistical. Statistics provides accurate and usable mathematical descriptions of the real world of the soil, both in the laboratory and in the field.

For soil scientists with an agricultural background the subject of statistics often conjures up a picture of experiments carefully designed to compare crop varieties or the effects of fertilizer treatments on yield. The measurements from these are subject to analysis of variance, a mysterious process whose culmination and climax is a test of significance. What joy ensues when an F ratio emerges blessed with three stars to confirm our hypothesis, or prejudice! This is unfortunate. Significance tests have a perfectly proper place, but in soil survey they will usually be secondary, superfluous, or even inappropriate to the main purpose of the investigation. In soil survey and soil systematics statistical methods provide means of condensing data into economical descriptions of variable material. They enable us to predict and to estimate the confidence that we may place on prediction. They enable us to identify relationships and structure in our data and to display these. Thus some tasks are probabilistic while others are not. If a significance test is appropriate we should apply it since it could prevent our drawing unwarranted conclusions from sample evidence. But the precise level of probability at which we test is less important, and is to some extent a matter of personal choice.

Aims and means

Much of the first half of the book concerns soil survey. But the reader who has become accustomed to regard soil survey as the recognition of soil types and their display on maps might find himself on unfamiliar ground. He will discover that soil classification is not a necessary prerequisite to mapping nor mapping essential to the purpose of survey. Soil survey is presented simply as the means by which information about the soil of areas of land is obtained. Soil classification is very often a means by which survey can be carried out more economically or its findings presented. It is a convenient tool. Neither survey nor classification is an end in itself, and the investigator is urged to decide just what he wants to know before considering how to go about finding it out. Once an investigator is clear about his goals, and only then, he is in a position to choose the means for reaching them in the most direct way, by designing a survey specifically for the purpose. In some instances this will entail classification and mapping; in others these will be unnecessary or even unhelpful.

In this connection it has seemed to me that sampling is the weakest feature of current practice in many soil surveys and much field research. Much of the data that are obtained only with difficulty in laboratory and field are of little use because the original sampling was unsatisfactory. If the reader finds the emphasis on sampling obstrusive, I offer no apology.

The latter part of the book deals with multivariate methods. Although these can serve very specific purposes, they are also exploratory tools: for identifying relationships between soil profiles and classes of soil; for experimental classification; and for suggesting hypotheses that can be tested by other techniques. These methods have become practicable only with the advent of computers to perform the complex or very long calculations involved. Soil scientists have had little experience with the methods, and most studies reported to date have been made on familiar data collected for other purposes. This has been necessary to give confidence, but with that experience behind us, we are ready to apply the methods in unfamiliar situations.

In addition to these two main groups of topics I have included a chapter introducing computers and programming, and other reviewing quantitative mapping.

Scope

A book of this size cannot deal with all the mathematical techniques that a soil surveyor or systematist might need. I have had to make a selection. In doing so I have tried to cover those topics that soil scientists most often ask about and that I have found useful. Although most are described in statistical texts, soil scientists find it difficult for one reason or another to link the statistical theory to their work. I have tried to provide that link here, especially with the examples. It seems that few students of soil science have studied mathematics since leaving school, and I have constantly borne this in mind in presenting the material. For this reason, and for compactness, I have omitted most derivations and proofs. But the reader who fights shy of symbols must discipline himself to mastering them.

I have assumed that the reader is thoroughly *au fait* with the physical or biological aspects of his work and the methods of measurement in the laboratory or field.

The reader who wishes to apply the methods in his own investigations will often need to consult one or other statistical table. Many standard statistical texts include tables and it has not seemed necessary to duplicate them here. The statistical tables compiled by Fisher and Yates, first published in 1938 and now in their 6th edition (Fisher and Yates 1963), are available to soil scientists in agricultural institutes and research laboratories all over the world. For this reason I have referred to them freely. However, Lindley and Miller (1953) include all the elementary tables, while the Biometrika tables (Pearson and Hartley 1966, 1972) are more comprehensive and provide more advanced tests.

The reader will notice that I have chosen most of the illustrative examples from my own experience. This is not because they are necessarily more suitable than the work of others, but simply that I already had the data and intermediate workings to hand.

A note on terminology and symbols

A number of common English words have a somewhat restricted or special meaning in statistics. Some of these occur frequently throughout this book, and are introduced here.

Attributes and variables. When a property of the soil (or anything else) is recorded qualitatively it constitutes an *attribute*. If, for example, we record calcium carbonate as either *present* or *absent* in the soil at a number of sites, calcium carbonate is an attribute of the soil at those sites. We may also use the term to refer to properties that can occur in more than two qualitative states — the shape of structural aggregates, for example, can be platy, prismatic, blocky, granular, and so on. On the other hand, when a property varies from one place to another and is measured it is termed a *variable*. If, instead of recording calcium carbonate only as *present* or *absent*, we measure how much there is, calcium carbonate becomes a variable. It is convenient to be able to use the word *character* to embrace both attribute and variable. A random variable is termed a *variate*. When applied to soil, the term usually means a set of measured values of some property in which there is more or less random variation.

Parameter. A *parameter* is a quantity that is constant in the case being considered, though it may differ in other cases. In statistics it is generally reserved for quantities, such as means and standard deviations, of whole populations (q.v.), and is distinguished from estimates of them made by sampling, for which the word *statistic* is used. In computing, a parameter is usually a quantity that is held constant for a particular run of a program. Parameter is not synonymous with variable or character, and the current fashion for using the term with this sense is to be deprecated.

Population. The whole set of individuals or material under study in a particular instance is referred to as a *population*. A population can be either finite – for example, a set of described soil profiles – or infinite – for example, the soil of a district, which can be considered as made up of an infinite number of soil profiles.

Sample. A *sample* is a small set of individuals or a collection of material taken from a larger population about which information is wanted. In soil laboratories the term sample often refers to a single bag (disturbed) or core (undisturbed) of soil taken from the field. In the statistical sense it more often refers to several bags or cores, and applies equally to a set of sites where the soil has been or is to be described or measured without any soil necessarily being collected.

Survey. In the statistical sense a survey simply means a type of investigation in which a situation is observed as it is without alteration other than that unavoidably incurred in sampling. It differs from an *experiment*, in which the investigator changes some feature of the situation on purpose so that he can study effects of the change. The meaning of survey in statistics also differs somewhat from its meaning in soil survey, in which it has implications of mapping and classification.

Classification. This is the act of dividing a population, or agglomerating individuals, into groups. It can also be the set of classes that result from such action. The nouns *class* and *group* are treated as synonyms in this book. *Allocation* is distinguished from classification and is used to mean the assignment of individuals to classes or the *identification* of individuals as belonging to those classes.

The common mathematical symbols will be familiar to the reader, but there are several other conventions that might need explaining.

Summation. Summation is one of the most frequent operations in statistics. If there are n values, $x_1, x_2, x_3, \ldots, x_n$, their sum can be written as $\sum\limits_{i=1}^{n} x_i$, where

$$\sum_{i=1}^{n} x_i = x_1 + x_2 + x_3 + \ldots + x_n.$$

Mean. The arithmetic mean is also much needed, and is usually signified by placing a bar over the symbol for the variate concerned. Thus for the n values of variate X, the mean $\bar{x}$, which is read 'x bar' is

$$\bar{x} = \sum_{i=1}^{n} x_i/n.$$

Product. The product of a set of values is occasionally needed and is symbolized by capital Π. The product of n values of X are thus

$$\prod_{i=1}^{n} x_i = x_1 \times x_2 \times x_3 \times \ldots \times x_n.$$

Combination. The number of ways of choosing r items out n is

$$\frac{n!}{r!(n-r)!}$$

where $n!$ (factorial n) is $1 \times 2 \times 3 \times \ldots \times n$. It is conventionally abbreviated to $\binom{n}{r}$.

Several lower case Greek letters are widely used: μ (mu), σ (sigma), and ρ (rho) indicate the mean, standard deviation, and correlation coefficient of populations respectively, while the sampling estimates of the last two are denoted by Roman equivalents s and r. The letter χ (chi), as χ^2 (chi square), is used for the distribution with this name. Capital lambda, Λ, is used for Wilks' criterion, while in the lower case it usually refers to latent roots.

Matrix notation. Many multivariate procedures are most economically and clearly expressed in matrix form, and this practice is followed in Chapters 7 to 11. A brief account of matrix algebra and symbolism is given in the Appendix.

2. Data handling and computing

Whatever task lies to your hand,
do it with all your might.
ECCLESIASTES 9:10

The investigator who embarks on any kind of quantitative survey of soil or study of soil classification will want to collect information, and having collected it, to sort it and perform calculations on it. At its simplest a survey might cover two or three soil properties at a few tens of sites only, and calculation involve no more than adding, counting, and finding means. Pencil and paper will suffice to arrange the information and to record the steps in the arithmetic. A small desk or pocket calculator might be a useful aid. More complex studies can involve measuring fifty or more soil properties at hundreds or thousands of sites and examining relations among them; and the same data might need to be screened, analysed, and presented several times in different ways. Here a computer is essential, and many valuable techniques of analysis and display have become practicable only with the advent of computers.

Tasks of intermediate size can often be carried out on a desk calculator provided it has at least one memory or register to hold sums of squares or products. However, it is tedious; and though undue repetition can be avoided by using a programmable calculator, an increasing proportion of work is being done on general-purpose computers as they become cheaper and more readily accessible to the soil scientist. The computer is fast becoming the general work horse for information processing, and we should expect it to be in everyday use by soil surveyors in the not too distant future. So this chapter will outline the workings of the modern computer and the measures a scientist must take in order to use it.

The computer

The modern computer is electronic and digital, in the sense that it works by discrete electronic impulses on information presented to it and stored by it in the form of discrete electrical states. Information from almost every field of study or walk of life can be handled in this way, and it is this that makes the computer so generally useful. There are analog computers, but they are usually designed for specific purposes and we shall not consider them further.

A computer consists of a number of functional parts, known as *hardware*, whose relations to one another are symbolized in Fig. 2.1. The most important is perhaps the central processor, which contains an *arithmetic* or *logic unit*, and a *control unit*. Closely associated with the central processor is the *memory unit* or *high-speed store*. This consists of many small elements, each of which can be set in either of two states corresponding to the two values, 0 and 1, of a binary digit. Until recently the memory was built of ferrite rings or cores, each of which could be magnetized in either direction, and so it became known as the *core store* or just *core*, and this name has stuck. The elements of the core, each of which can be made to represent a binary digit, or *bit*, are linked into groups to form *words*. The number of bits per word varies from one machine to another, and can be as few as 12 or as many as 96. In general, the smaller machines have fewer bits per word than the larger ones. A small computer might have a store of only 4000 words, a large one over 100 000 words. In some machines bits are grouped in series of eight to form *bytes*, which can uniquely represent all the alphabetic and numeric characters, and special symbols for arithmetic and punctuation. The word is the most important combination of elements to the scientist, since each will hold one number of reasonable size or one command. Computer languages are written in such a way that each word may be identified and addressed individually.

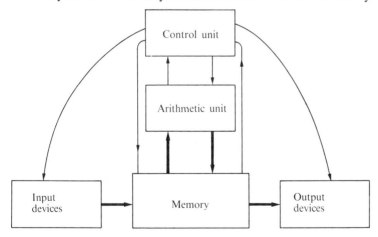

FIG. 2.1. The functional parts of a computer. Broad arrows indicate the transfer of the user's information. The thinner lines show how control is maintained.

Attached to the central processor are a number of peripheral devices that enable data, programs, and other instructions to be entered (*input*), results to be obtained from the machine (*output*), and provide auxiliary storage.

The arithmetic unit consists of a set of circuits, *logic circuitry*, that performs arithmetic and logical tests. The arithmetic units in some machines also have special circuits to determine functions such as square roots and logarithms. The purpose of the control unit is to control the operations within the central processor itself, as well as in the core store and peripheral units, by interpreting programmed instructions and ensuring that they are carried out in their proper sequence.

The machine has a console, usually consisting of an array of switches and a typewriter keyboard, from which the operator instructs the computer. Other input devices include paper-tape and card readers, magnetic tape and disc units, and remote terminals. The most familiar output is that produced on the line printer, which assembles and prints one line of print at a time. Each line may contain a maximum of 120 to 160 characters, and may be printed at the rate of 600 to 1000 lines per minute. Other output devices include paper-tape and card punches, graph plotters, cathode ray tubes, magnetic tape and disc, and remote terminals.

The amount of immediately accessible store, the core, is strictly limited even in the largest computers, so large quantities of data must be stored on an alternative and cheaper medium. Data, and also frequently-used programs, intermediate results, and information that is to be transmitted from one program to another, are usually held in an auxiliary store or *backing store*. Backing store can consist of magnetic tape, disc, or drum. Of these magnetic tape is the cheapest but also the slowest. Nevertheless all allow much faster transfer of information between them and the main store than could be achieved with cards or paper tape.

Files and keyboard terminals

In many modern computers jobs are not run directly from cards or paper tape. Instead, data and programs presented to the computer in this form are read and converted to *files*, which are then held on disc. The information in such files usually retains the same format as that on the cards or tape, and such files are said to have *card-image format*. Jobs are run from the disc.

A machine that operates in this fashion has one or more keyboard terminals by which a user can communicate with it. Terminals can have a range of equipment, but basically each consists of a typewriter keyboard with a few additional controls, and a printer or cathode ray tube display (CRT). The user 'speaks' to the computer by typing what he wishes to say; the machine replies on the printer or CRT. Terminals can be situated next to the computer, in a nearby room, or many miles away. Some have permanent lines to their parent machines, others are linked as required through the public telephone network.

Terminals additional to the operator's console provide the computer user with much wider scope and flexibility than would otherwise be available, especially in allowing interactive computing. However, for the kind of work described in this book, the most valuable feature of a terminal is that it enables the user to interrogate his files, to modify them while they are held in the computer, and to instruct the computer to carry out jobs using them.

Programming

A *program* (the American spelling is common usage) is a series of instructions written so that a machine can perform some desired computation. Ultimately these instructions must be available to the computer in binary code, or *machine code*; only then will it obey them. Every operation must be exactly specified, and the address of every item of data and every result must be given. Writing in machine code is therefore very laborious. It requires an intimate knowledge of the particular machine, the command of a very cryptic code, and meticulous attention to detail. Few scientists have either the time or inclination to master a machine language.

The difficulties inherent in programming in machine code can to some extent be overcome using an *assembly language*. Assembly languages differ from machine code in two main ways: (i) there is a mnemonic code for each operation, and (ii) addresses can be identified by symbols — the machine keeps its own record of the actual addresses. Otherwise there is in general a one-to-one correspondence between instructions in assembly language and their equivalents in machine code. Useful though they are, assembly languages are nevertheless strongly oriented towards the machine rather than the scientist, and several languages have been developed that enable scientists to write programs in a notation similar to that of mathematics and English. These are known as *high-level languages*, and include Algol, Fortran, and Basic. Cobol is another high-level language, but was designed for business purposes.

Programs written in either high-level or assembly language (*source programs*) have to be translated into machine code (*object code* or *object programs*) before they can be obeyed. The computer itself does the translation using another program known as a *compiler* (or *assembler* if the source program is in assembly language). The compiler reads the source program, which it treats as data, and converts it into machine code. It will usually output the compiled version to backing store. The source may be a complete program or one or more sub-programs; the importance of the latter alternative will become apparent later. Some machines have *in-core* compilers. With these a source program is compiled directly into the core of the computer ready for immediate use. For this reason the program submitted must be complete apart from standard facilities provided in the machine's library. The Watfor (Waterloo Fortran) compiler is perhaps the best known in-core compiler.

Many compilers not only translate source programs into machine code, but also provide information to the programmer. These are known as *diagnostic compilers*. They identify errors in the source language and in the execution of the program when it is run with data. If desired, some will list all identifiers (names) used in the program and their internal addresses in the computer.

A substantial advantage of high-level languages is that programs can be written as a set of sub-programs, or modules containing one or more sub-programs, each of which can be compiled and tested separately. A *link editor* or *composer* later joins the compiled sub-programs into a complete working program.

High-level languages

Whereas machine code and assembly languages vary substantially from one computer to another, most high-level languages can be used on any machine for which a compiler has been written. They are said to be *machine-independent*. Unfortunately they are not strictly so, and when a program is transferred from one machine to another it will usually require at least minor alteration. Some computer manufacturers have written and implemented very effective high-level languages for their own machines. There are also high-level languages for specific kinds of work — and we shall discuss one of these, Genstat, later. The main features of the more important high-level languages are described briefly below, and programming manuals for them are listed in the section on further reading.

Algol (<u>Al</u>gorithmic <u>L</u>anguage) is the most logical and powerful language in this group. It was devised by an international committee as a means of communicating algorithms, and is maintained and developed under the guidance of the International Federation for Information Processing. It enables the steps in a computation to be written so that they are both intelligible to a computer and easily read by a person. Many algorithms and complete programs, written by acknowledged experts in their fields, have been published in Algol, and so are readily available to other workers. There were some serious limitations in the early versions of the language, including the widely used Algol 60. These have been largely removed in the current version, Algol 68. The most unfortunate feature of Algol is that procedures for input and output are unspecified. Each manufacturer can therefore devise his own procedures, and the programmer must learn a fresh set of rules for each computer on which he works. Likewise, programs written for one machine must have all their input and output instructions altered if they are to be used on another.

Fortran (Formula Translator), less powerful than Algol, is nevertheless more widely used. Its popularity stems in part from the fact that it was devised by IBM, the world's largest computer manufacturer. Other manufacturers have written Fortran compilers for their own machines in order to remain competitive, and most computers now have good compilers for the language. Fortran has been steadily improved since its inception in 1957. In 1962 Fortran IV appeared, and a version was approved by the American National Standards Institute as standard in 1966. Standardization is perhaps its biggest single advantage: the many programs that have been written in Fortran to solve a wide variety of scientific problems can be transferred from one machine to another. Nevertheless, compilers have their idiosyncrasies: most have more facilities than specified in the standard. So a program written for one machine often requires some modification for use on another.

Fortran has inherited a strong influence from the Hollerith Company. Programs are written for punching with one instruction per card. The input facilities assume that data will be read from punched cards. Output, though mainly directed to line printer nowadays, is assembled into records of one line each as though for punching on to cards. Standard input and output are therefore somewhat inflexible. Time and technological innovation have revealed several other undesirable features.

The language PL/1, also developed by IBM, makes good the deficiencies of Fortran. It is both powerful and flexible, incorporating many of the desirable features of both Fortran and Algol, and also of Cobol (see below). Although intended for use in a wide field of applications spanning both science and commerce, it has not been implemented on many machines other than those made by IBM.

Basic (Beginners All-purpose Symbolic Instruction Code) is a simple but nevertheless powerful language developed at Dartmouth College in the United States. It was intended to be used mainly from keyboard terminals, and to provide a ready means for a user to communicate with the computer while his job was running. For this reason it is more concise than either Algol or Fortran. The language is easy to master. Programs can be typed into the computer from the keyboard, compilation is swift, and object programs are generally efficient. The user can obtain output at his terminal, make judgements in the light of the information presented, and respond to the computer, which will then continue its computation. Basic is thus a very attractive language for both interactive computing and teaching, and it can also be used for batch work.

Cobol (Common Business Oriented Language) was designed for use in business and commerce. Programs are written in a narrative style comprising passable English sentences. Scientists used to writing, for example, $Z = X - Y$, find the Cobol equivalent, SUBTRACT Y FROM X GIVING Z, unduly prolix and the language is scarcely used in science. However, its facilities for handling character strings and files have made it suitable for data management.

A set of concise yet powerful languages comprises the Autocodes, available on a number of British machines. The first of these was Mercury Autocode devised for the Ferranti Mercury computer in 1958. Users quickly appreciated its value; they modified and augmented it to make it more useful still. The most widely available development of the language is Extended Mercury Autocode (EMA), available on the Orion and Atlas computers, and now used on machines of the 1900 series. IMP, written at the Edinburgh Regional Computing Centre, is a further extension, incorporating several of the desirable features of Algol. It was developed as a convenient language for system programming as well as for general use. Like Basic, EMA and IMP can handle characters and operate on matrices using standard commands. Once the language has been learned, programs can be written economically and run efficiently.

Many special-purpose languages have been devised for particular tasks. Of these Genstat is most likely to interest readers of this book.

Nearly all the techniques described later in the book can be programmed using Genstat, and the results in several of the examples were obtained this way. Genstat was developed at Rothamsted Experimental Station by a team of statisticians led by Nelder (1973). It is itself written in Fortran IV, and is being made available at scientific computing centres in many countries.

A Genstat program consists of a series of declarations and commands. The declarations tell the computer what space to allocate to a problem, how it is to be organized to accommodate data and results, and how the data are structured and addressed. The commands instruct the computer to carry out the operations that the user desires in order to analyse the data. The language contains algorithms not only for many kinds of statistical analysis, but also for modifying data beforehand and tabulating them, and for storing results for later retrieval and use.

Genstat is a very powerful language indeed, enabling data to be handled with great freedom and analysed with remarkably concise programming. Its main weakness for soil survey is that it cannot accommodate very large sets of data at all easily. In this respect SPSS, Statistical Package for the Social Sciences (Nie, Bent, and Hull 1970) might be preferred, as it is designed for tabulating and analysing survey data. It has its own command language and is quite widely available. However, it is much less powerful than Genstat.

Writing a program

One of the most important decisions that the scientist must make is whether to write his own program (or have it written for him) or to use one already written: 'off-the-peg' as it were. There are numerous published programs for the more frequently required analyses, and many computing centres have libraries of programs for the same tasks. Perhaps the most generally available are the BMD programs (Dixon 1971) written by staff at the University of California for use in biological and medical research. Many more programs are available from their authors, most of whom are generous with their products and keen to see them used.

Clearly, there are advantages in using a standard program: it takes considerable time to write a program and ensure that it performs properly. But there are disadvantages, risks, and temptations of which the user should be aware. Many standard programs, especially those written in Fortran, have fixed array sizes and formats. These can unnecessarily constrain the user, who has to trim his data and arrange them in a way acceptable to the program. More seriously, the user might tailor his problem to what can be analysed by the programs that happen to be available to him, or even worse, use an inappropriate technique for the same reason. There is also the strong temptation to carry out an analysis just to see what happens: there is already a steady flow of unnecessary computing of this sort.

The user of other people's programs also runs other risks. The published listing of a program can contain misprints. These might be detected by the compiler, but equally they might not. Some programs are machine-dependent. Some programs contain logical errors, and in some the programmer has misunderstood the method. Many statistical programs use numerical methods that were developed for the desk calculator. Some of these methods, such as that commonly used to derive sums of squares and products, can incur serious rounding errors when used on a computer. Users of such programs therefore obtain results that are more or less erroneous, and the fact that a program is published is no guarantee against any of these defects.

A program may also be written without its author's foreseeing all the situations that can arise. Failures occur when the program runs and in many instances the computer provides singularly unhelpful diagnosis of the cause.

So the investigator should decide exactly what the problem is, what data are needed, and how they are to be analysed. He must consider hardware limitations, but should resist the temptation to gather data simply to feed the number-crunching monster to which he happens to have access. He should check whether an existing and authenticated program does exactly what is required. If it does then he should use it, but if not then he should prepare to write his own.

Writing a program is not necessarily difficult. The scientist must obviously learn a programming language. His choice of language will be determined largely by the compilers in use on the computer available to him, and he should seek advice from a member of the computing staff about this. The scientist must also understand the methods by which he will analyse his data. He should check that the methods he proposes to use are suitable for a computer: the textbook algebraic solutions to some problems are unreliable when used on a computer, and may give inaccurate and misleading results, if not catastrophic failure. He should find out whether appropriate numerical methods are already available as routines. Many computing centres hold libraries of efficiently programmed and properly tested algorithms that can be built into users' programs. The NAG library is one of the best. It was developed by the Numerical Algorithms Group for use in British universities and research institutes, and is now available generally. Thus, provided the scientist knows what mathematical treatment to apply, he can often call on library procedures when the arithmetic is difficult. But with few exceptions he can expect no such help with the organization of his data. He must be aware at all times where all his data and intermediate results are and must arrange the flow of information through the computer and its peripherals in a logical fashion. The wider the scope of the investigation, the more varied the sources of data, and the larger the quantities of data, the more important this aspect of computing becomes.

Apart from following the rules of the language, the programmer should bear other points in mind. He should write his program in a way that is easy to follow, using meaningful names as identifiers and a flowchart as aid. If a program is large he should divide it into *modules*, each of which performs a well-defined part of the whole task. Modules are best written as sub-programs so that they can be developed and tested independently. Repetitive parts of a program should be written once as modules and then called as often as needed. The programmer should be liberal with comment to explain what each part of the program does. Other users are likely to find this helpful, and he will too when he has forgotten the details. He should make his programs flexible so that they can handle other bodies of data with the minimum of change. He should try to trap errors in data, and anticipate snags like division by zero and extraction of roots of negative numbers, and in each case get the computer to print an informative message.

When a program is first written, unless it is a very short one, it will almost certainly contain errors or 'bugs' which must, of course, be corrected. Errors can be of several kinds. There are those in the language itself; faulty grammar and syntax. These must be put right before a program can be compiled. Part of the function of a compiler is to identify such errors and to inform the programmer accordingly. Once a program is acceptable to the computer there can still be logical errors in it, and the programmer should test his program thoroughly for these. He should use data that will explore every route through the program, and check the outcome in each case to see that it is correct.

Correcting the language is usually fairly easy for the programmer, because compilers on most modern machines will diagnose faults and list them. Logical faults are another matter: it is usually much more difficult to ensure that the computer is doing what is wanted. Provided the language is intelligible, the machine will do exactly as it is told. It will not rectify faulty logic. It will not identify implied intentions nor reliably resolve linguistic ambiguities. Nor will it check the good sense of an operation in unforeseen circumstances. A friend of mine recently told her son to fold his pyjamas neatly and put them under his pillow before leaving home for school. When she visited his bedroom some time later she discovered that he had done exactly that – only his pillow was on the floor. The lad had been inadequately programmed. Computers do not behave wilfully, though there are many instances when they seem unnecessarily stupid.

Data preparation

When the records from a small study are to be analysed by desk calculator, good sense directs that they be clearly written and neatly tabulated, but that is really all the preparation needed. Records to be processed by computer must also be converted to a form that can be read by the machine, but there are further stipulations and considerations. The machine will read exactly what it is given. It must be told how to recognize the end of one number and the beginning of the next, and which observation on one individual is to be compared with a similar observation on another. It will not unscramble badly tabulated data any more than assistants can be expected to punch cards or tape correctly from slovenly records. The investigator needs to plan the layout of his data with care.

At present, the individual scientist (for whom this book is written) is likely to use either punched cards or paper tape as his input medium. The choice depends to some extent on the kind of investigation and amount of data, the kind of machine (there would be no choice if the machine lacks either a paper-tape or card reader), whether the data are to be read by more than one machine, and whether the investigator intends to use a standard program with specific input requirements. Organizations that collect large quantities of data should also consider the use of other media, in particular *mark-sense* forms and optical character reading systems. The early difficulties experienced with these, especially their unreliability for recording in the field, are being overcome and their costs are decreasing. A recent review by Kloosterman (1975) provides guidance.

Paper tape

Information can be represented by holes punched in a continuous strip of paper tape. There can be 5, 6, 7, or 8 punching positions, known as *channels* or *tracks*, across the tape. Every character is represented by a particular arrangement of punched and unpunched positions – its paper-tape code. There are several standard sets of codes, even for a given number of channels. So anyone preparing data or programs on paper tape should ensure that the paper-tape code is the correct one for the computer he intends to use. Fig. 2.2 shows information punched on eight-channel paper tape. The small holes guide the tape through the punch and reader.

Programs and data are transferred from written records to paper tape by means of a punch controlled from a typewriter keyboard with special control characters. In addition much laboratory equipment is now fitted with direct reading devices that record measurements automatically on paper tape. A computer reads paper tape by sensing the pattern of holes photo-electrically for each character in turn. Reading speeds of 1000 characters per second are common.

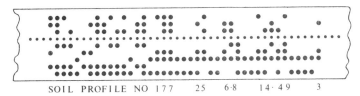

SOIL PROFILE NO 177   25   6·8   14·49   3

FIG. 2.2. A length of 8-track punched paper tape

Punched cards

Information can also be punched on to cards, and the most usual kind of card, the 80-column Hollerith card, is illustrated in Fig. 2.3; it bears the same information as the paper tape in Fig. 2.2. A card has 80 columns, each of which can be punched in one or more of 12 positions. The punch code for the numerals 0 to 9 and letters is standard for all machines, though the representations of other characters vary.

Punched cards can be prepared on a small hand-operated key-punch, but they are usually punched on larger machines in which, again, punching is controlled from a typewriter-like keyboard. Cards can be punched in the field using a 'Portapunch'. This consists of a frame that holds an 80-column card. On its front there is a grid of rectangular holes that exactly match the punching positions of the card, except

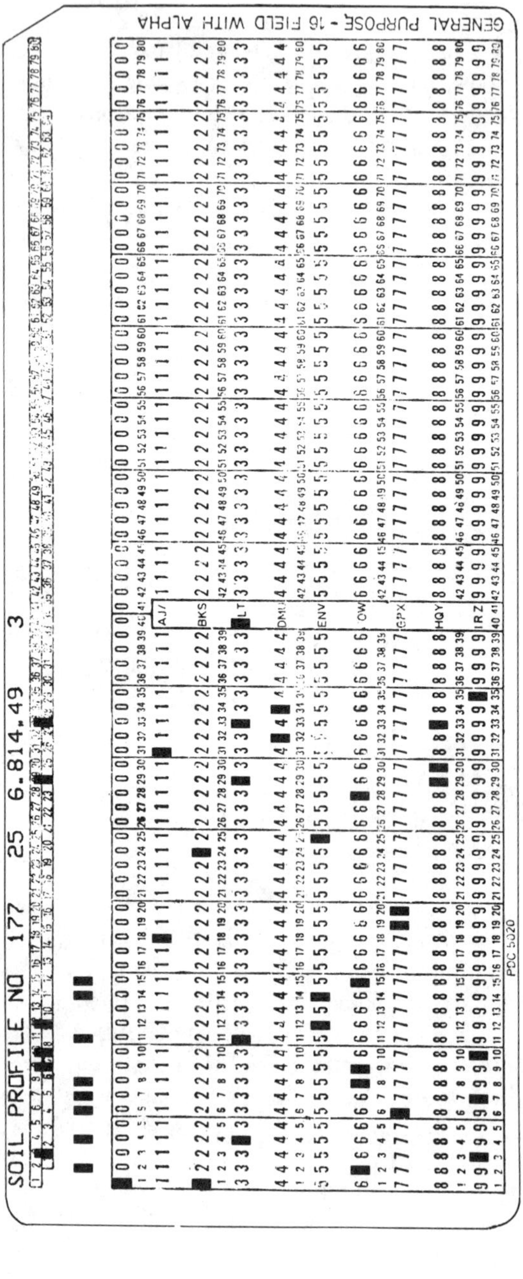

FIG. 2.3. A punched 80-column card

that only alternate columns of the card are exposed. The cards themselves are pre-treated by perforating the edges of the punching positions so that the small rectangular centres can be readily and cleanly pushed out using a small stick. Portapunch has been used successfully for forest soil surveys in Sweden where fairly few soil properties are of interest. It has been found too cumbersome for recording many properties.

An alternative to Portapunch is a mark-sense card that is similar in appearance to the punched card. The positions to be punched are marked with a pen or pencil in the field or laboratory. Afterwards they are passed through a machine that senses the marks and interprets them as if they had been punched.

Format

The way in which data, and to some extent programs, are laid out is known as their *format*. When every column of a line has a specific meaning, the format is said to be *fixed*. Then each piece of information, say, the observed value of some soil property, is recognized by its position in the line. The antithesis of fixed format is *free* or variable format, in which entries are distinguished from one another by *separators*, that is, characters by which the computer recognizes the end of an entry. Fig. 2.2 shows the values 25, 6·8, 14·49, and 3 of four properties of soil profile no. 177 separated from one another by one or more spaces. In Fig. 2.3 there is a field of five columns allocated to each entry and each value is right justified within it. The format is fixed, otherwise the string of characters 6·814·49 would be nonsense. In both examples the data are punched in a defined order. Data can be punched in variable order provided each data value is preceded by a label identifying the property concerned. This method corresponds most closely to the traditional way of recording in field notebooks. It is usual to prepare data for cards in fixed format, and to punch data on paper tape in free format. Data entered from a keyboard terminal are also most conveniently entered in free format.

Comparison of paper tape and punched cards

The relative merits of paper tape and cards have been contested vigorously, and it is difficult to distinguish the intrinsic merits of each from the personal whims and experience of their devotees on particular equipment, and manufacturer's bias. In North America cards have been used almost to the exclusion of paper tape. On the other hand in

Britain, and more generally in Europe, the bias has been somewhat the other way.

To the soil scientist the factors that matter are:

(i) *Bulk*. The data from a moderate-sized survey can be appreciable: the field and laboratory records of 400 sites might well require 4000 punched cards. The same data could be held on two moderate-sized reels of paper tape that would be easier to handle and require much less space to store. Cards are dearer for the same volume of information.

(ii) *Security*. Punched cards can easily get out of order and individual cards lost. Anyone who has had to retrieve his cards from the machine-room floor, or more seriously from the puddle outside the computer laboratory, will know this to his cost. Records on paper tape cannot get out of order accidentally and a section of a reel of paper tape is very unlikely to go astray.

(iii) *Flexibility*. Punched cards can be renewed and replaced if they become dog-eared. They can be rearranged as desired in any order: new cards can be inserted and existing ones removed. Files of data and programs can be edited by hand readily. Because the numerals and letters have a standard punched code, data held on cards can be processed on almost all makes of computer. These are the two biggest advantages of cards. Tape has neither. Cards, however, have lines of fixed length. If they are not filled then space is wasted and the data are still more bulky than necessary.

Experience suggests that field survey data are best punched in fixed format on cards from field records. However, this advice will need to be reviewed in the light of developments in mark-sense and similar recording techniques for use in the field. The laboratory worker can already choose more widely. The would-be user should therefore consult a member of staff at the computer installation where his work will be done before finalizing his choice. For any large study it will pay handsomely to do this and to design a form on which to record data *before* they are collected. The data can then be recorded directly, whether in the field or the laboratory, on the forms from which cards or tape can be punched. This eliminates transcription from one form to another and the attendant delay and risk of additional errors.

Error detection and prevention

All recording, whether in the field or laboratory, whether manual or automatic, and whether by novices or experts, is prone to error. In soil studies a major contributor to the total error is sampling error, which derives from the variability of the soil itself. We shall discuss this in a later chapter. A smaller contribution stems from our inability to read instruments exactly. For example, we might read a pH as 6·1 or 6 when we should read 6·13, or we read 6·1 when the true value is 6·2. This is usually trivial, though we should ensure that any instruments we use are properly calibrated. Our main concern here, however, is with mistakes, which we all make from time to time. We might read the pH correctly as 6·13 but write 6·23 or 0·13 or 913. Or we might originally have written 6·13 in our laboratory notebook but the value was transcribed or punched wrongly. When we have few data and analyse them mentally or on a desk calculator, we spot the obvious anomalies and correct them as we proceed if they are wrong. But when data are treated automatically there are no such checks unless we take positive steps to make them. It is doubtful whether there is any large body of scientific records free from human or machine errors. Nevertheless, even though mistakes are inevitable we clearly want to keep them to a minimum and to eliminate any substantial ones from the data we finally analyse.

Prevention is better than cure, and we should first consider ways of avoiding errors. A few have been mentioned already. Write neatly, forming characters well. Distinguish ambiguous digits and letters by a firm convention, eg 0, 1, 2 for digits; Ō, I, Z for letters. Beware of the symbol ∅. In some conventions it signifies the letter o, in others the digit zero, while on Scandinavian keyboards it is a letter in its own right. Restrict the digit 0 to mean zero and do not confuse it with 'missing' or 'inapplicable'. Other symbols can be used for the latter. Cut out transcription if at all possible. Record on proformas designed for the purpose of the investigation with clear headings and ample space, and from which the data can be punched. A simple tabular layout on standard 80-column recording forms will usually serve well for small sets of data. Qualitative data ultimately need to be coded for analysis, and there is much to be said for encoding them at source, especially those recorded in the field. It is a lot quicker to be able to write '4' instead of 'SUB-ANGULAR BLOCKY' and it uses much less space on a recording sheet. However, it is also easy to write '5' by mistake, and to continue doing so every time sub-angular blocky structure is encountered. Coding is a potential source of error, and when it is decided to encode data, have a list of codes ready for reference and use it.

Having described a soil profile or recorded observations in the laboratory, check them there and then.

Punching is an obvious source of error, and much careful thought has been devoted to the detection of punching errors so that they can be virtually eliminated by verification, as follows. The cards or paper tape on which data have been punched are transferred to a verifier, a machine with the same kind of keyboard as the punch. The data are keyed a second time on this machine. Any mismatch between the original punching and the current keying is signalled to the operator, who can then ensure that a correctly punched card is inserted or that the new paper tape being generated is right. A listing, that is a paper printout, can be obtained from both cards and paper tape for checking. Further mistakes can arise when cards or tape are read into the computer, though they rarely pass undetected.

Despite our efforts to prevent mistakes and to correct those we do make, some errors will almost certainly find their way into the computer. If any of these are large they could make nonsense of analysis, cause loss of confidence in the data or the computing system, lead to false conclusions, and vitiate the investigation. Clearly we want to avoid this. Fortunately, most serious errors can be easily detected, either by the system software or by our own programs. Faults like numbers with two decimal points and letters where digits are expected will cause the machine to terminate any job involving them. Program the computer to print out minimum and maximum values for each variate, and see whether each is reasonable. If there are logical limits on some measurement or attribute, check whether the values and codes are within the permitted range. Display the data graphically if possible. A set of percentages can be summed and flagged if the sum exceeds 100. Check whether depths down a profile follow in sequence. Such checks can be programmed separately or built into programs for analysis. In either event they should enable the offending errors to be identified and corrected, or removed if correction at this late stage is impossible. Small errors will usually escape detection, and will simply swell the errors due to sampling and observation. Nevertheless, if we have done our best to eliminate mistakes as outlined above, we should be able to rest assured that any errors remaining will neither invalidate analysis nor lead us to wrong conclusions.

3. Quantitative description of variable material

Not chaos-like, together crushed and bruised,
But, as the world harmoniously confused:
Where order in variety we see,
And where, though all things differ, all agree.

A. POPE
Windsor Forest

It would be a simple matter to describe soil if it were everywhere the same. But soil is not like that: there is almost endless variety. So when we wish to describe the soil of an area quantitatively, we must not only be able to describe the soil at individual observation points but must also know how to deal with the differences between points that we shall surely find. In this chapter we shall consider the kinds of observation and measurement that we can make on the soil at any one place, and then how to summarize sets of measurements and describe variation that occurs within any one set.

Scales of measurement

Binary variables – attributes

In the introduction we saw that qualitative terms are often quite adequate to describe clearly distinct states of soil. There are places where the soil changes abruptly from sand to clay, and others where it changes equally abruptly from red to black. For all practical purposes only two states of the soil need be recognized in each case. So, for example, sand and clay can be regarded as points on a *binary* scale and given the values 0 and 1. Characters that are either present or absent, for example the presence or absence of litter, calcium carbonate, manganese concretions, or earthworms, can also be recorded on binary scales. If the character is present, it is given the value 1, otherwise it takes the value 0. Such characters are also known as *attributes*, and division of a population according to the presence or absence of an attribute constitutes the simplest form of classification. Binary scales are sometimes known as *dichotomies*.

Multi-state characters and ranked variables

Properties such as the shape of structural aggregates are also described in qualitative terms; granular, blocky, prismatic, platy, and so on. When there are more than two states they are said to constitute a *manifold*, or a *nominal* scale. They are also known as *multi-state characters*, and when there is no sense in which they are ordered they may be termed *unordered* multi-state characters. For computing purposes it is usually convenient to identify each state by a number, but one must avoid subsequently mistaking them for quantitative values.

Other multi-state morphological characters include dry, slightly moist, moist, wet, waterlogged and non-plastic, slightly plastic, plastic, that describe moisture state and plasticity of the soil respectively; the terms to describe the degree of structural development are also multi-state. But each of these sets is ordered. They are sometimes referred to as *ordered multi-state characters*, or more often as *ranked* variables.

Continuous variables

Properties are recorded in a fully quantitative way when they are measured and assigned values on a continuous scale with equal intervals. Examples include the thickness of horizons (dimension length), organic carbon content (proportion), shear strength (dimensions, mass $\times$ time^{-2} $\times$ length^{-1}), and water held at 50 mbar (proportion). The Munsell colour scales may properly be regarded as fully quantitative since they have been arranged as far as possible in steps of equal perception. It is sometimes important to distinguish between those scales that have an absolute zero and those for which the zero is arbitrary. Most scales on which soil properties are measured do have absolute zeros, even though some, like those mentioned above, rarely attain zero in nature. Others, such as the proportion of stones and calcium carbonate often do, of course. Measurements made on scales that have an absolute zero are said to be *ratio* measures. It is meaningful to compare values as multiples or ratios of one another. For example, soil that contains 4 per cent of calcium carbonate may be considered twice as calcareous as soil that contains only 2 per cent. Some scales have only arbitrary zeros. Colour hue and longitude are examples. In practice both are represented in soil survey by small segments of circular scales. The zero of the pH scale is also arbitrary. Such scales are usually known simply as *interval* scales.

We need not distinguish between interval and ratio scales for most purposes. Data recorded on both are amenable to all kinds of mathematical operation and to many forms of statistical summary and analysis. They are the most tractable and informative of all data. Most soil properties can be measured on such scales, as distinct from being recorded qualitatively, either in the field or in the laboratory. Measurement usually requires more effort than qualitative description, but the investigator who seriously seeks a quantitative description or analysis should be prepared to make the effort. He is likely to be well rewarded if he does.

Coarse stepped scales and estimates

Although these quantitative scales are continuous, there are practical limits to the minimum interval on any scale. In the laboratory this is usually determined by the sensitivity of an instrument or the accuracy of its calibration. In either case the minimum interval is negligibly small for practical purposes. However, refined instrumentation is often too expensive for routine field survey, and properties measured in the field are often recorded in coarse increments on short scales. Soil colour provides an example. On the Munsell scales, colour value (lightness) extends from 1 to 9, and the test charts provide steps of 1; chroma (intensity) ranges from 0 to 8 in steps of 1 or 2. Hue (spectral composition) has a longer scale, but in areas where the greenish and bluish greys are absent, hue rarely extends over more than five increments, e.g. from 10R to 5Y with intermediate values 2·5YR, 5YR, 7·5YR, 10YR, and 2·5Y. In high latitudes the range is usually less than this. It is possible to estimate values between those in the Munsell charts, but such interpolation needs good lighting and very careful perception, and so is not common practice. The pH of the soil can be measured reasonably quickly with universal indicator, but a surveyor is unlikely to be able to judge values to better than 0·5 of a pH unit. So, although records of pH and colour are quantitative and can legitimately be treated by most mathematical and statistical techniques, results might be somewhat crude.

There are also other properties observed in the field for which time-consuming measurement is often replaced by rough estimation, but on scales related purposefully to measurable quantities. Examples include root density, carbonate content, and soil strength. The steps of their scales are not necessarily equal in terms of measured values, but have been chosen as the best compromise between increments of equal practical significance and increments whose limits can be detected consistently. Such assessments need to be treated with some caution, but there are many instances where data so derived can be treated as fully quantitative, especially where the central limit theorem applies (see Chapter 4).

Counts

An attribute can sometimes be given quantitative character by counting. Instead of recording roots as present or absent, or giving a rough estimate of their frequency, we can count those cut by a particular cross section of the soil. Similarly it is common practice to count grains of particular species of heavy mineral in studies of soil provenance. Counts can be treated by many of the methods used for continuous variables, though care is needed to ensure that the treatment and results are sensible.

Circular scales

Although colour hue and latitude and longitude are circular, treating them as linear has no serious consequences when only a small part of each scale is used in any particular study. The situation is different when a whole circle or a large part is represented. In soil survey this most often arises in records of the direction faced by the land surface − its slope azimuth or aspect. Aspect may quite properly be recorded in degrees from 0 to 360°, or coded 1 = north north-east, 2 = north-east, . . . , 16 = north. But absurd results will almost certainly follow if such records are treated as though they were linear. The orientations of stones and sand grains in soil are also directional. Special methods are needed to summarize and analyse directional data. They are not mentioned further here, and readers can find details in Mardia (1972).

Representing variation: frequency distributions

The soil is a continuously varying material, and measurements of almost any property made at different places will differ more or less. Likewise, replicate measurements made in the laboratory on a single sample (bag) of soil will vary. This *experimental* or *observational error* can often be diminished to negligible proportions by mixing and sub-sampling the soil carefully and by using well-maintained instruments and good laboratory technique. It cannot be eliminated completely. Variation in the soil from place to place is a fact of nature and is substantial. It is a major source of uncertainty in soil survey, and causes many of the difficulties of applying mathematics to the study of the soil. It is in fact the main reason why this book was written. In the rest of this chapter we shall see how to treat the variation present in sets of measurements.

TABLE 3.1.

Values of soil matric suction at 38 cm in Oxford Clay on 18 May 1963 in centimetres of water and as pF (= $log_{10}cm$ water)

cm water	pF	cm water	pF	cm water	pF
53·3	1·73	5·7	0·76	9·8	0·99
19·3	1·29	6·9	0·84	22·4	1·35
15·5	1·19	4·4	0·64	34·9	1·54
13·0	1·11	4·5	0·65	40·2	1·60
13·0	1·11	7·0	0·85	4·9	0·69
10·5	1·02	20·9	1·32	15·0	1·18
11·9	1·08	12·0	1·08	22·5	1·35
10·7	1·03	16·1	1·21	11·2	1·05
23·3	1·37	8·5	0·93	30·1	1·48

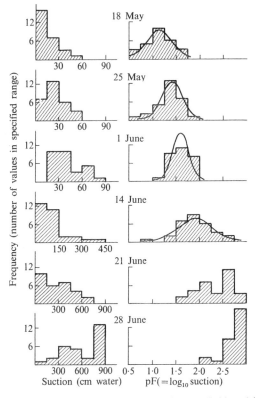

FIG. 3.1. Histograms of suction in centimetres of water (left) and pF = log_{10} cm (right). Curves of the normal distribution are fitted to the first four pF histograms. (From Webster 1966)

The histogram

One of the first steps in studying a set of measurements is to divide it into a manifold. To do this we choose values at equal intervals as limits of successive classes within the observed range. The number of individual values falling within each class is counted and is the *frequency* for that class. The frequencies for all the classes constitute the *frequency distribution* for the set. A graph can be drawn of the distribution, with frequency on the ordinate and the variate values on the abscissa, and with contiguous bars representing the frequencies of the classes. Such a graph is known as a *histogram*. Several examples are shown in Fig. 3.1; the first pair are derived from the values in Table 3.1.

Choosing the class interval is a matter of judgement and experience of the particular soil property and locality. Generally speaking the fewer observations there are, the fewer the classes and the wider the class interval to give a reasonable picture. With thirty observations five or six classes will probably serve best, increasing in number to around ten for 60 to 100 observations, and perhaps as many as twenty-five for populations of three hundred or more. Little is to be gained by having more than about 30 classes however many observations there are. The locations of the intervals, i.e. the class limits, are a matter of convenience. In some studies it is helpful if the class limits are round numbers. They obviously must be if the variate is a count. However, it is important that there should be no ambiguity about the assignment of individuals with values falling on a borderline. Such ambiguity is best avoided by assigning all individuals with borderline values to the classes immediately below or all to the classes above. A similar result can be obtained by defining class limits to one further place of decimals than that present in the recorded measurements. When the recorded values have already been rounded it may be better to assign individuals lying on a particular borderline alternately to the class above and the class below.

Although histograms are commonly drawn by plotting the number of observations as the ordinate, it is important to note that it is the *area* beneath the horizontal top of each bar that actually represents the class frequency. When class intervals are equal, the bars of any histogram drawn this way automatically have their areas proportional to the class frequencies. If class intervals are not equal then the heights of the bars must be calculated so that the areas of the bars are proportional to the frequencies. Note that a histogram is not appropriate for a discontinuous variable such as a count. For such variables frequencies are best represented as isolated vertical bars.

Other ways of displaying frequency distributions are by *frequency polygons* and cumulative frequency diagrams. The latter are often used to present the results of particle size analysis. A frequency polygon differs from a histogram in that the ordinates at the centres of the classes are joined to their neighbours by straight lines instead of being stepped. Its disadvantage is that the area under the graph is no longer exactly equal to the frequency.

Valuable though frequency tables and histograms are, they need summarizing further for most practical purposes. We shall now consider what are perhaps the two most important characters of distributions of soil measurements, representing the position and spread of the values on the measurement scale respectively.

The arithmetic mean

The position of a distribution can be represented by its centre or average, and there are several measures that may be used, each appropriate in certain circumstances. The most useful is the *arithmetic mean*, or simply the *mean*. Suppose we have a set of N observations, $x_1, x_2, \ldots, x_N$, then the mean μ is defined as

$$\mu = \frac{1}{N} \sum_{i=1}^{N} x_i. \tag{3.1}$$

As a measure of position the mean has several advantages: it takes account of all the observations; it can be treated algebraically to compute, for example, totals and to combine averages from several sets of observations; the mean of a sample is an unbiased estimate of the population mean, a point that will become clearer in the next chapter.

Median and mode

Two other measures of the position of a distribution are the *median* and the *mode*. The median is the central value of the variate when the observations are ranked in order from smallest to largest. Thus there are as many observations with values less than the median as there are with values greater than it. Mathematically it is less tractable than the mean. When a property is recorded on a coarse scale the median is likely to be only a rough estimate of the true centre.

Its main advantage is that it is not disturbed by the size of extreme values. Suppose soil is sampled at several places to determine its potassium status. If a bag of fertilizer had been spilt at one of the sampling points or there had been a bonfire, then the potassium value there might be one or more orders of magnitude larger than the rest. Its inclusion would influence the mean greatly, but could leave the median unaffected. In some instances extreme values are suspect because the instrument used for measurement is insensitive in that part of the range, or they are unobtainable because the true values lie beyond its range. Again the median is not upset in this situation whereas the mean is. This situation is illustrated in Fig. 3.1 and Table 3.2, taken from a study in which soil matric suction was measured at weekly intervals by tensiometers placed at 38 cm in soil on a small plot of land (Webster 1966). On the logarithmic pF scale of measurement, the distribution is symmetrical and the median closely approximates the mean for the first four sets of readings. However, the tensiometers could not measure suctions more than about 710 cm water, pF 2.85, and as the soil dried out an increasing number of them failed to provide reliable values. This is illustrated in the last two histograms on the right-hand side of Fig. 3.1. The values bunch at the high end of the scale. The centre of the true pF values on 21 June was probably nearer to the median, pF 2.41, than to the mean, pF 2.33. On 28 June the median is a much more realistic estimate of the true average suction than the mean, though by then even that might have been too low.

The idea of the mode is familiar enough to field pedologists. The mode is the most frequent or the typical value. It implies that the distribution has a single peak. Some distributions have more than one peak and may be termed *multi-modal*. Although we may intuitively identify what we think is the mode, its numerical value is difficult to determine in practice. If the class interval can be made very small and the class frequencies still increase and decrease smoothly, then the mid-value of the most frequent class would probably be a good approximation. But such a procedure is likely to work only if many observations have been made. The alternative is to fit to the frequency values an ideal frequency curve whose peak would then be the mode of the distribution.

For any symmetrical distribution with a single peak, the mean, median, and mode coincide. In asymmetric distributions the median and mode lie further from the longer tail of the distribution than the mean, and the median lies between the mode and the mean. The formula

$$\text{mode} - \text{median} = 2\,(\text{median} - \text{mean})$$

provides a rough guide to their relative positions. The mean and median of the suction values in cm water given in Table 3.2 illustrate the difference:

mean   16·6 cm,

median 11·9 cm.

The mode is difficult to judge on so few data. The histogram shows
it to lie somewhere between 0 and 15 cm. It seems to be less than
11·9 cm, the median, but the the value of 2·5 cm given by the above
formula is obviously too low.

Dispersion

As with the position of a distribution, so there are several measures
for describing its dispersion or spread. They include the *range*, the
interquartile range, the *mean deviation*, and the *standard deviation*.
Of these the standard deviation and its square, the *variance*, are without
doubt the most valuable. The variance of a set of observations or finite
population, $x_1, x_2, \ldots, x_N$, is often defined as

$$\sigma^2 = \frac{1}{N} \sum_{i=1}^{N} (x_i - \mu)^2 \qquad (3.2)$$

where μ is the mean as above. In Chapter 4 and later in the book we
shall define the variance slightly differently by replacing N in the
denominator of this expression by $N - 1$. The reasons for this will be
made clear then.

The variance and standard deviation, like the mean, are based on all
the observations; they can be treated algebraically and are the least
affected by sampling fluctuations. They are both special cases of
important quantities in the theory of errors. Suppose u is some particular value of the property about which we have N measurements,
then the quantity

$$s^2 = \frac{1}{N} \sum_{i=1}^{N} (x_i - u)^2$$

is known as the *second moment* of the distribution about u. If u is μ,
then the second moment about the mean is the variance. Its square
root s is called the *root-mean-square deviation*. The merit of these
quantities will become more apparent when we apply theoretical distributions to soil data. Until then we can gain a 'feel' for the standard
deviation by matching the histograms in the right-hand side of Fig. 3.1
with the values of the standard deviation given in Table 3.2. In the first
four distributions at least, and in many other reasonably symmetrical
distributions, we shall not go far wrong if we assume that about two
thirds of the observations lie within one standard deviation of the mean.

TABLE 3.2.

Means, standard deviations (s), coefficients of variation (CV), and medians of soil matric suction expressed as pF (= $\log_{10}$cm water) at 38 cm recorded by thirty tensiometers in 1963

Date	Mean	s	CV (per cent)	Median
18 May	1·13	0·29	25·5	1·11
25 May	1·41	0·23	16·2	1·39
1 June	1·58	0·18	11·1	1·59
14 June	1·91	0·38	20·0	1·90
21 June	2·33	0·35	15·1	2·41
28 June	2·73			2·85

Coefficient of variation

The standard deviation expresses dispersion in the same units as those in which the variable is measured, and takes no account of the position of the distribution in relation to the zero of its scale. Sometimes we wish to express variation in relative terms. Suppose we have measured some property of the soil at a number of points in two different regions. The standard deviations of the two sets of measurements, σ_1 and σ_2, are equal, but there is a two-fold difference in their means; $\mu_1 = 2\mu_2$. Relative to its mean, the soil of the first region is twice as variable as in the second. The *coefficient of variation* CV, which equals the standard deviation divided by the mean, expresses this. It is usually given as a percentage:

$$CV = 100\frac{\sigma}{\mu}\%$$

It is a useful measure for comparing variation in different sets of observations, but care is needed to ensure that its use is appropriate. In particular, it is unlikely to be helpful for scales with arbitrary zeros.

Skew and kurtosis

The mean and variance of a set of observations describe their position and spread. We sometimes wish to describe other characters of a distribution, in particular its degree of symmetry, or *skew*, and its peakedness, or *kurtosis*. These are derived from the third and fourth moments about the mean respectively.

Considering skew first, we compute the third moment

$$m_3 = \frac{1}{N}\sum_{i=1}^{N}(x_i - \mu)^3. \tag{3.3}$$

For symmetrical distributions m_3 is zero, since the positive deviations balance those that are negative. A distribution with its peak nearer the low end of the range and large values extending far above the mean has a positive value of m_3. It is said to be *positively skew*. If a distribution has a long tail at the low end of its scale, then m_3 is negative and the distribution has negative skew. Skew is usually measured by a dimensionless quantity $\beta_1^{1/2}$ or γ_1, defined as

$$\beta_1^{1/2} = \gamma_1 = \frac{m_3}{m_2 m_2^{1/2}} \qquad (3.4)$$

where m_2 is the second moment about the mean, i.e. the variance.

Soil variables often have skew distributions, and the left-hand sides of Figs. 3.1 and 3.2 both show examples of positive skew. The suction data for Wytham are more skew (γ_1 for 18 May is 1·51) than the values of aluminium at Ginninderra ($\gamma_1 = 0·87$).

The fourth moment about the mean is

$$m_4 = \frac{1}{N} \sum_{i=1}^{N} (x_i - \mu)^4. \qquad (3.5)$$

The importance of m_4 relates especially to the normal distribution, which we shall discuss next, and for which the ratio

$$\beta_2 = \frac{m_4}{m_2^2} = 3. \qquad (3.6)$$

The quantity γ_2 is then defined equal to $\beta_2 - 3$, so that $\gamma_2 = 0$ for normal distributions. Distributions that are more peaked than normal have positive values of γ_2, and distributions that are flatter than normal have negative values. They are said to be *leptokurtic* and *platykurtic* respectively.

The Normal Distribution

We now come to a feature of data that is central to statistical theory, namely the *normal distribution*. This theoretical distribution was discovered independently by De Moivre, Gauss, and Laplace in the eighteenth century. It was found to describe remarkably well the errors of observation in physics and particularly in astronomy. Its equation is

$$y = \frac{1}{\sigma\sqrt{2\pi}} \exp\left\{-\frac{(x - \mu)^2}{2\sigma^2}\right\} \qquad (3.7)$$

where π and exp are constants with their usual meaning, and μ and σ are the mean and standard deviation of the particular variable. The shape of the distribution is characteristically that of the cross section through a bell. Several graphs of the normal distribution are shown in Figs. 3.1, 3.2, and 3.3. They show the kind of graphs that we might expect to obtain if we had very many measurements of the properties in question, made the class intervals very small, and then joined the class frequencies to form frequency polygons.

The normal curve has a number of features of interest. It is continuous and symmetrical, with its peak at the mean of the distribution. It has two points of inflexion, one on each side of the mean at a distance equal to the standard deviation σ. The ordinate y at any given value of x is a measure of the probability of that value of x occurring, and is known as the *probability density* at x. Since the peak of y is at μ, the mean is the most likely value of x. The area under the curve is equal to 1, the total probability of the distribution, i.e. the probability that x takes any of its possible values. The area under any portion of the curve, say between x_1 and x_2, represents the proportion of the distribution lying in that range. Some useful figures to remember are: slightly over two thirds of the distribution lies within one standard deviation of the mean, i.e. between $\mu - \sigma$ and $\mu + \sigma$; about 95 per cent of it lies in the range $\mu - 2\sigma$ to $\mu + 2\sigma$; and 99·74 per cent of the distribution lies within three standard deviations of the mean. When considering a particular set of data, it is natural to think of frequencies rather than probabilities, in which case the above probabilities or proportions are simply multiplied by N, the number of observations.

The reader may well ask what this has to do with soil. Now it is another remarkable fact that very many variables, not only of soil, but also of other natural materials, plants and animals, and manufactured articles are distributed in a way that closely approximates the normal curve. Many measurements that are not normally distributed can be made so by transforming their measurement scales. The matric suction data of Table 3.1 are just such. The original measurements in cm of water are very skew, but their common logarithms (pF) match the normal distribution closely. Other transformations will normalize some non-normal measurements. Canarache (see especially Canarache and Vintilâ 1970) and associates have done much empirical survey in Romania to confirm this picture for soil. Even for variables that are far from normally distributed and cannot be normalized by transformation, their sample averages tend to become more nearly normal as the size of the sample is increased.

For these and other reasons the normal distribution has been intensively studied. It is very well understood, and though it never describes exactly any real distribution of a soil variable, it can usefully and reliably be applied to many tasks involving estimation, prediction and comparison of soil in one or more regions. Further, tables of its ordinates and integrals have been accurately prepared, and are available in many standard texts. Thus the investigator is likely to have the strong backing of statistical theory and practice when he measures the soil properties of interest.

Other distributions

The normal distribution is one of several distributions that we shall come across in this book. In the next chapter we shall see that proportions are distributed somewhat differently; they follow the *binomial distribution*. Certain mathematical quantities, when calculated for random samples, are distributed in their own characteristic way and are known by their own names. They include *Student's t*, χ^2 (*chi square*), and the *F ratio*. These distributions have been worked out and are published in sets of tables, see for example Fisher and Yates (1963).

Transformations

Sets of observations that are not normally distributed give rise to difficulties that are absent with normally distributed sets. We have already seen that we are in some doubt as to which measure of the centre we should use when the distribution is skew. Other results that depend on normality cannot be applied, or can be applied only roughly. Comparisons between means of different sets of observations (see Chapter 5) are especially unreliable if the variable is skew, for the variance changes from one set to another. Our estimate of the proportion of a population lying in any given range could be erroneous if we assumed normality when there was appreciable kurtosis. These difficulties can often be overcome by transforming the scale of measurement so that the distributions on the new scale are normal. Further, it is often found that the same transformations also make the variances of samples less dependent on the mean, and they are therefore often made mainly to stabilize the variance.

Measurements of soil properties are often skewed on their original measurement scales. Matric suction measured in cm water, or more usually nowadays in bars, is one example. Content of exchangeable cations, available phosphorus, electrical conductivity, and microbial

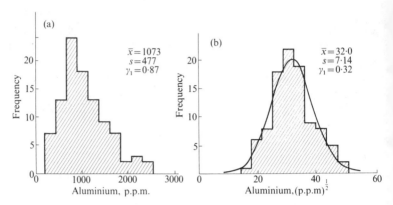

FIG. 3.2. Histograms of extracted aluminium in parts per million (a) and transformed to $(p.p.m.)^{1/2}$ (b). The normal curve is fitted to (b). (Data from study by Webster and Butler 1976)

activity are often positively skew. If the skew is only slight, no transformation need be made, and results of a statistical analysis are unlikely to be misleading. But for more pronounced skew some transformation is desirable, and the investigator has several options.

Square root transformation

Moderate skew can often be removed by taking square roots of the measurements. Fig. 3.2 shows an example of this.

Logarithmic transformation

A more powerful transformation than taking square roots can be obtained by taking logarithms, either to base 10 or e as desired. Care is needed to ensure that there are no zero or negative values in the data. If there are, then a small value should be added to each measured value to ensure that the smallest is just positive. Fig. 3.1 shows how well matric suction values can be normalized in this way. It is worth noting here that means calculated on transformed values are transforms of the geometric means of the original data. Thus if

$$\bar{g} = \left\{ \prod_{i=1}^{N} x_i \right\}^{1/N}$$

then

$$\log \bar{g} = \frac{1}{N} \sum_{i=1}^{N} \log x_i. \tag{3.8}$$

Reciprocals

Still more powerful is the reciprocal transformation, though this is rarely needed in soil studies. If the transformation is made, it is again worth noting that the mean of the reciprocal data is the reciprocal of the harmonic mean of the original data.

Angular and logit transformation

Data that consist of proportions are clearly confined in the range 0 to 1, or 0 to 100 if expressed as percentages. Their distributions are often compressed near 0 and 1. The aim of the angular transformation is to spread the distribution out near the ends of its range. If the proportion is p then the transformation is

$$\phi = \sin^{-1} p^{1/2}, \tag{3.9}$$

i.e. the angle whose sine is $p^{1/2}$. For this reason the transformation is also known as the *arcsine* transformation. The circumstances in which this transform is likely to help are fairly clear.

The transformation is appropriate where the proportions are based on counts, and follow the binomial distribution (see Chapter 4). It is widely used in biology. In soil studies it is likely to apply to proportions of mineral species based on counts of sand grains. However, it can also be applied empirically to other measures expressed as proportions, such as particle size fractions. Fig. 3.3 shows an example.

When the observed values fall in the range 30 to 70 per cent, there is very little to be gained by the transformation, and it is unlikely that

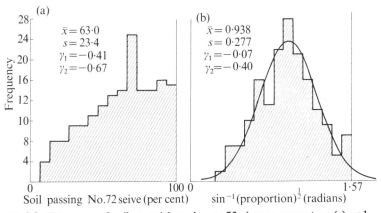

FIG. 3.3. Histograms of soil material passing no.72 sieve as percentage (a) and transformed to arcsine (b). The curve of the normal distribution is fitted to the right-hand graph. (Data for Berkshire kindly provided by M.G. Jarvis)

there will be much gain when only a small proportion of the observations fall outside this range. However, it should be noted that the arcsine scale is still constrained between 0 and $\pi/2$. If observations are concentrated close to 0 or 1 then the *logit* transformation might spread them out to approximate normality. If p is an observed proportion and $q = 1 - p$, then its logit is

$$Y = \log_e (p/q), \tag{3.10}$$

and its scale ranges from $-\infty$ to $+\infty$. As with the logarithmic transformation, if any value is exactly 0 or 1 then some small value should be added or subtracted to keep the logit within a manageable range. There is no report of logits having been used on soil data to the best of my knowledge, but the transformation should be borne in mind when dealing with proportions.

Faced with all these options for transformation the soil scientist might well wonder which, if any, he should use. To some extent it is a matter of good judgement that comes with experience. The beginner should therefore be prepared to compare histograms of original observations with those transformed in several ways and fit normal curves to them after calculating their means and standard deviations. He will not go far wrong if he transforms to a scale on which his data 'look' normally distributed, and does not transform data when he has doubts about it. Bartlett (1947) provides further guidance in a useful review.

Correcting for positive skew is often necessary with soil data, and is a little more problematic than arcsine transformation. The best transformation for a single set of observations can be judged as above. When several sets of observations have been made, especially if they have been on soil of different types, or from different regions, or on which different treatments have been applied, there is an additional way of forming a judgement. Differences between the groups of soil will usually be reflected in differences among the mean values of the variable concerned, and if there is skew the variances of the sets will also tend to differ. If the skew is positive, then the larger the mean, the larger the variance is likely to be, and the most appropriate transformation can be determined from the relation between the means and variances. Jeffers (1959) suggests a neat approach, as follows. On double logarithmic graph paper plot the variance of each set of observations against the mean for that set and note any trend. If the plotted points fall approximately on a line through the origin with a slope of 1, i.e. 45°, then the variance increases in proportion to the mean and the original values should be transformed to their square roots. If the trend passes through the origin and has a slope of 2, the standard deviation is proportional to the mean, and the logarithmic transformation should be used. If the slope of the line is 4, i.e. the variance increases as the fourth power of the mean, then data should be transformed to their reciprocals.

Transformation enables many sets of measurements to be analysed and results to be applied confidently. However, the results are not so readily understood as are those from data that do not need transformation. It is helpful to transform means back to the original scales, and sometimes to express standard deviation as two values, the back transforms of $\mu - \sigma$ and $\mu + \sigma$. Confidence limits (see Chapter 4) should be treated similarly.

Transformation might smack of 'cookery'. In one sense there is an analogy: transformation renders data more digestible, and hence more useful than they would otherwise be. But as Moroney (1956) wisely remarks, the natural scientist regards it as entirely proper if he makes the transformation himself, for example, from hydrogen ion concentration to pH. It is equally proper when a transformation is done for the purpose of analysis.

4. Sampling and estimation

Truth lies within a little and certain
compass, but error is immense.
> HENRY ST. JOHN
> *Reflections on exile*

We have already seen that we cannot measure any property of the soil everywhere. If we want to know what the soil of any area is like we must be satisfied with measurements made on a part of it, that is, on a sample. However, such information is of little practical value unless we can use it as a reliable description of the area as a whole. We want information that is truly representative of the area, and a means of sampling that will ensure this, bearing in mind that soil is very variable.

Over the last forty years statisticians have devoted much attention to the theory of sampling, which now provides a base for sound sampling in many spheres. The results of this work are recorded in several standard texts. Those by Cochran (1963) and Yates (1960) are especially recommended. In this chapter we shall consider how to apply the theory to obtain good samples from an area, how to use the information from a sample when we have it, and the special difficulties that arise in soil survey. Not all of the theory is crucial to an understanding of soil classification, and readers whose main interest is in classification might skip pp.56–70 on first reading.

The population

When we want to learn something about soil we have first to decide which soil: which of all possible soil is to be included in the investigation. The kinds of question that must be asked and answered are:

(i) Is the study to be of the whole soil profile, or just the topsoil, or the material below 45 cm?

(ii) What is the area to be covered in the investigation: the experimental station, or the neighbouring locality; the administrative district or the national territory?

(iii) Is the study to be of one or a few particular kinds of soil only: brown earths, or brown earths and podzols; soil developed from granite; soil used for agriculture; or 'undisturbed' soil?

(iv) Is the study to be restricted to soil material already collected or to a set of data from an earlier investigation?

If the answer to the last question is yes then, of course, there is no sampling problem. The investigator should know how the sample was obtained, since this might affect his conclusions. The other questions might seem equally obvious and easy enough to answer, but a little reflection will show that they are not so, especially questions (i) and (iii). For example, we can well understand an agronomist's interest in the topsoil, but when we come to measure its properties we need to know more precisely what constitutes topsoil. Is it to be the A horizon, or the plough layer, or that part of the soil that would be cultivated if cultivation were undertaken? And what constitutes the 'whole soil profile?' Despite years of debate this question is almost impossible to answer in many instances. If we wait for it to be resolved on pedological grounds we may never begin our investigation. We might decide to consider all the soil down to rock. In some areas this would be feasible, but in others it would not. We might instead decide to consider that part of the soil containing plant roots: the bottom of the soil will be that depth beyond which there are no roots. This too might be unsatisfactory if we have some soil under grass and some under forest. So we might quite arbitrarily decide to take the top metre, or two, or three metres. What is needed in each case is a workable definition of the soil to be included in the study; a rule that can be easily applied and is reasonable and appropriate in the circumstances.

Once the investigator is quite clear what soil he wishes to include in the study and can define it operationally, that soil becomes the *population* for the purpose of the study.

Question (ii) involves somewhat different problems and pitfalls. For example, suppose it is desired to assess the potential productivity of the soil in an area of several thousand square kilometeres, but it turns out to be impossible to carry out trials uniformly over such an area and to prevent depredations, whether by insects, game, or the local people, far from base. So the investigation takes place on local experiment stations instead. Or information about the soil of a national territory is desired, but because the area is large and manpower scarce, only a small portion can be visited, or has been surveyed when the data come to be analysed. Or a disease like foot and mouth disease breaks out and access is denied to part of the area. These are factors that should become apparent at the planning stage, though some, like an outbreak of disease, might occur during execution. The result in each case is that the population actually sampled is not the population that the investigator originally intended to study. The latter is sometimes known as the *target population* to distinguish it from the actual population.

Although the soil exists as a continuous mantle, when we sample it we have to regard it as made up of a number of elements or individuals, some of which we shall actually observe or measure in the field or in the laboratory. What constitutes an individual is more or less arbitrary and determined largely by convenience. Individuals are often sampling cores from the topsoil or from the whole profile with finite size in three dimensions. They might be pedons, though the pedon (the volume of soil beneath a metre square of the soil surface) is usually too large for practicality, and its extended definition to cover short range cyclic variation is statistically unsound (Arnold 1964). Or they might be faces of pits with length and depth and just sufficient thickness for their morphology to be ascertained. The size of the individual might less arbitrarily be chosen as the volume of soil occupied by the roots of a single plant, or the volume of soil deformed under a given load. In one sense it is immaterial what the individuals are, for in any large area there are so many that we may regard their number as infinite, and this simplifies the statistical treatment. However, the degree of variation that we observe from one individual to another depends very much on the size of the individuals. Variation among 2 cm auger cores could include substantial effects caused by burrowing small animals. Such variation is likely to be smoothed out if the individuals are 1 m cubes. It is important, therefore, to decide what the individual is to be, to adhere to that decision throughout a survey, and to state it when reporting results.

Usually in a particular study we are not interested in the whole soil so much as certain characters of it; its pH or colour or clay content, for example. We may therefore regard the soil population as a set of individuals each possessing a limited number of characters.

Sampling

Having defined the population for the purpose of a study the next task is to choose a method of sampling it. One way is for someone familiar with that soil to select 'typical' or 'average' occurrences. Measurements can then be made on these. Such sampling is sometimes known as *purposive sampling*, and is often used to describe individual classes of soil. When a population is very variable and resources allow the soil at only one or two sites to be examined, this method can provide a more accurate description than others. It relies heavily on personal judgement. There is no knowing just how good that judgement is, and no way of communicating the expert's confidence in his choice.

Further, there is a strong risk that an expert's choice will be to some extent biased; that is, it will give preference to some part of the population at the expense of the rest. Bias is almost always present in human judgement, and it cannot be avoided either by training or by conscious effort. Yates's (1935) work on bias at Rothamsted showed how serious this risk is. Selection of the 'typical' is not a safe way to sample.

Neither is sampling from 'convenient' spots satisfactory. Soil surveyors are well aware how atypical the soil is near to gates and other places of access to agricultural land. And if parts of an area are avoided because they are too inconvenient to reach, then the sampled population is not the target population.

The only sure way of avoiding bias is by *random* or *probability* sampling. In common parlance random tends to mean haphazard or casual. For example, a participant in a card trick might be asked to 'take a card at random'. A soil sample chosen casually is quite as likely to be biased as one chosen purposively, and will not do. Random sampling means choosing individuals from a population so that all members of that population have an equal chance (probability) of being chosen.

Although it is easy to state this principle, it is far from obvious how to achieve random sampling in practice, and, paradoxically it can be achieved only by following firm rules.

To sample soil randomly we need two things: first, a means of identifying individuals in the soil population; second, a means of selecting individuals once we have decided how to identify them. If the population consists of pots of soil in a greenhouse or fields in a parish, each pot or field is identified by a unique number. These numbers are then matched to a sequence of random digits, which may be read from one of the several published tables of random digits (e.g. Fisher and Yates 1963; Rand Corporation 1955), or may be generated by machine for the purpose. There are several well-tried computer routines for producing pseudo-random numbers. Thus, if there are 240 pots in a greenhouse from which we wish to choose 10 at random we number the pots from 1 to 240. Then we can take a row of digits in a table and read off digits in sets of three until we have ten unqiue three-digit numbers less than or equal to 240 and excluding 0. The pots with these numbers then constitute the random sample.

When the population is the soil of an area and the individuals are sampling cores or profile pits, this technique is too cumbersome. An area of $100 \, \text{km}^2$, for example, contains 10^{10} disjoint $10 \, \text{cm} \times 10 \, \text{cm}$ elements that we might choose; and there is in principle an infinite number of profile faces that we could expose. The most convenient alternative is to regard the individuals as points in a plane and to identify them by reference to a rectangular grid whose origin and orientation are known. Points to be included in a sample can then be chosen by selecting pairs of numbers from a table of random digits, and using these as the coordinates of the points on the reference grid. The result is a *simple random sample*. Other ways of obtaining unbiased samples that are more efficient, give more even coverage, and are preferred for mapping are described later.

The degree of resolution, that is the number of significant digits in the coordinates, requires some thought. Referencing to 10 cm is needed to give equal probability of selecting $10 \, \text{cm} \times 10 \, \text{cm}$ elements once the position of the grid is fixed. For areas of more than 1 ha this is impracticable and unnecessary. Resolution to one thousandth of the length of either axis of the grid is more than adequate for any one area, since this will give nearly one million possible sampling points. Too fine a resolution will also make it difficult to find sampling points in the field. If a surveyor cannot locate himself to better than 100 m there is no point in his obtaining more precise coordinates than this. Nor is it necessary to locate points with great accuracy provided bias is not introduced at this stage and an accurate map is not to be constructed from the observations.

It can be very convenient to identify sampling points by reference to a standard geographic grid. The British National Grid is one such. It is an orthogonal square grid with principal divisions on most British maps at 1 km intervals. Latitude and longitude may also be used, though if the area is very large the parts nearest the poles will be more densely sampled than those nearer the equator, and some compensatory adjustment will be needed either to the sampling procedure or to the results of the survey. It is also worth noting that once it is decided to use a particular grid and degree of resolution, most potential sampling points are excluded from the sample. This is scarcely likely to matter.

Location in practice

Having decided on a sampling scheme and chosen where each observation is to be made, we then have to find each point in the field. This can be done accurately by triangulation, but as already noted such accuracy is rarely necessary and, provided we avoid bias, we may use more rough and ready methods. The following procedure will usually suffice. Choose from a map or air photograph some easily recognizable feature that is near the sample point to be reached, and go there. Estimate from the map the direction and distance to the sample point. Then, using a compass to give direction, measure out the estimated distance. If the ground surface appears uniform the sample point may be located by pacing. But if the ground is variable, especially close to the sample point, then beware of introducing bias by shortening or lengthening paces to avoid what may seem atypical, unpleasant (e.g. swamp or thicket), or difficult to dig or record (e.g. stony ground). It is safer to use a chain or tape in these circumstances.

Inevitably snags arise, and the investigator must be prepared in advance to deal with them. *Ad hoc* decisions made in the field as they arise can easily lead to bias. One of the commonest difficulties occurs when a sampling point happens to be on a road, in a river, or on a farm building. What should the surveyor do? The answer depends on the nature of the investigation. If the aim of the survey is even in part to assess *how much* soil there is or what proportion of an area is usable soil, then such sample points must be accepted and the findings there recorded. If the survey is solely concerned with, say, agricultural soil then the investigator has a choice. He may simply ignore the point. Alternatively, he may follow a predetermined rule for choosing a substitute near by. Such a rule might be: when the selected site is not on agricultural soil choose as substitute a site x metres away on a bearing θ degrees. The values of x and θ may themselves be chosen from a table of random numbers and replaced by a new pair when once used. Or x may be fixed and θ chosen as 0, 90°, 180°, 270° in turn. The distance x should be kept to a small proportion of the average distance between neighbouring sampling points. This procedure is of little advantage if simple random sampling is used, and the first course is safest. But it is valuable when even coverage is desired for mapping.

A surveyor may less consciously go astray when a sample point lies in a hedgerow or gateway, or near a ditch that has recently been cleared or deepened. It is easy to regard such situations as atypical and to omit them from the sample. The matter must be resolved by deciding in advance whether such sites are part of the target population. If they are, then they are accepted when they occur in the sample, otherwise they are rejected.

Another difficulty arises when a land-owner refuses to grant access to his land. If only a few selected points cannot be visited for this reason, then they may be omitted from the sample without serious consequence. If several land-owners deny access, the investigator should consider whether there is some relation between the kind of land and owners' attitudes to survey. This is by no means as silly as it might at first seem. If there is any such relation then, as above, the population actually sampled will not be the target population, and the fact should be recorded. The same holds if any large tract of land cannot be visited for this or other reasons.

Yet other problems arise when a farmer is willing to cooperate but with restrictions. The investigator might reasonably comply with a request not to dig up the front paddock where the horses are kept. To keep out of the standing crops, on the other hand, could bias results, and the investigator should consider returning there after harvest. Numerous small snags such as these can occur during a survey and prevent the sample being truly random. The course taken over many of them is unlikely to affect the outcome seriously provided the investigator is always on the look-out for bias.

Estimation and confidence

Quantitative data from a sample can be summarized just like those from any other set of individuals. Thus, we can calculate the mean and variance to express the central position and dispersion in the sample. However, provided the sampling is sound, we can use these values to *estimate* the corresponding parameters in the population. Using Greek letters for population parameters and Roman ones for the sample values, $\bar{x}$ estimates μ and s^2 estimates σ^2. The estimates apply strictly to the population that was actually sampled, and if that differs from the target population, then any inference extended to the target or other population rests solely on the judgement of the investigator.

In a sample of variable material such as soil there are inevitably differences between individuals included in the sample and those excluded. As a result, sample estimates differ more or less from the true population values. In a random sample such differences are attributed to sampling error, and are distinguished from errors due to bias. Sampling error can usually be reduced by increasing the size of the sample, so that the estimate converges on the population value. Similarly, in the absence of bias the average of sample estimates converges to the true value as the number of samples is increased.

We must now make a formal distinction between two kinds of bias. That mentioned so far is the systematic error that arises from faulty selection. When present it is a constant source of inaccuracy that is unaffected by the size of the sample. The same kind of bias can result from slack laboratory technique and the use of poorly calibrated instruments. The second kind of bias is that associated with an estimator. An estimator is said to be biased if its average value taken over all possible random samples differs from the population parameter being estimated. An unbiased estimator is one which gives the true value on average, and is generally regarded as desirable.

Since sampling error is inevitable, we need to be able to assess it and take it into account when applying sampling estimates to populations. Sampling error is usually expressed as the standard deviation of the sample mean, or *standard error*, and is obtained from the sample variance s^2. In a sample of n individuals with mean $\bar{x}$, the estimated standard error $s_{\bar{x}}$ is

$$s_{\bar{x}} = \left(\frac{s^2}{n}\right)^{1/2} \tag{4.1}$$

where

$$s^2 = \frac{1}{n-1} \sum_{i=1}^{n} (x_i - \bar{x})^2. \tag{4.2}$$

It represents the variation in $\bar{x}$ that would occur if repeated samples of size n were taken. The standard error of a total, s_T, is sometimes needed and is given by

$$s_T = s n^{1/2}. \tag{4.3}$$

Finite population correction

The above expression for standard error assumes that the sample is drawn from an infinite population. If the population is finite — say pots of soil in a greenhouse — and the sample is more than about one-twentieth of the population, then a correction should be applied. For a sample of size n drawn from a population of N individuals, the sampling fraction is

$$f = \frac{n}{N}.$$

The standard error is then corrected by multiplying it by $(1-f)$. The quantity $1-f$ is known as the *finite population correction*, or f.p.c. Its effect is to diminish the calculated standard error somewhat. The populations of concern in soil survey are usually infinite, or practically so, and in this case the f.p.c. can be ignored. We shall ignore the f.p.c. in the remainder of this chapter.

Degrees of freedom

Eqn. (3.2) for the variance of a finite population contains N alone in the denominator. By analogy we might have expected to replace it by n when calculating the variance of a sample. But in eqn. (4.2). we use $n-1$, and this needs explanation. The variance of a population is the average of the squares of deviations from the population mean μ. However, when sampling we do not know μ but have only our sample estimate $\bar{x}$, which is more or less in error. Further, calculation of the mean as

$$\bar{x} = \frac{1}{n} \sum_{i=1}^{n} x_i$$

ensures that $\sum_{i=1}^{n} (x_i - \bar{x})^2$ is less than it would be if $\bar{x}$ were replaced by any other value, and in particular is less than $\sum_{i=1}^{n} (x_i - \mu)^2$. Thus, if variance is calculated from sample data using n instead of $n-1$ in eqn. (4.2), it will underestimate

$$\sigma^2 = \frac{1}{N} \sum_{i=1}^{N} (x_i - \mu)^2:$$

it is a biased estimator of the population variance. Eqn. (4.2) ensures that σ^2 is estimated without bias.

It might help to grasp the difference between the variance of a finite population and a sample estimate if we consider what happens in the limit when $N = 1$. If we have a population consisting of a single measurement it clearly has zero variance: $x_1 = \bar{x}$, $(x_1 - \bar{x})^2 = 0$, and the whole expression $(x_1 - \bar{x})^2/N$ is zero. If we have a sample of size 1 the fact that its variance is zero tells us nothing about variation in the parent population. The formula

$$\frac{1}{n-1} \sum (x_1 - \bar{x})^2$$

reduces to 0/0, which expresses this lack of information.

The quantity $n-1$ is known as the number of *degrees of freedom* in the estimate of the variance. This concept arises as above because the variance is calculated from the squares of deviation from the sample mean, which is itself calculated from the same sample data, and so leaves one fewer independent quantities than there are individuals in the sample. Using degrees of freedom also simplifies the mathematics in more complex analyses of data and in tabulating sampling distributions. We shall use it in the remainder of this book for calculating both population variances and their sampling estimates.

Central limit theorem

Before considering how we can use the standard error, we shall discuss another important feature of sampling. When samples are drawn at random from a population, their means tend to be distributed in a more nearly normal fashion than do the individual values. Further, however the original population is distributed, provided its variance is finite, the distribution of the sample mean approaches normality as the size of the sample increases. This result is known as the *central limit theorem*, and its importance lies in its allowing a large body of statistical theory to be applied to practical problems even though the underlying population distributions are far from normal.

Confidence limits

The standard error measures the precision attained in a survey. We can use it to determine the range within which the true population mean can be said to lie with any desired degree of confidence. Assuming that the sample is large and its mean $\bar{x}$ is normally distributed, then confidence limits for the population mean are

$$\bar{x} - z\left(\frac{s^2}{n}\right)^{1/2} = \bar{x} - zs/n^{1/2} = \bar{x} - zs_{\bar{x}}, \text{the lower limit}$$

and

$$\bar{x} + z\left(\frac{s^2}{n}\right)^{1/2} = \bar{x} + zs/n^{1/2} = \bar{x} + zs_{\bar{x}}, \text{the upper limit.} \qquad (4.5)$$

The quantity z is the value of the normal deviation for the desired level of confidence, and can be obtained from tables. Frequently-used values are

Confidence (per cent)	75	80	90	95	99
z	1·15	1·28	1·64	1·96	2·58

For example, the probability that the interval $\bar{x} - 1·64s/n^{1/2}$ to $\bar{x} + 1·64s/n^{1/2}$ embraces the true mean is 0·9, and we can be '90 per cent confident' that the true mean lies in this range.

When n is small, confidence limits may still be obtained in this way if a precise estimate of the population variance, σ^2, is already available, as it might be from a previous study. However, when the only estimate of σ^2 is s^2, the sample variance, then z must be replaced by Student's t. The quantity t is the deviation of the estimated mean from the population mean as a ratio of $s/n^{1/2}$, thus

$$t = \frac{\bar{x} - \mu}{s/n^{1/2}}. \qquad (4.6)$$

We cannot calculate t because we do not know μ, but the sampling distribution of t has been worked out, and values can be obtained from published tables for n up to 120. So, for example, to find the 90 per cent confidence limits for a mean estimate from a sample of size 10, we find the corresponding value of t with $n - 1 = 9$ degrees of freedom. It is 1·83, and confidence limits are therefore

$$\bar{x} - 1{\cdot}83s/10^{1/2} \quad \text{and} \quad \bar{x} + 1{\cdot}83s/10^{1/2}.$$

The question naturally arises: how small is 'small'? It has at least two aspects. The first concerns whether to use t instead of z. For n greater than about 60, z and t are so nearly equal that it is largely immaterial which is used. It is worth noting, however, that the t distribution holds exactly only when the individual values are normally distributed, though moderate departure from normality does not seriously affect it. The second aspect is that if the original population is not normally distributed, then the distribution of the sample mean might not be sufficiently close to normal to justify basing confidence limits on it. The sample must be large enough for probabilities calculated for the normal distribution to apply. There is no easy answer to this aspect of the question, but in most instances involving measurements on soil the problem can be avoided by applying a normalizing transformation to the original data beforehand.

In some instances only one confidence limit is of interest. For example, a mining company might sample the soil of an area with a view to ore extraction (for example bauxite for aluminium). There would be some critical concentration, say c, of the metal below which extraction would be uneconomic and above which extraction would be profitable. If the sample mean exceeded c, the company would wish to know the probability of the true mean exceeding this value. Thus it would calculate the value for z or t to satisfy

$$c = \bar{x} - zs_{\bar{x}} \quad \text{or} \quad c = \bar{x} - ts_{\bar{x}}, \tag{4.7}$$

and would determine from the appropriate table the corresponding level of confidence. If this exceeded 99 per cent it might proceed to extract. If not, then the company would probably carry out further sampling to increase the precision of the estimate. A public health authority, on the other hand, might be more interested in toxicity of a metal in soil. It too could have some critical level of metal that served as a warning light, though in this instance the authority would become increasingly alarmed the nearer the upper confidence limit approached the critical value.

Note that when calculating single confidence limits, the probability of the true mean lying beyond one limit is half that of its lying beyond both limits. Thus, in the example above with $n = 10$, the probability of the true mean being less than $\bar{x} - 1{\cdot}83(s^2/10)^{1/2}$ is 5 per cent.

Chi square and confidence limits of variance

In many investigations the mean values of the properties studied are clearly the important ones, and variances are of interest only in so far as they provide measures of confidence. In soil survey and classification the variances themselves are often of interest, and we then wish to know how precisely we have estimated them. The sampling distribution of variance is closely related to the theoretical distribution, known as the *chi square* (χ^2) distribution, which is introduced now.

Let $z_1, z_2, \ldots, z_m$ be m values drawn at random from a normally distributed population with a mean of zero and unit variance. The quantity χ^2 is then the sum of their squares, that is

$$\chi^2 = \sum_{i=1}^{m} z_i^2. \tag{4.8}$$

If sets of m values are drawn repeatedly and independently from such a population, then the values of χ^2 will be distributed in a characteristic way, the chi square distribution with m degrees of freedom. This distribution is continuous. Its shape depends only on the number of degrees of freedom, which is also the mean of the distribution. For a small number of degrees of freedom it is very skew: since it is a sum of squares it cannot be less than zero, and occasional large values of z, in absolute terms, give it a long upper tail. But as the number of degrees of freedom increases it becomes less skew. For m exceeding 30 the distribution of $(2\chi^2)^{1/2}$ is close to normal with a mean of $(2m-1)^{1/2}$ and variance of 1. The chi square distribution has many applications, and is tabulated in several standard texts.

The relation between the distribution of χ^2 and variance will be clear if we consider a sample of size n from a normal population with known mean μ and variance σ^2. Then

$$s^2 = \frac{1}{n} \sum_{i=1}^{n} (x_i - \mu)^2. \tag{4.9}$$

If we divide through by σ^2 we have

$$\frac{s^2}{\sigma^2} = \frac{1}{n} \sum_{i=1}^{n} \left(\frac{x_i - \mu}{\sigma} \right)^2 \tag{4.10}$$

The term in brackets is a random normal deviate, hence

$$s^2/\sigma^2 = \frac{1}{n}\chi^2$$

and

$$\chi^2 = \frac{ns^2}{\sigma^2} \tag{4.11}$$

with n degrees of freedom. Usually μ is estimated by $\bar{x}$ and s^2 is an estimate with $n-1$ degrees of freedom. In these circumstances

$$\frac{(n-1)s^2}{\sigma^2} = \chi^2. \tag{4.12}$$

This quantity is distributed as χ^2 with $n-1$ degrees of freedom, and we can use the expression to determine confidence limits for variances, provided the original population is normal.

The published chi square tables contain the values of χ^2 that are exceeded with given probabilities. Table IV of Fisher and Yates (1963), for example, lists χ^2 for fourteen probabilities P ranging from 0·99 to 0·001.

If we read values of χ^2 given for $P=0·95$ and $P=0·05$, the probability that a randomly chosen value lies between these two is 0·90, i.e. 0·95 – 0·05. If now we rearrange eqn. (4.12), we have

$$\sigma^2 = (n-1)s^2/\chi^2 \tag{4.13}$$

and by inserting the 0·95 and 0·05 values of χ^2, we obtain a 90 per cent confidence interval for σ^2 as

$$\frac{(n-1)s^2}{\chi^2_{0.05}} \leqslant \sigma^2 \leqslant \frac{(n-1)s^2}{\chi^2_{0.95}}. \tag{4.14}$$

Incidentally, since the mean value of χ^2 is equal to $n-1$, the number of degrees of freedom, eqn. (4.13) shows that s^2 is an unbiased estimator of σ^2.

As an example consider the pF values in Table 3.1 as a sample from the plot of land in which the instruments were inserted. The sample variance is 0·08297 and there are 26 degrees of freedom. The values of χ^2 at $P=0·05$ and $P=0·95$ are respectively 38·90 and 15·38. Ninety per cent confidence limits for σ^2 are therefore

$$26 \times 0·08297/38·90 = 0·0554$$

and

$$26 \times 0·08297/15·38 = 0·1402.$$

Their square roots are the corresponding limits for the standard deviation; thus with $s = 0.29$, σ lies between 0·235 and 0·374 unless we have been unlucky enough to obtain a sample with unusually small or unusually large variance, the chances of which are one in ten.

The standard error in planning

When planning a survey an investigator naturally wants to know what effort is likely to be required – how big a sample should he take? When he wants to estimate the mean value (or total value) of some soil character the above methods can often help. The investigator must make two decisions. He must decide what degree of confidence he wishes to place in the estimate, and how wide a confidence interval he can tolerate. He also needs a prior estimate of the population variance σ^2. Assume that the investigator is happy with a 90 per cent level of confidence and sets limits l on either side of the mean. Then

$$l = 1.64\sigma/n^{1/2}, \tag{4.15}$$

which can be solved to find n. Often his estimate of σ^2 is little better than a guess, so no great accuracy can be expected.

The relation between standard error and sampling effort is illustrated in Fig. 5.1. Precision can be increased substantially by modest increases in the size of small samples. But once the sample size is more than ten to fifteen, the standard error declines very slowly in response to increases in sample size.

Area sampling schemes

Simple random sampling

Fig. 4.1 is an example of a simple random sample of 49 points. The coordinates of the points were taken from the first four columns of Fisher and Yates's (1963) table of random digits. The first pair of digits in each row identifies the x-coordinate and the second pair the y-coordinate for each point. Notice how the points seem to cluster, and that two parts of the area, bottom centre and in the upper half just right of centre, are comparatively sparsely sampled.

Uneven coverage often makes simple random sampling inefficient (in a sense to be explained later) for describing areas, and several techniques are available for choosing points more evenly.

Stratified random sampling

In this method the total area is divided into cells (they are usually squares, but can be elongated rectangles, triangles, or hexagons),

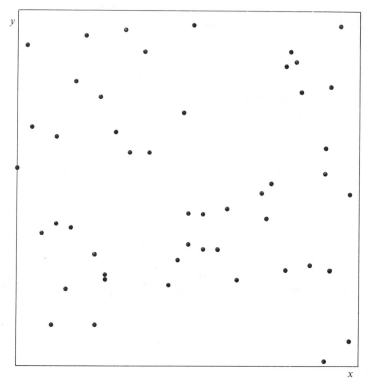

FIG. 4.1. A simple random sample of 49 points

within each of which one or more points are chosen at random. Each cell can be regarded as a stratum for sampling, and the method is one example of a more general technique known as *stratified* random sampling. Fig. 4.2 is an example with two points in each of 25 squares chosen using columns 1 for x and 3 for y from p.134 of Fisher and Yates's tables. Cover is still somewhat uneven. Several groups of points appear to be clustered, and there seems to be one substantial gap (just below centre).

Provided all cells are equal in area and contain the same number of sample points, the mean $\bar{x}$ of all observations estimates the population mean without bias, as before. However, the standard error is now

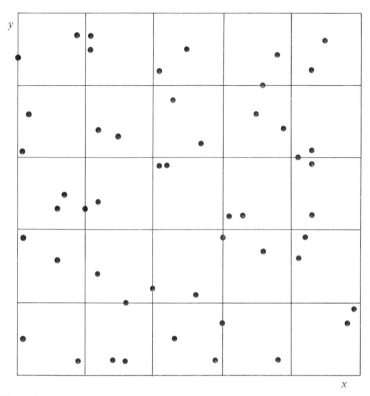

FIG. 4.2. A stratified random sample of 50 points with two points chosen randomly within each of 25 squares

estimated from the pooled within-cell variance according to

$$s_{\bar{x},\text{st}} = \frac{1}{h^{1/2}} \left(\frac{\sum\limits_{k=1}^{h} s_k^2}{n_k} \right)^{1/2} \qquad (4.16)$$

where h is the number of strata (cells), s_k^2 is the variance of n_k observations within each stratum, and the subscript $\bar{x}$, st refers to the mean of the stratified sample. There must be at least two points per cell to estimate it.

The term $(1/h) \sum\limits_{k=1}^{h} s_k^2$ represents the pooled variance *within cells*, which we may denote by s_w^2, and replaces s^2, the variance for the whole sample, in the formula for the standard error. Thus, the sampling error in a stratified sample derives solely from variation *within* the strata. Differences among strata make no contribution. Generally speaking, the smaller the area of land the less the soil varies within it. So when an area is divided into cells as above, s_w^2 is usually less than s^2, and $s_{\bar{x},\text{st}}$ is less than $s_{\bar{x}}$ for the same-sized sample. This represents a gain in precision that results from stratification, and may be expressed as $s_{\bar{x}}^2/s_{\bar{x},\text{st}}^2$, the *relative precision* of the method. It also means that fewer individuals are needed to achieve a given standard error by stratified sampling than would be required in a simple random sample. In this sense stratified sampling is the more efficient, and its efficiency may be expressed as $(n_{\text{random}}/n_{\text{stratified}})$.

Experience suggests that of the total variance of many soil properties in areas of 10 to 1000 ha, as much as a quarter, or even a half, can occur within a few square metres. Surveyors should therefore expect modest rather than dramatic gains in precision or efficiency from stratification.

Systematic sampling

Completely even coverage, and potentially greater efficiency, can be obtained by systematic sampling, in which sampling points are located at regular intervals on a grid, as in Fig. 4.3. Systematic samples are the easiest to select, and if the sampling grid is aligned with the map grid, they are the most easily located and indexed. The preparation of maps from the data is also easier from regular spaced observations than from irregular ones. However, as many statistical texts take pains to warn, there could be regular periodicities in the population. If these coincide with the period of the grid, or are some simple multiple or fraction of it, then dire results would surely follow. The risk of introducing bias in this way when sampling an orchard or plantation is clear. But the period of variation and its direction are equally obvious, and a grid can be chosen with quite unrelated spacing and orientation. A field that has been underdrained may possess a less obvious pattern, and systematic sampling of it could be hazardous. It is less often realized that if a systematic sample is small, with say 20 members, its period does not need to be at all closely tuned to the period of variation in the population or its harmonics for bias to occur. But when a survey extends over much larger areas than the single field, orchard, or plantation, and the sample is large, the taboo on systematic sampling seems quite unjustified. No regular soil variation with a period of more than a few tens of metres or of more than local extent has so far been identified. Bias can also occur when systematic sampling is applied to an area across which there is some general trend.

There is another disadvantage of systematic sampling. The method gives no entirely valid estimate of the sampling error, since the sampling points are not located at random within the strata. Nevertheless, there is considerable empirical evidence to show that systematic sampling is usually more precise than simple random sampling and comparable with stratified random sampling or even better. Theoretical studies by Yates (1948) and Quenouille (1949) support this experience in certain circumstances, and interested readers can follow the matter further in those papers. If an estimate of sampling error is required, the approximate methods given by Yates (1960) and Cochran (1963) should be adequate.

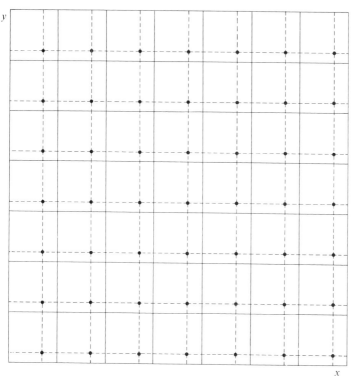

FIG. 4.3. A systematic sample of 49 points. The coordinates of one point are chosen at random; all others are at fixed intervals equal to the cell width in both horizontal and vertical directions

Clearly it is impossible to say categorically that systematic sampling should or should not be used in any or all circumstances. Each case should be judged on its merits. A wise course is to consult a sympathetic statistician when systematic sampling is being contemplated.

Unaligned sampling

Unaligned sampling or, to give its full name, *stratified systematic unaligned sampling*, combines the advantages of a regular grid and randomization. The sample is constructed by dividing the survey area first into cells (again usually square) by means of a coarse grid. A fine grid is superimposed on each cell in turn as a reference system. Starting in one of the còrner squares, say top left, a horizontal coordinate x and a vertical coordinate y are chosen randomly and the point located by means of the reference grid. The reference grid is moved to the next cell of the top row, the *horizontal* coordinate is retained but a new random value for y is chosen, and the point in this cell then located. The procedure is repeated for all remaining cells in the top row, keeping the x coordinate constant but choosing y afresh each time. For example, in Fig. 4.4, a square area is divided into 49 square cells. The reference grid for each cell is 10×10 with its origin at the bottom left corner. The x and y coordinates of the point in the top left cell are 0 and 4. The x coordinate of all cells in the top row is 0, but y changes along the row and has values 4, 7, 7, 5, ... Sample points are chosen similarly in the left hand column, but this time holding the vertical coordinate constant and varying x. In Fig. 4.4 $y = 4$ and x is 0, 9, 1, 1, ... The position of the point in each remaining square is then determined by the x coordinate of the point in the left-hand square of its row and the y coordinate of the point in the uppermost square in its column. There is thus a constant interval both along the rows and down the columns, and this ensures even coverage without alignment.

This method provides unbiased estimates of means. As with systematic sampling, there is no simple way of estimating the sampling error, though Quenouille (1949) and Das (1950) have shown that unaligned sampling can be more precise than either stratified random or regular grid sampling in some circumstances.

Unequal sampling

In the methods described above all points initially have equal probability of being chosen. However, if one part of an area is known beforehand to be more variable than the rest, then intuitively it makes

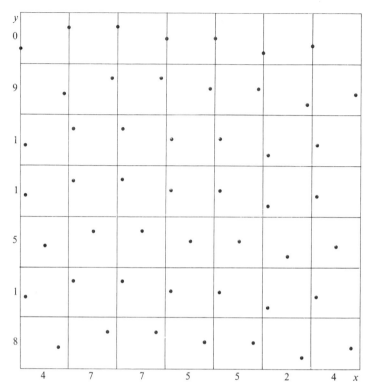

FIG. 4.4. An unaligned sample. The horizontal coordinate in each cell is constant for any one row and is given in the left-hand margin. The vertical coordinate is constant for any one column as is given along the bottom of the figure

sense to give this part more attention. The corollary is even more evident: to sample a seemingly uniform and endless plain at the same intensity as would be needed for an area of intricately dissected and contrasting sediments makes no sense. Clearly it is desirable to be able to vary the sampling intensity. This can be done, retaining all the advantages that probability sampling confers, provided that the different probabilities of selection are known for each part of the area. This is another case of stratified sampling. In Chapter 5 we shall discuss other kinds and uses of stratification.

Suppose we divide an area on its visual appearance (or geology or relief, or some combination of these) into several strata, $k = 1, 2, \ldots, h$ which we sample with different intensities. To combine data from several strata we assign a weight w_k to each stratum such that

$$w_k = \frac{\text{area of stratum } k}{\text{total area}}$$

Then the mean $\bar{x}$, for the whole area is given by

$$\bar{x} = \sum_{k=1}^{h} w_k \bar{x}_k \tag{4.17}$$

where $\bar{x}_k$ is the mean for the kth stratum. Its standard error is given by

$$s_{\bar{x},\text{st}} = \left(\sum_{k=1}^{h} \frac{w_k^2 s_k^2}{n_k} \right)^{1/2} \tag{4.18}$$

where s_k^2 is the variance and n_k the number of sample points in the kth stratum.

Sampling for proportions

A sample survey can often be undertaken to determine the proportion or amount of land in a region that possesses some attribute or belongs to some particular class of soil. For example, what proportion of the soil is calcareous or how much land is suitable for irrigation, or for growing wheat, or whatever is of interest? Answers to questions of this kind are especially important in economic planning. They can be answered by a sample survey, provided, of course, that for each sampling point the surveyor can decide whether the soil possesses the attribute of interest.

Let us assume that an area has been sampled at random, n sites have been recorded, and a sites possess some attribute X. Then $p = a/n$ is the proportion of observed sites possessing X, and this is an unbiased estimate of the proportion, P, of the area possessing X. We shall define $Q = 1 - P$ as the proportion lacking X, and $q = 1 - p$ as its sampling estimate.

Since we can regard an attribute as a variable that takes only the values 1 (when the attribute is present) and 0 (when it is absent) the proportion p is equivalent to the sample mean

$$p = \frac{a}{n} = \frac{1}{n} \sum_{i=1}^{n} x_i = \bar{x}. \tag{4.19}$$

It can then be shown algebraically that the variance of p is PQ/n, and its estimate is

$$s_p^2 = \frac{pq}{n-1}. \tag{4.20}$$

Its standard error is therefore s_p.

Cochran (1963) points out that the variance of a proportion is usually given as pq/n, but that this is biased. However, as we shall see, n usually needs to be large and so the difference between results calculated by the two formulae is then so small that it can safely be ignored.

Binomial distribution

When samples of size n are drawn from a population in which the proportion possessing a given attribute is P, the probability $\Pr_a$ of obtaining any given number of individuals a possessing the attribute can be calculated as

$$\Pr_a = \frac{n!}{a!(n-a)!} P^a Q^{n-a}. \tag{4.21}$$

The probabilities for all possible values of a are the successive terms in the expansion of $(P + Q)^n$, in which the first part of each is the familiar binomial coefficient. The distribution of a, and therefore of p, is said to follow the *binomial distribution*.

Confidence limits

Confidence limits for P from sample evidence can be obtained by calculating the probabilities of each value of a from the above formula. Alternatively, the probabilities can be obtained from published tables (National Bureau of Standards 1950; Romig, 1952; Harvard Computation Laboratory 1955). Note that since a must be integral, the exact level of confidence cannot be chosen in advance.

If n is at all large, the method is cumbersome even when the probabilities are read from tables, and it is usual to determine approximate limits from the normal distribution instead. This gives limits for P as

$$p \pm \left\{ z \left(\frac{pq}{n-1} \right)^{1/2} + \frac{1}{2n} \right\}$$

where z is the normal deviate for the chosen probability. The normal distribution is continuous whereas the binomial distribution is not, and the term $1/2n$ represents a correction for continuity.

TABLE 4.1.

The smallest value of np and sample size for use of the normal approximation (from Cochran 1963)

p	np, or $nq = n(p-1)$, whichever is the smaller	n
0·5	15	30
0·4	20	50
0·3	24	80
0·2	40	200
0·1	60	600
0·05	70	1400

The central limit theorem guarantees good approximation to the normal distribution when n is large or when p is between about 0.3 and 0.7. Table 4.1, taken from Cochran (1963), indicates when the normal approximation may safely be used. It shows especially the importance of taking a large sample if P is near 0 or 1, when the binomial distribution is very skew.

When the normal approximation is likely to mislead, confidence limits can be calculated from the binomial distribution or read from Table VIII of Fisher and Yates (1963).

Size of sample for estimating proportions

We now come to a question of some importance when estimating proportions, namely how big a sample should we take? For a continuous variable, confidence limits were $l = \bar{x} \pm z\sigma/n^{1/2}$. Assuming that the normal approximation holds, the limits for a proportion are similarly

$$p \pm z \left(\frac{PQ}{n} \right)^{1/2} . \qquad (4.23)$$

As before, we decide our level of confidence, and hence z, and the degree of error we can tolerate. We do not know P, and initially have to make a guess. Having done so, we can then solve for n.

We now consider the consequences. Suppose that a very attractive dam site (from an engineering point of view) has been identified, and that water from the dam, if built, could irrigate some 2000 km^2 of land by gravity. Not all the land that it commands has soil that is suitable for irrigation, and the extent of suitable soil will decide whether building the dam would be a sound investment. So we need a fairly precise estimate of the area of irrigable soil in the region. The suitability of soil for irrigation is determined largely by characters such as its clay content, permeability, and exchangeable sodium. To measure these or to collect soil for laboratory analysis, sites must be visited. Sampling and laboratory analysis will be expensive, and we shall therefore wish to know the minimum number of sites to record to provide a reliable estimate of the extent of irrigable soil.

We start with the best prior estimate that we can obtain. Someone with a general knowledge of the region says that about 30 per cent of the soil is likely to be suitable, i.e. 60 000 ha. We then choose a tolerance and the probability that the true area lies within the chosen tolerance. Suppose our tolerance is 10 000 ha on either side of the estimate, i.e. confidence limits are 60 000 ha ± 10 000 ha, and that we accept a chance of 1 in 10 that the true area lies outside these limits. Thus our estimate of P, $\hat{P}$, is 0·3, $\hat{Q} = 1 - \hat{P} = 0·7$, the permitted error, l is 0·05, and z at the 90 per cent level is 1·64. Inserting these in eqn. (4.23) and rearranging, we have

$$n = \frac{z^2 \hat{P}\hat{Q}}{l^2} = \frac{1·64^2 \times 0·3 \times 0·7}{0·05^2} = 226.$$

This is a fairly substantial number. But a planner could well want more confidence in the result — say 95 per cent instead of 90 per cent. If so n would be 323. Or, if he wanted narrower confidence limits — say, ± 5000 ha — then 904 sites would need to be recorded.

Table 4.2 gives some examples of the size of sample required to

TABLE 4.2.

Size of sample required to estimate P within limits P ± 0·05 for three levels of confidence, calculated from the normal approximation

	n		
P or $(1 - P)$	80 per cent	90 per cent	95 per cent
0·5	164	269	384
0·4	157	258	368
0·3	136	226	323
0·2	(105)[†]	(172)	245
0·1	(59)	(97)	(139)
0·05	(31)	(71)	(101)

† Values in parentheses should be replaced by values from the binomial distribution

estimate P within limits $P \pm 0.05$ for different values of P and three levels of confidence. It shows how greater confidence can be bought by increased sampling, and also that a smaller sample will suffice to estimate P near 0 (or near 1) than is needed with P near 0·5 for the same tolerance. This is equivalent to stating that the standard error of p is largest when $P = Q$ (or $p = q$) and decreases as P approaches either 0 or 1. In fact, n varies in proportion to PQ, as is obvious from eqn. (4.23). If nothing is known about the size of P to start with, then setting $\hat{P} = 0.05$ will ensure an adequate sample size and, if P happens to be in the range 0·3 to 0·7, will not entail serious over-sampling.

When we want an estimate of an area, however, it is more appropriate to express our tolerance in terms of a percentage of the true value. A tolerance of $\pm 10\,000$ ha might be acceptable if the true area is about 60 000 ha. If the area were only 10 000 ha we should almost certainly regard the same confidence interval as too wide to be helpful, and would want the interval to be much smaller, perhaps 1000 to 2000 ha. Table 4.3 shows how expressing tolerance as a constant percentage of the true value affects sample size. Confidence limits are set as 10 per cent of the likely value on either side of the proportion. The sample size now depends not on PQ but on PQ/P^2, i.e. Q/P, and clearly rises dramatically as P decreases. A very large sample is needed to estimate the area of a scarce soil type with reasonable accuracy if it is chosen in a simple random fashion.

Here we note two points. A single observation of an attribute carries little information. It can take only one of two values, and this is partly why samples for estimating proportions must be so large.

TABLE 4.3.

Size of sample required to estimate P within limits $P \pm 0.1\,P$ for three levels of confidence, calculated from the normal approximation

P or (1 − P)	Confidence limits	n		
		80 per cent	90 per cent	95 per cent
0·5	± 0.05	164	269	384
0·4	± 0.04	245	331	576
0·3	± 0.03	382	627	896
0·2	± 0.02	655	1075	1536
0·1	± 0.01	1474	2420	3456
0·05	± 0.005	3112	5109	7296

Second, it clearly pays to have good prior estimates of the proportions of land possessing the attributes of interest when attempting to determine areas. A sample survey designed to estimate the area of a soil type covering 10 per cent of a region could cost several times too much if the type turned out to cover 30 per cent.

Increasing efficiency

Sampling for attributes can often be made more efficient, and therefore less costly, by using one of the alternatives to simple random sampling described earlier. We saw that several sampling designs in which the sample points were more evenly spread gave more precise estimates of means of continuous variables than simple random sampling. The same applies to estimates of proportions.

We shall consider first the advantages of stratified random sampling. In the simplest case we divide the region to be sampled into square cells by a grid, randomly choose an equal number of points in each cell, and observe whether each point possesses the attribute of interest, X. Using the same notation as before,

$$p = a/n \tag{4.24}$$

is an unbiased estimate of P, and if in the kth cell a_k points out of n_k possess the attribute, then

$$p_k = \frac{a_k}{n_k} \quad \text{and} \quad q_k = 1 - p_k \tag{4.25}$$

and

$$p = \frac{1}{h} \sum_{k=1}^{h} p_k = \frac{1}{h} \sum_{k=1}^{h} \frac{a_k}{n_k}. \tag{4.26}$$

The variance of p is, as before, a function of the variance within cells, and is estimated by

$$s_{p,\text{st}}^2 = \frac{1}{h^2} \sum_{k=1}^{h} \frac{p_k q_k}{n_k - 1} \tag{4.27}$$

and the standard error is its square root.

If the cells are not of equal area, then the formula becomes

$$s_{p,\text{st}}^2 = \sum_{k=1}^{h} w_k^2 \frac{p_k q_k}{n_k - 1} \tag{4.28}$$

where w_k is the ratio of the area of the kth stratum to the total area.

Within small cells the soil will tend to be all of one type, and either to possess the attribute everywhere or to lack it everywhere. Thus $p_k q_k$ is likely to be smaller for most cells than pq for the whole population, and as a result $s_{p,\text{st}}^2$ is likely to be smaller than s_p^2, the variance for the simple random case.

The early survey of soil and fruit in the Vale of Evesham (Osmond *et al.* 1949) provides an example. The report suggests that the best types of soil for all-round fruit production are the heavy, but not poorly drained, ones, namely the Worcester, Evesham, Chadbury, and Hipton Hill series. Assuming the soil series map to be correct, we can estimate the proportion of the region surveyed that is good for fruit growing and the area that it covers. The map was divided into 2 km × 2 km cells. Some 1 km² squares near the edge of the map were not included in the 4 km² squares, and were grouped into 4 km² cells of different shapes. Four points were then chosen at random in each cell, i.e. one point per km². The results were as follows

$$n = 344$$
$$a = 163$$
$$p = 0 \cdot 474,$$

i.e. 34 400 ha, of which 16 300 ha are estimated as good for fruit growing. The standard errors are

$$s_{p,\text{st}} = 0 \cdot 022$$
$$s_{\text{area,st}} = 760 \,\text{ha},$$

giving P and A and their 90 per cent confidence limits as

$$P = 0 \cdot 474 \pm 0 \cdot 036$$
$$A = 16\,300 \pm 1245 \,\text{ha}.$$

Had the same values of a and p been obtained from a simple random sample we should have had

$$s_p = 0 \cdot 027$$
$$s_{\text{area}} = 926 \,\text{ha},$$

with correspondingly wider confidence limits than those actually obtained.

Sampling was repeated with the map divided into cells 2 km × 1 km and two points chosen per cell. The results, summarized in Table 4.4,

TABLE 4.4

Estimated proportion and area, standard errors, and 90 per cent confidence limits for two stratified random samples of the Vale of Evesham

		Stratification	
		4 points/2 × 2 km²	2 points/1 × 2 km²
	Count	163	166
	Area, ha	16 300	16 600
	Proportion	0·474	0·483
Standard	proportion	0·022	0·021
Error	area, ha	760	712
90%	proportion	± 0·036	± 0·034
confidence			
limits	area, ha	± 1245	± 1168
Efficiency compared with			
	random	1·5	1·7

are very similar to those for the 4 km² cells. Both stratified samples represent modest improvement over simple random sampling for the same effort.

If we regard the standard error of 0·027 as acceptable we can determine roughly the extent to which sampling could be reduced by inserting $s = 0.027$ for the tolerance, l, in eqn. (4.28) and rearranging. Since $w_k = n_k/n$, the value of n is obtained from

$$n = \frac{1}{l^2} \sum_{k=1}^{h} w_k n_k \frac{p_k q_k}{n_k - 1}.$$

For the 2 km × 2 km strata this gives a sample size of 230, and for the 2 km × 1 km strata, 207, and efficiencies relative to simple random as approximately 1·5 and 1·7 respectively. These represent worthwhile savings. These estimates are somewhat optimistic, because with fewer sampling sites the cells would be bigger and the variances within them would therefore also tend to be larger. However, the difference between the variances within the 2 km² and 4 km² is small, and the estimates of efficiency are likely to be good enough for planning purposes.

Comparison of sampling designs was taken one stage further for the Vale of Evesham. The soil map was re-sampled using unaligned and and regular systematic schemes, and this was repeated eight times. The points in the unaligned design were chosen by random coordinates within the kilometre squares of the National Grid. A kilometre grid with a fresh random origin and orientation was laid over the map to obtain each systematic sample. The results are summarized in Table 4.5. They show that unaligned sampling is about three times as precise as the stratified random scheme for the same sampling effort, and that systematic sampling is about five times as precise. And, of course, both are even more precise than simple random sampling. The result for the systematic sampling agrees closely with that predicted by Yates (1948) from purely theoretical considerations. With the proviso already noted, we should expect comparable improvements in efficiency from these two sampling designs. For the record, we may note that sampling at 1 km intersections of the National Grid gave a count of 163: hardly an indication of bias.

TABLE 4.5

Estimated proportion and area, standard errors, and 90 per cent confidence limits for unaligned and systematic sampling of the Vale of Evesham

		Design	
		Unaligned	Systematic
Count		162·5	164·25
Area, ha	Average of eight	16 250	16 425
Proportion		0·472	0·477
Standard errors	Proportion	0·012	0·0093
	Area, ha	424	319
90% confidence limits	Proportion	± 0.020	± 0.015
	Area, ha	± 695	± 523

In a similar study carried out by Berry (1962), stratified sampling with only two observations per cell reduced the standard error much more than in this one. Berry also found that systematic and unaligned sampling performed better still. The improvement was comparable to that obtained in the Vale of Evesham.

Systematic or unaligned sampling will usually be the most efficient schemes for estimating proportions, and are recommended except where a precise estimate of sampling error is needed.

In the next chapter we discuss other forms of stratification that should increase efficiency still further.

5. Generalization, prediction, and classificatio

Classification is easy: it is
something you just do.
                    F.C. BAWDEN

The descriptive measures and sampling methods discussed in the last
two chapters enable us to generalize with confidence about a soil
population, whether a set of soil specimens or profiles or the soil of an
area. Thus, if we have measured the pH of the topsoil at 100 sites and
found that on average the pH is 5·6 and the standard deviation is 0·3
we can say that in general the soil at those sites is moderately acid.
Assuming normality, some 95 per cent of the observations fall within
2 standard deviations of the mean; i.e. in the range pH 5·0 to 6·2.
Provided the sites were chosen probabilistically from an area, we may
say the same about the soil of that area with considerable confidence.
With 100 sites the standard error of the mean is 0·03 pH units, giving
very narrow confidence limits. It is obviously useful to be able to
generalize in this way.

If, on the other hand, the observed pH ranged from 4·5 to 9·7 with
a mean of 7·0 and standard deviation of 2·0, it would be a good deal
less sensible to attempt to generalize. It is undoubtedly true that the
soil is neutral on average; but this hides the fact that an appreciable
proportion of the soil is acid, and a similar proportion alkaline, and
associated properties will be very different. In these circumstances some
division of the population is needed. Distinguishing just two classes,
acid and alkaline, might be enough to allow useful generalization.
Adding a third, say, neutral, could well allow generalization to be even
more useful.

Exactly the same philosophy applies in sampling the soil profile.
If the pH or other properties of interest are much the same all the way
down, then their values may be averaged for the profile. If they are not,
and, of course, there is often an important change in some property,
then values are best kept separate and averaged only for particular
horizons.

Prediction

Prediction in the context of soil survey usually means predicting
the state of the soil at some place or places where the soil has not

previously been observed and often where it cannot be observed for one reason or another. Since soil is continuous, and we can observe it, at least in depth, at only a finite number of sampling points, it is clearly important to be able to predict. The same techniques enable us to do this.

Suppose a soil property (a variable) has been measured at several randomly chosen sites in an area. If the variable has a symmetric distribution then the most likely value for any site is the mean value of the variable, and we may use the sample mean as its predictor without bias. Further, if the distribution is normal we can set confidence limits to our prediction. These limits are often termed *prediction limits* to distinguish them from the confidence limits of a parameter. Returning to our first pH illustration above, to predict the pH at some site that we had not measured we could say that its pH was more likely to be 5·6 than any other value and that the chances are 95 in 100 that its value lies in the range 5·0 to 6·2, i.e. $\bar{x} - 2\sigma$ to $\bar{x} + 2\sigma$. In general, symmetrical prediction limits on a prediction are $\bar{x} \pm z\sigma$ where z is the standard normal deviate corresponding to the confidence we choose, i.e. approximately 1·0 at 66 per cent, 1·28 at 80 per cent, 1·64 at 90 per cent, 1·96 at 95 per cent, and so on.

Often we are concerned with only one prediction limit, say a critical strength of the soil, and we wish to know the likelihood that the soil strength is less than this value. We can estimate this likelihood if we have a sample mean and know σ or have a precise estimate of it. The value of z corresponding to the critical value, c, is calculated as

$$z = \frac{|c - \bar{x}|}{\sigma} \tag{5.1}$$

and the probability of obtaining a value larger than or equal to z can be found from tables, e.g. Table III of Fisher and Yates (1963).

As mentioned in the last chapter, our value of the standard deviation is usually itself an estimate based on the sample, and so subject to error. Prediction limits are therefore wider than they would be if we knew σ precisely, especially when samples are small. So as before, we replace z by Student's t with the appropriate number of degrees of freedom. With samples larger than 60 there is little difference, but for smaller ones there is, and t should be used instead of z.

Consider now the second illustration where the mean and standard deviation are 7·0 and 2·0 respectively. Our best prediction of the pH is 7·0 but reasonable confidence intervals are wide. Thus, even at the

80 per cent level of confidence the lower and upper limits are approximately 4·4 and 9·6. Intervals as wide as this are clearly unhelpful. The interval must be narrowed to achieve worthwhile prediction, and this can often be done by classifying the soil.

In some instances the spread of values is not only large, but the frequency distribution of the variable of concern has more than one distinct peak. The population is then almost certainly heterogeneous. If it is some property of the soil that has been sampled, the sample almost certainly consists of a mixture of two or more soil types. The population cannot be represented adequately by a single mean, nor can knowledge of its standard deviation lead to confident prediction. Each type of soil needs separate recognition, usually with a separate estimate of its mean, and perhaps of its standard deviation.

So even when we measure soil properties instead of describing them qualitatively, soil classification can have an important role in generalization, prediction and, as we shall see later, estimation. In the remainder of this chapter we shall consider kinds of soil classification and how they enhance the value of the data or the efficiency of the survey.

Kinds of soil classification

Dissection

When a single soil property is all-important, classes of soil, each with strictly limited variation, can be created by dividing its range at certain fixed points. These critical values can either be determined by technological need or be chosen more arbitrarily at convenient points to achieve some desired number of groups. The process is often known as *dissection*. Dissection implies neither that the soil is hetereogeneous nor that the divisions are in any sense 'natural'. The only consideration is that the classification be useful for the purpose in hand.

An example arises when using alkaline soil, especially for irrigated agriculture. Ease of management and plant growth depend critically on the exchangeable sodium percentage (E.S.P.) of the soil; that is, the amount of exchangeable sodium as a proportion of all exchangeable cations. Soil with more than about 15 per cent E.S.P. readily deflocculates and is difficult to make and keep permeable. It needs ameliorative treatment before it can be used for agriculture. Soil with E.S.P. in the range 7·5 to 15 per cent is usable but needs careful management, and in particular, care is needed to ensure that its E.S.P. does not increase when irrigated. Where the E.S.P. is less than 7·5 per cent, sodium has no appreciable effect on the soil. The critical dissection values are thus 7·5 and 15 per cent.

Fertilizer recommendations are often based on measurements of the available nutrients in the soil. Relations between measurements and responses are rough, and there is little justification for having more than four or five levels of recommended treatment for any one crop, and sometimes no more than three – high, medium and low, corresponding to no fertilizer, a moderate dressing, and a heavy dressing. For example, Cooke (1975) divides the scale of soluble phosphorus (in parts per million) into four groups: < 5, $5-10$, $10-15$, and > 15, and indicates for each group suitable fertilizer dressings to grow cereal crops. The limits of each class are not critical, but are round numbers that conveniently divide the range.

If use of the soil depends largely on two or three properties, then classes can be created by dividing all their measurement scales at critical or convenient values.

When a soil survey is undertaken to divide land for different forms of use or management, or to resolve competing claims for its use several, many properties of the soil are perhaps recorded. All are thought to be relevant, but none are critical. The number of kinds of land use or management envisaged will normally be few, and it is convenient if the soil can similarly be classified into a few groups, but ones based on all the measurements. Clearly if every scale were divided, even into two, the number of groups would be unmanageable. Much effort has been devoted to the solution of this problem. It has involved the search for close relations between sets of variables in the hope that division on one scale might effectively divide others also. Until recently there was no generally satisfactory solution. The advent of computers stimulated research on this problem, and there are now numerical methods for classifying soil from such data without creating a plethora of groups and in ways that reflect relationships in the data and are generally useful. Several of these are described in later chapters.

General-purpose classification

Much soil classification is not at all like the above. At the local level soil is usually divided into classes intuitively, based on what the observer can see on the surface and in profile and any supplementary information that he might gain in the laboratory. The way the observer classifies soil can be influenced by what grows on the land and by relations apparent between soil and its environment. The scientist is here simply extending the layman's approach. The observer forms in his mind 'notional types', and as his experience grows these become his standards or nuclei around which classes grow. We may call the result 'typological' classification. Alternatively the observer might approach a new area or set of profiles with a fairly clear idea of the types he wishes to recognize, and attempt to divide the new soil into the same groups.

Classification based purely on intuition can be very fluid and is not easily communicated. Organizations with large staffs often feel the need to define standard classes using criteria that everyone can apply consistently. The classes might initially be recognized intuitively, but their definitions become explicit. Such classifications can be called 'definitional'. Classes are usually disjoint, and in a number of schemes soil profiles are grouped at different levels, or categories, in a hierarchical fashion like the Linnaean classification of plants and animals. The soil classification used by the Soil Survey Staff (1960) of the U.S. Department of Agriculture is the most meticulously defined of these. Others include those by Avery (1973) for England and Wales, and by Northcote (1971) for Australia.

Definitional classifications dissect the scales of the properties on which definition is based. But they rarely produce a disjoint division of the scales of other properties: there is almost always some overlap in the latter, and when used to predict these other properties, they present much the same problems as intuitive classifications.

Both intuitive and definitional classifications are often said to be 'natural', either because they take account of many properties of the soil, or because they divide the population at natural discontinuities in the soil, or because they are generally useful, or some combination of these. For much the same reasons they are also called *general-purpose classifications*. In this chapter we shall use this term for such classifications and shall distinguish them from dissection.

Horizons, profiles, and areas

Soil in the field is classified in three main ways: into horizons, into classes of profile, and into area parcels or groups of parcels. The recognition of A, B, C horizons or others without conventional labels is a classification of the soil in profile. Its aim is to enable the soil in part of the profile to be described more precisely than could the whole soil.

Likewise the soil of a region can be divided into parcels within any one of which the soil seems reasonably similar and different from its neighbours. Distant parcels that possess similar soil are grouped to form classes that are usually known as *mapping units*.

Both horizons in a profile and mapping units in an area are separated by boundaries in space. The classification of soil profiles is a little more abstract, in that profiles in the same group can be near or far away on the ground. Their proximity is immaterial in principle, though in practice classes of profile are often recognized because the particular range embraced happens to occur in sizeable tracts of country. Profile classification often derives from mapping exercises. In other instances attempts are made to delineate areas containing previously recognized types of profile. The mapping unit is then an attempt to display the extent of that particular class of profile. In either event there is a duality in the classification, and the same names or labels are usually given to classes of profile and to their corresponding classes of area. In general discussion the two kinds of class need not be distinguished. But in more critical work, especially that concerned with sampling and quantitative appraisal, the investigator must be quite clear which kind of classification he means.

General-purpose soil classifications are most obviously appropriate for resource inventories and surveys for multiple land use. The classes are intended to convey a wide variety of information. However, a similar approach is often taken for more specific purposes, and the reasons are primarily economic, and sometimes logistic. A few examples will make this clear.

1.   Much agricultural land in Britain can be or has been improved by underdraining to remove 'surface' water from impermeable soil. If a drainage engineer has measurements of the hydraulic conductivity of soil that needs draining, he can design a suitable drainage scheme for that soil. But because individual drainage schemes are small (only about 5 ha on average) and the likely economic benefits also small, the cost of measuring hydraulic conductivity (which is large) cannot usually be justified (Thomasson 1975). An economically feasible alternative is to classify the soil on its appearance and on cheap measurements, paying special regard to characters that seem related to hydraulic conductivity. Conductivity is determined at a few sites on each class of soil, and is predicted elsewhere according to the classes present.

2.   Establishing productive forest on land where there is none or planting with exotic species is expensive and takes a long time. It could be risky and potentially very wasteful to plant the whole of a large area without prior indication of the performance of the tree species to be used. Records of previous experience are therefore assembled. If these are insufficient to allow a firm decision, then trials are carried out on small sample areas. Provided the species are suitable for the climate,

their growth is likely to depend on the soil. So the results of experience and experiment are indexed according to the type on which they were obtained, and are used to forecast the performance of the same species on the same soil types elsewhere. The soil classification is again the means by which information from a few sites is extrapolated to many. The same philosophy is often applied to agricultural development. General soil survey is followed by field trials on representative sites of each soil type that is not obviously unsuitable, and these in turn are followed by land settlement or reorganization to produce crops on the kinds of soil on which they grew successfully in the trials.

3.   When land is accessible only with difficulty, either because it is remote or in the military context because it is held by an enemy, or when large areas must be covered by few staff, the assessment of soil conditions relies heavily on air-photo interpretation. In most instances interpretation involves first, a classification of the photo image into relatively homogeneous regions, and secondly, sampling on the ground at representative sites for each class of region. Soil conditions at inaccessible or unvisited sites are then predicted from the measurements made at sites of the same class. Photo interpretation has been especially successful in civil engineering for predicting the foundation qualities of soil for roads and airfields and for identifying construction materials.

The problem common to all three examples is this. The soil is known to vary too much for it all to be treated similarly. The properties that determine how it can be used are known – hydraulic conductivity, yield of timber, bearing strength, etc. – but they cannot be measured everywhere. Classification is seen as a solution whereby generalization and prediction are based on sample evidence for each class separately. Variation within any one class is, or is hoped to be, less than that in the whole population and small enough for generalization or prediction to be useful. Success depends on the extent to which this is so. We should note that the same criterion of success, namely utility for specific purposes, applies to any general-purpose classification. For although a person may create a classification that he intends to be generally useful, it is difficult to imagine a general-purpose user. Any individual user will usually have a specific interest to which a few specific soil properties relate.

Effects of classification: analysis of variance

Dissection clearly and predictably limits the range of the variable or variables concerned. Its effects on other variables are much less predictable. Similarly, though variation of some properties within classes of a general-purpose classification will be less than that in the population as a whole, the degree of variation is far from predictable. For other properties variation can be no less within classes than it is in the whole population. The variation present must be determined empirically.

Just as we measured the variance and standard deviation for whole soil populations, so we can for each class separately. Thus for a class i, sampled at n_i places with sample mean $\bar{x}_i$, the variance σ_i^2 is estimated by

$$s_i^2 = \frac{1}{n_i - 1} \sum_{j=1}^{n_i} (x_{ij} - \bar{x}_i)^2. \tag{5.2}$$

If s_i^2 is small enough, we can usefully generalize about that class and can use $\bar{x}_i$ as the class predictor with limits calculated from s_i.

Now, consciously or otherwise, when an investigator classifies soil at a particular level, he tends to create classes within which the degree of variation is much the same. Thus, all soil series recognized in a survey project, however much they differ in their mean values, might reasonably be expected to have approximately the same standard deviation of any one variable (transformed if necessary); experience bears this out. When this is so, we can obtain a precise estimate of the within-class standard deviation, σ_W, by pooling them. This is done by taking averages of the *variances*, weighted by their corresponding degrees of freedom, to give a pooled variance, from which the standard deviation is derived. For k classes this is precisely equivalent to:

$$s_W^2 = \frac{\sum\limits_{i=1}^{k} \sum\limits_{j=1}^{n_i} (x_{ij} - \bar{x}_i)^2}{\sum\limits_{i=1}^{k} (n_i - 1)}. \tag{5.3}$$

In addition to the total and within-class variances, σ_T^2 and σ_W^2, there is a third variance that is often of interest: it is the variance among class means. These three variances and the relations between them can be used to evaluate and compare classifications. Their estimates can all be obtained by *analysis of variance*, which is at once one of the most powerful and elegant techniques in statistics, and was developed by R.A. Fisher in the 1920s.

The basis of analysis of variance is that variances are additive, and that the total variance is the sum of variances from two or more independent sources. The aim of the analysis is to estimate these separately. We know already how to estimate the total variance and the pooled within-class variance, two of the quantities we need. Let us suppose that the classes do not differ with respect to the variable of interest. Then s_T^2 and s_W^2 both estimate the same population variance, $\sigma_T^2 = \sigma_W^2$. We can also obtain a third estimate of the variance from the sample means of each class. As we saw in the last chapter, each mean is an estimate of the population mean with a variance σ_T^2/n_i, where n_i is the number of observations in the ith class. So the sum of squares of deviations of the class means from the general mean, each multiplied by the sample size, and divided by the number of degrees of freedom, gives us our third estimate. Thus

$$B = \frac{1}{k-1} \sum_{i=1}^{k} n_i(\bar{x}_i - \bar{x})^2. \tag{5.4}$$

This is usually laid out as in Table 5.1.

If, however, the classes differ in their means μ_i, then σ_T^2 and σ_W^2 are not equal and B estimates σ_W^2 plus a contribution from the variation between classes. Put another way, the variance among the sample means,

$$V_B = \frac{1}{k-1} \sum_{i=1}^{k} (\bar{x}_i - \bar{x})^2,$$

TABLE 5.1
Analysis of variance

Source	Degrees of freedom	Sum of squares	Mean square
Between classes	$k-1$	$\sum_{i=1}^{k} n_i(\bar{x}_i - \bar{x})^2$	$\dfrac{1}{k-1} \sum_{i=1}^{k} n_i(\bar{x}_i - \bar{x})^2 = B$
Within classes	$N-k$	$\sum_{i=1}^{k}\sum_{j=1}^{n_i} (x_{ij} - \bar{x}_i)^2$	$\dfrac{1}{N-k} \sum_{i=1}^{k}\sum_{j=1}^{n_i} (x_{ij} - \bar{x})^2 = W = s_W^2$
Total	$N-1$	$\sum_{i=1}^{k}\sum_{j=1}^{n_i} (x_{ij} - \bar{x})^2$	$\dfrac{1}{N-1} \sum_{i=1}^{k}\sum_{j=1}^{n_i} (x_{ij} - \bar{x})^2 = T = s_T^2$

N is the total size of the sample
k is the number of classes, the ith class containing n_i observations
$\bar{x}$ is the mean for the whole sample
$\bar{x}_i$ is the mean for the ith class.
B, W, and T are convenient symbols for the three mean squares.

estimates the variance among the population means plus the sampling variances of the means, $s_W^2 n_i$. Thus if all n_i are equal $(n_i = n)$, then

$$V_B = s_B^2 + s_W^2/n$$

$$B = nV_B = ns_B^2 + s_W^2$$

and

$$s_B^2 = (B - s_W^2)/n. \qquad (5.5)$$

If the n_i are not equal, then n is replaced by n_0 (Snedecor and Cochran 1967), where

$$n_0 = \frac{1}{k-1} \left(N - \frac{\sum\limits_{i=1}^{k} n_i^2}{N} \right) \qquad (5.6)$$

and

$$s_B^2 = (B - s_W^2)/n_0 \qquad (5.7)$$

The meaning of s_B^2 is not always easy to appreciate, and in some instances is a matter for debate. It depends very much on the nature of the sampling in relation to the classification. Two distinct situations can be recognized.

Fixed effects

The first occurs when we have classified the soil in an area into several groups, every one of which is sampled. The aim is usually to estimate the means μ_i for each class $i = 1, 2, \ldots, k$. The deviations between the group means and the general means are fixed quantities, and though s_B^2 estimates, $\dfrac{1}{k-1} \sum\limits_{i=1}^{k} (\mu_i - \mu)^2$, it is not usually of much interest.

Random effects

In studies of classification and sampling schemes individual classes are not of prime interest. Schemes are devised so that replicate samples are obtained for some classes, but it is largely immaterial which. The actual classes included depend on chance, and the differences between the class means and the general mean, $\mu_i - \mu$, are subject to random variation. In this event s_B^2 estimates the variance among a larger population of means, usually denoted by σ_B^2 and termed a *component of variance*, and is of considerable interest.

Intraclass correlation

The size of σ_B^2 in relation to σ_W^2 can be used as a measure of the effectiveness of a classification. The relation can be expressed as the intraclass correlation ρ_i, defined as

$$\rho_i = \frac{\sigma_B^2}{\sigma_W^2 + \sigma_B^2},$$ (5.8)

and estimated by

$$r_i = \frac{s_B^2}{s_W^2 + s_B^2} = \frac{B - s_W^2}{B + (n-1)s_W^2}.$$

The last expression enables r_i to be calculated swiftly from the analysis of variance table. The term derives its name from the fact that it expresses the 'correlation' among the individuals within the same class.

Clearly, r_i has a theoretical maximum value of 1 when each class is uniform ($s_W^2 = 0$). In practice, there is always some variation within classes in a measured variable, so r_i never actually attains 1. The minimum value of r_i is more problematic. The minimum value of σ_B^2, and hence of ρ_i, is zero. However, their sampling estimates s_B^2 and r_i are often negative, and this disconcerts investigators. In the analysis of variance it appears as $B < W$, and in soil survey the cause is simply sampling error in situations where the differences between classes are small.

A simpler but closely related way of expressing the effect of classification is by the ratio s_W^2/s_T^2, sometimes called the *relative variance*. Its complement, $1 - s_W^2/s_T^2$, can be regarded as the proportion of variance accounted for by classification. When both the total sample size and the number of groups are large, its value is very similar to that of r_i.

Example

Some years ago the Royal Engineers wished to know whether classifying soil or land according to features visible on photographs would improve their ability to predict engineering properties of soil. This example is drawn from a study of the situation (Beckett and Webster 1965a, b). The land in south central England had been classified largely on its air-photo appearance. Seventeen of the classes were sampled by choosing sites within each class in as nearly random a way as circumstances would allow. Several soil properties were then measured at each site. The following is the analysis of variance for the plastic limit of the soil at 5 inches (13 cm) taken from a single 10 cm auger core at each site.

The mean plastic limit for the region was estimated as 38·1 with a variance per site of 245·7 and hence a standard deviation of 15·7. Confidence limits for prediction are somewhat wide. The variance was then partitioned for the classification, and details are given in Table 5.2. The F ratio is well in excess of that at the 0·001 level of probability, and we conclude that there are highly significant differences between classes. Table 5.3 gives the means. Classes 9.1 and 9.2, river flood plains, have organic-rich soil with the largest values; classes 12, 13.1, and 13.2 lie on the Corallian formation with predominantly sandy soil and the lowest plastic limits. Confidence limits for prediction are obtained for each class from the class mean and the pooled within-class standard deviation, which is 11·5.

The estimate of the between-classes component of variance is 121·1, and intraclass correlation is therefore

$$r_i = \frac{121 \cdot 1}{121 \cdot 1 + 132 \cdot 4} = 0 \cdot 477.$$

This compares with the simple estimate of variance accounted for,

$$1 - s_W^2 / s_T^2 = 0 \cdot 461.$$

This is a fairly typical result. About half the variance in the physical properties of soil in a region can be attributed to differences between

TABLE 5.2
Analysis of variance for the plastic limit at 5 inches

Source	Degrees of freedom	Sum of squares	Mean square	F
Between classes	16	15 837	989·8	7·48
Within classes	105	13 900	132·4	
Total	121	29 737	245·7	

TABLE 5.3
Sample size and mean plastic limit for 17 classes

Class	Sample size	Mean	Class	Sample size	Mean	Class	Sample size	Mean
1	6	27·0	8·2	6	38·0	13·1	5	23·6
2	8	36·4	8·3	11	44·1	13·2	4	19·8
3	6	26·3	9·1	6	67·9	13·3	11	33·9
4	17	32·8	9·2	6	60·5	14	3	29·0
5	10	41·5	10	6	36·3	15	6	39·7
8·1	7	51·9	12	4	25·0			

TABLE 5.4
Means, $\bar{x}$, within-class variance, s_W^2, and intraclass correlations,
r_i, of topsoil properties for a classification of 1000 km^2
in south central England

Property	$\bar{x}$	s_W^2	r_i
Clay (%)	37·2	90·2	0·61
Mean matric suction in summer (pF$_1$)	2·66	0·07176	0·66
Mean matric suction in winter (pF$_1$)	1·82	0·00402	0·61
Mean soil strength in winter (cone index)	138	510	0·70
Liquid limit (%)	68·0	309·8	0·48
Organic matter (%)	9·8	9·48	0·28
pH	7·09	0·326	0·33
Available P (%)	0·031	0·00114	0·09
Available K (%)	0·013	0·0000939	0·06

classes in a fairly simple classification of soil based on profile appearance, physiography, or geology. A few other results from the same study originally reported by Webster and Beckett (1968) are given in Table 5.4. Experience suggests that chemical properties are less easily differentiated by such simple classifications, and that between-class components of variance are likely to be only about one tenth of the total variance.

The example has another feature that is not obvious but could be important. One aim of the survey was to obtain a reasonably precise estimate of the mean for each class sampled, and in the context of the survey all classes were equally important, whatever their extent. From the air-photo analysis and prior field work, it seemed that some of the classes were more variable than others. These classes also happened to include the ones of smallest extent, the spring lines (class 2) and small valley floors (classes 8.1, 8.2, and 8.3), in addition to the river flood plains (classes 9.1 and 9.2). Further, to obtain good estimates of their class means, some of these very variable classes were sampled more than the more uniform ones. These variable classes therefore contribute disproportionately to the within-class variance in the above analysis, both because of their small extent and above-average sampling. If classes are represented more nearly in proportion to their extent, class 2 is eliminated and classes 8.1, 8.2, and 8.3 are represented by only two sites each. The total variance of the reduced sample remains much the same, but the within-class variance is substantially less and the intraclass correlation correspondingly larger, as follows:

total variance	253·7
within-class variance	99·32
between class component	167·5
intraclass correlation	0·63

Except in the classes mentioned that are more variable than average, the confidence intervals are narrower than would have been judged from the first analysis, since the within-class standard deviation is now 10·0.

Short cuts

The reader will note that the number of degrees of freedom (d.f.) between classes and the d.f. within classes add up to the total d.f.

$$(k - 1) + (N - k) = N - 1. \tag{5.10}$$

Likewise the entries in the sums of squares columns for between classes and within classes sum to the total. This can provide a useful check on the arithmetic. However, when computing is done on a desk calculator, normal practice is to calculate the sums of squares for the total and between classes and to derive the within-class sum of squares as the difference. This saves time.

It is also easily shown that

$$\sum_{i=1}^{k} \sum_{j=1}^{n_i} (x_{ij} - \bar{x})^2 = \sum_{i=1}^{k} \sum_{j=1}^{n_i} x_{ij}^2 - \frac{1}{N} \left(\sum_{i=1}^{k} \sum_{j=1}^{n_i} x_{ij} \right)^2 \tag{5.11}$$

and

$$\sum_{i=1}^{k} n_i (\bar{x}_i - \bar{x})^2 = \sum_{i=1}^{k} n_i \bar{x}_i^2 - \frac{1}{N} \left(\sum_{i=1}^{k} \sum_{j=1}^{n_i} x_{ij} \right)^2. \tag{5.12}$$

This enables further time to be saved, since deviations from the general mean no longer need to be calculated separately. They are taken into account in the second term on the right in the above equations. This term is known as the *correction for the mean.*

Many textbooks recommend these short cuts. However, there are two hazards. The first is that the investigator loses track of the meaning of the terms he is calculating. The very slickness of the computation blinds him. The second hazard is that the terms on the right-hand sides of eqns. (5.11) and (5.12) are often very large quantities with small differences between them. When the arithmetic is performed by computer these quantities can easily be rounded and large errors introduced into their differences (see Nelder 1975). These methods are therefore best avoided when using a computer.

Significance

We now come to an important and often mystifying aspect of analysis of variance, and of statistics generally, namely tests of significance.

In the last chapter we saw that sample estimates of a population mean μ were not all equal. They deviated more or less from μ. Provided sampling was unbiased, we regarded this as sampling error. When several samples are taken there is variation from sample to sample, and as we have seen this is measured by the between-classes mean square B in the analysis of variance. If the samples are drawn from different classes and the term B is larger than s_W^2, i.e. $s_B^2 > 0$, the question arises: how should we decide whether this result is a chance effect of sampling or a reflection of real differences between the classes? The problem is resolved by adopting a *null hypothesis*. We begin by assuming that all class means are the same – there are no differences among them, that $\sigma_B^2 = 0$ if we are dealing with random effects, and that if s_B^2 is larger than zero it represents sampling error. When s_B^2 is small this assumption is reasonable, but the larger s_B^2 is, the less reasonable the assumption becomes. Eventually we decide that it is too large to attribute to chance and that it represents real differences among the classes. We then reject the null hypothesis, and the differences between means are said to be *significant*. The criterion for deciding whether to accept or reject the null hypothesis is the ratio $F = B/W$ in the analysis of variance. Its sampling distribution was worked out, actually as $z = \log_e F^{1/2}$, by R.A. Fisher and is tabulated in many statistical textbooks. The calculated F is compared with the tabulated values for the same degrees of freedom, $k - 1$ and $N - k$, and the probability of obtaining that value of F or a larger value is thereby obtained. Convention is to regard an F ratio or value of s_B^2 as significant if the probability P of its occurring by chance were less than 0·05. An investigator who feels this is too stringent a test may choose a somewhat larger value of P, say 0·1. If he does, he runs more risk of judging classes to differ when they do not. He may on the other hand choose a smaller value of P, say 0·01. In that event the risk of chance variation being regarded as real variation between classes is less, but real differences are less readily detected.

There are published tables of F values for probabilities 0·25, 0·1, 0·05, 0·025, 0·01, 0·005, and 0·001. The precise level of probability is to some extent a matter of choice, and in making that choice an investigator should consider the consequences of his judgment. Is it a matter of life or death, as it might be if a land-settlement scheme fails or a military convoy gets bogged? Or is it a situation in which a mistaken judgement could readily be corrected or recovery from ill-advised action fairly painless? The proper course in all cases is to report the probability associated with the estimate of σ_B^2 or the F ratio and number of degrees of freedom. The user of the information can then make his own judgement.

Even when a significance test is essential at the end of an investigation, and we quote the value of P, that is not the only important result. The class means, s_W^2, s_B^2, and r_i matter more. It is worth noting that when comparing recognizable classes of soil the null hypothesis is nearly always highly implausible — there are nearly always some differences in whatever property we happen to measure. So, however small and trivial such differences are, we can find them significant if we take a large enough sample.

Statistical method embraces many kinds of test for significance. The F ratio in the analysis of variance leads to just one. However, the feature common to all is that we have results for a sample, but wish to make inferences about a population. To do that the sample must be drawn without bias from the target population. If $s_B^2 > 0$ for a sample, then that is a fact: but the extension to the population, i.e. $\sigma_B^2 > 0$, is a matter of judgement. Life is uncertain, the real world an uncertain place, and significance testing is one of the means whereby we can make decisions against the background of uncertainty.

Homogeneity of variances

We noted earlier that classification at some particular level of generalization results in classes each having much the same variance. This is the intention. However, in an actual survey it is not always possible to achieve this. Even detailed maps of the soil of some areas show parcels of varying complexity. If the classes are not equally variable with respect to the property of interest it is as well that we know, since we shall wish to apply different confidence intervals to them.

Clearly we can sample each class and determine its variance. We shall obtain different values for each class, and as with the differences between means we may test for significance. If we have only two classes we calculate their variance ratio

$$F = s_1^2/s_2^2.$$

If s_2^2 is the larger variance, then we invert the expression. The resulting value of F is compared with those tabulated to find its probability. It should be noted that most published tables, e.g. Table V of Fisher and Yates (1963), are for 'one-tailed' tests. The probabilities given assume that we know in advance which variance is the larger. In the present situation where either σ_1^2 or σ_2^2 for which we have estimates may be the larger, the test is 'two-tailed', and the probability that $\sigma_1^2 \neq \sigma_2^2$ is double the published values.

With more than two classes we can use a test due to Bartlett (1937). We compute

$$M = \log_e s^2 - \sum_{i=1}^{k} (n_i - 1)\log_e s_i^2 \tag{5.13}$$

and

$$C = 1 + \frac{1}{3(k-1)} \left\{ \sum_{i=1}^{k} \frac{1}{n_i - 1} - \frac{1}{N - k} \right\} \tag{5.14}$$

The quantity M/C is distributed approximately as χ^2 with $k - 1$ degrees of freedom, and calculated values can readily be compared with those tabulated for the desired level of probability.

The F test for two variances and Bartlett's test are sensitive both to real differences of variance and to departures from normality. Analysis of variance is much more robust, and even when significant differences are found among variances, the investigator is often quite justified in proceeding with analysis of variance on the assumption that the variances are equal.

Estimation

When classification divides a population into classes within which variance is less than the variance in the population as a whole, we can use the classification to generalize more usefully and predict more precisely than we could otherwise. Nevertheless, we may still be concerned about a whole population. For example, we may wish to know the total amount of bauxite in a district, or the area of land suitable for irrigation. Classification can be helpful here too.

We saw in the last chapter that the standard error (s.e.) of a mean and its associated confidence intervals vary inversely as the square root of the sample size, n. In principle, therefore, we could reduce the s.e. to any desired level simply by increasing n. Fig. 5.1 shows that very large samples are needed to diminish the s.e. to much less than one fifth of the population standard deviation.

We also saw in Chapter 4 how to improve the precision of an estimate by stratifying a population. If an area was divided into cells and the soil

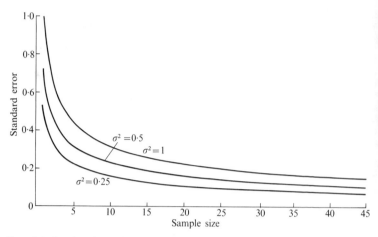

FIG. 5.1. Graphs of standard error for samples of varying size drawn from populations with variances of 1, 0·5, and 0·25

of each cell sampled separately the sampling error depended on the variation within the cells, which is generally less than that in the whole area. Sampling strata need not be regular cells, but can be created by any classification of soil. When the variation within such classes is less than in the population as a whole, population parameters can be estimated more precisely or more efficiently by sampling the classes independently. If, for example, the variance within strata is half that in the population as a whole then, other things being equal, the sample need be only half the size to achieve the same standard error. If simple division of an area into regular cells achieves this, then the advantage is pure gain. If, on the other hand, we have to make subsidiary observations of the soil or recognize and delineate soil boundaries, the effort involved must be set against the advantages of the resulting smaller variance.

In many instances investigators do not know what precision to aim for, nor can they forecast how effective a soil classification will be. They cannot easily decide what effort to commit either to classification or to sampling, and have to do what seems reasonable in the circumstances. Graphs like those in Fig. 5.1 are then useful aids. Assuming the population variance is 1, it might seem unreasonable to carry out expensive trials at 25 sites to reduce the standard error to 0·2, and so in the absence of other information an investigator might settle for s.e. = 0·29 from 12 sites. If with modest effort he could recognize soil classes within which the variance was 0·5, he might consider it worthwhile devoting that effort to classification and still sample at 12 sites to give a s.e. only slightly more than 0·2. If an estimate of the sampling error is to be obtained from the sample there should be some replication within the classes, of course. When sampling is dear and classification cheap, the options are represented mainly in the left of the figure. When sampling is cheap and classification dear attention should be focused on the upper graph but can extend to the right and beyond.

Experience to date suggests that the variances within the classes of a typical general-purpose soil classification of an area range from about half the total variance for physical and mechanical properties to less than one tenth for some chemical properties. It is unlikely that the within-class variance will be reduced to a quarter of the population variance without very substantial effort. Some attributes are closely associated with particular classes of soil; for example, some types of soil are well suited to agriculture, others quite unsuited. A survey intended to determine the proportion of land suitable for agriculture could be carried out efficiently after a preliminary stratification.

Is classification worthwhile?

We have seen some of the effects and potential advantages of classification and how to measure them. We have also noted that classification does not always confer advantages, and it will be salutary to end this chapter with some guidance for action.

First, the soil within classes must be less variable with respect to the properties of interest than in the whole population. Otherwise prediction can be no more precise and generalization no more useful than if no classification were made, and the classification is irrelevant.

Second, the classification must be easy and cheap to create or to use. If it costs more to identify the class of soil than to measure the soil property of·interest, then it is better to measure the soil directly than to attempt prediction.

Many situations are not clear cut. Classification allows somewhat better generalization, and somewhat more precise prediction and estimation. But the effort needed to classify or identify the soil is substantial, even though less than that required for direct measurement. The investigator must attempt to balance the costs of classification against the benefits that he can expect from it. If in doubt, he will probably do best to limit classification to the most obvious differences and to increase sampling as far as resources allow.

6. Nested classification and sampling

As I was going to St. Ives
I met a man with seven wives.
Each wife had seven sacks,
Each sack had seven cats,
Each cat had seven kits . . .
                    NURSERY RHYME

The partition of variance into that present within classes and that attributable to differences between classes is the simplest form of analysis of variance. It is quite possible with more complex sampling schemes to identify other sources of variation in a soil population, and to make use of the information gained to plan surveys efficiently. In this chapter we shall consider some of the possibilities offered by nested sampling designs.

Nested design

If a population is divided into several classes, and these are in turn divided into smaller classes, we have a *nested* or *hierarchical* classification with two levels. If we wish, we can subdivide further so that we have three or more levels. The classification at each level may be a formal level of a systematic classification scheme such as order, main group, subgroup, family, or series. Alternatively the levels might be soil type, district, farm, field; or more simply long-, medium-, and short-range separation. The important point is that in all cases we have small groups within bigger groups, etc; and that an individual observation belongs to one and only one group in each level.

If we now replicate sampling within the groups at the lowest level of subdivision we can by analysis of variance determine how variable classes are at each level, and what proportion of variance is contributed by each level.

Youden and Mehlich (1937) were among the first workers to apply this kind of analysis to soil survey, and we shall begin by studying one of their examples.

Variance in the Culvers gravelly silt loam

A soil survey of Broome County in New York State showed that a part of it was dominated by a particular type of soil, the Culvers gravelly

TABLE 6.1

Hierarchical sampling scheme for determining the pH of the Culvers gravelly silt loam

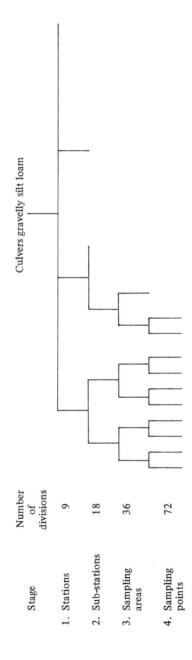

Stage	Number of divisions
1. Stations	9
2. Sub-stations	18
3. Sampling areas	36
4. Sampling points	72

silt loam. The surveyors wished to characterize the soil by laboratory determinations, and to sample in a way that would allow this and at the same time reveal any regional differences. They therefore devised the following scheme. They chose nine primary stations with approximately one mile (1·6 km) between adjacent stations. At each station two sub-stations were chosen 1000 feet (305 m) apart. At each sub-station two sampling areas were chosen 100 feet (30·5 m) apart, and in each area two points were located 10 feet (3·05 m) apart. There were thus $9 \times 2 \times 2 \times 2$ sampling points. Soil was taken from 0–6 inches (approx. 0–15 cm) at each sampling point and its pH determined. The sampling scheme is an example of *multi-stage sampling*, and it can be represented as a hierarchy (Table 6.1).

Each level in the hierarchy constitutes a stage and makes a contribution to the total variance. There are 71 degrees of freedom, $n - 1 = n_1 n_2 n_3 n_4 - 1$, and the immediate aim of analysis of variance is to apportion these properly and to calculate the sums of squares for each stage. The number of degrees of freedom (d.f.) between stations is straightforward: it is 8, i.e. $n_1 - 1$. There are 18 $(= n_1 n_2)$ sub-stations and therefore 17 d.f. However, differences between stations account for 8 of these, and there remain 9 d.f. for differences between sub-stations within stations (stage 2). In other words each pair of sub-stations contributes one degree of freedom from which to estimate the variance due to differences between sub-stations within stations. By similar reasoning there are 18 d.f. for differences between areas within sub-stations (stage 3), and 36 d.f. for differences between sampling points within areas (stage 4).

The entries in the sums of squares column are calculated without difficulty provided we are quite clear about the meaning of each. The total sum of squares is, as before, the sum of squares of deviations of individual observations from the general mean. Similarly the between-stations sum of squares is the sum of the squares of deviations of the station means from the general mean, each multiplied by the number of observations that make up the station mean. Entries for the intermediate stages are determined as follows. For each class at any given stage g, the difference between its mean and the mean of the class to which it belongs at the stage immediately above, $g - 1$, is squared and multiplied by the number of observations in that class. The sum of these values is the appropriate sum of squares. The computations are laid out in Table 6.2. As before, the sums of squares of the individual stages sum to the total sum of squares. Mean squares are obtained by dividing the

TABLE 6.2
Terms in the analysis of variance of four-stage sampling of Culvers gravelly silt loam

Source	Degrees of freedom	Sums of squares	Components of variance estimated by mean square
Stage 1 Between stations	$n_1 - 1$	$\sum_{i=1}^{n_1} n_2 n_3 n_4 (\bar{x}_i - \bar{x})^2$	$\sigma_4^2 + n_4 \sigma_3^2 + n_3 n_4 \sigma_2^2 + n_2 n_3 n_4 \sigma_1^2$
Stage 2 Between sub-stations within stations	$n_1(n_2 - 1)$	$\sum_{i=1}^{n_1} \sum_{j=1}^{n_2} n_3 n_4 (\bar{x}_{ij} - \bar{x}_i)^2$	$\sigma_4^2 + n_4 \sigma_3^2 + n_3 n_4 \sigma_2^2$
Stage 3 Between areas within sub-stations	$n_1 n_2 (n_3 - 1)$	$\sum_{i=1}^{n_1} \sum_{j=1}^{n_2} \sum_{k=1}^{n_3} n_4 (\bar{x}_{ijk} - \bar{x}_{ij})^2$	$\sigma_4^2 + n_4 \sigma_3^2$
Stage 4 Between sampling points within areas	$n_1 n_2 n_3 (n_4 - 1)$	$\sum_{i=1}^{n_1} \sum_{j=1}^{n_2} \sum_{k=1}^{n_3} \sum_{l=1}^{n_4} (x_{ijkl} - \bar{x}_{ijk})^2$	σ_4^2
Total	$n_1 n_2 n_3 n_4 - 1$	$\sum_{i=1}^{n_1} \sum_{j=1}^{n_2} \sum_{k=1}^{n_3} \sum_{l=1}^{n_4} (x_{ijkl} - \bar{x})^2$	

For each stage g, n_g is the number of subdivisions within each class of stage $g - 1$, and σ_g^2 is the component of variance. Group means at each stage are indicated by appropriate subscripts, and the general mean by $\bar{x}$. Note that in sampling the Culvers soil, the same number of subdivisions are made of every class at any one level. If classes are sampled unequally then the factors $n_2, n_3 n_4, n_3 n_4$ and n_4 in the sums of squares for stages 1, 2 and 3 are replaced by m_i, m_{ij} and m_{ijk}, the numbers of individual observation within the classes i, ij, and ijk respectively. Estimation of the components of variance is more complex (see text).

TABLE 6.3

Analysis of variance of pH at 0–15 cm in Culvers gravelly silt loam

Source	Degrees of freedom	Sum of squares	Mean square	F	Probability of obtaining this or larger value by chance
Stage 1 Between stations	8	2·753	0·3441	2·90	< 0·1
Stage 2 Between sub-stations within stations	9	1·067	0·1185	4·75	< 0·01
Stage 3 Between areas within sub-stations	18	0·4491	0·02495	1·79	< 0·1
Stage 4 Between sampling points with areas (residual)	36	0·5008	0·01391		
Total	71	4·770	0·06718		

sums of squares by the degrees of freedom, as before, and Table 6.2 gives the components of variance that they estimate. Notice that the mean square at any stage apart from the lowest contains a unique contribution from that stage, plus contributions from the components in all stages below. This enables each component to be estimated separately, and to be tested to judge whether it is larger than zero by computing the F ratio:

$$F = \frac{\text{mean square at stage } g}{\text{mean square at stage } g + 1}$$

The results of the analysis of pH of the Culvers soil are laid out in Table 6.3 and the components of variance listed in Table 6.4. They provide a useful picture of the way pH varies in this soil. The total variance is estimated by the sum of the components, i.e.

$$\hat{\sigma}_T^2 = s_1^2 + s_2^2 + s_3^2 + s_4^2. \tag{6.1}$$

Of these the largest is $s_1^2 = 0.02819$, the between-stations component. It accounts for almost 40 per cent of the total. The between-substations (1000 ft) component is the second largest, accounting for almost a third of the variance. The variance between sampling points at the 10 feet spacing is third largest (nearly 20 per cent of the total) and the variance contributed from the 100 feet spacing is least. The result is shown in Fig. 6.1, in which the variance is accumulated and

TABLE 6.4

Components of variance of pH at 0–15 cm in Culvers gravelly silt loam

Source	Component
Between stations	0·02819
Between sub-stations within stations	0·02340
Between areas within sub-stations	0·005518
Between points with areas (Residual)	0·01391

plotted against the logarithm of distance. The variance increases substantially as the distance between sampling points is increased. This seems entirely reasonable. However, this is not the pattern everywhere, and Fig. 6.2 (taken from a study by Webster and Butler (1976)) shows different patterns of change in an area of the Australian Capital Territory. A feature of some of the graphs is that the variance appears to converge on a finite value, not zero, as the separating distance approaches zero. This is partly because the graphs are drawn with distance represented logarithmically. Nevertheless this feature of sampling

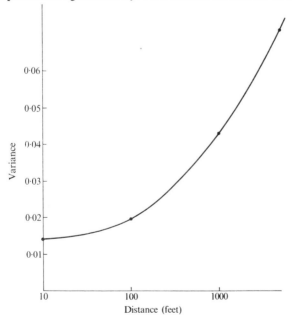

FIG. 6.1. Graph of variance in pH with varying distance for the Culvers gravelly silt loam

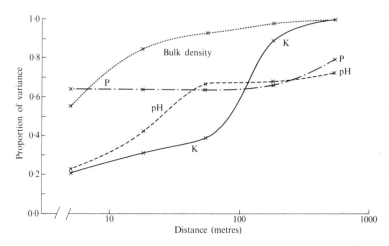

FIG. 6.2. Graphs of variance (as a proportion of the total) of bulk density, pH, available phosphorus (P), and potassium (K) at Ginninderra in the Australian Capital Territory (from Webster and Butler 1976)

often occurs in ore assessment and mineral exploration, where it is known as the *nugget effect*. It is difficult to imagine that adjacent cores of soil are not very similar indeed, yet the sampling evidence suggests that they are not. The true situation is hidden, and can be revealed only by sampling more closely.

On this sampling of the Culvers soil, the probabilities that σ_1^2 (between stations) and σ_3^2 (between areas) are zero are less than 10 per cent but greater than 5 per cent. The probability that $\sigma_2^2 = 0$ is less than 1 per cent. Note that the largest component is not the most significant because its test is based on the fewest degrees of freedom.

We now consider the precision with which pH was determined in the survey of the Culvers soil. The mean of each area (stage 3) was determined from two sampling points, so the variance of an area mean is estimated by

$$V_{\text{area}} = \frac{s_4^2}{2}. \tag{6.2}$$

The mean of a sub-station was determined from two area means, each composed of values from two sampling points. Its estimated variance is

$$V_{\text{sub-station}} = \frac{s_4^2}{2 \times 2} + \frac{s_3^2}{2} = \frac{s_4^2 + 2s_3^2}{4}. \tag{6.3}$$

By similar reasoning, the estimated variance of a station mean is

$$V_{station} = \frac{s_4^2}{2 \times 2 \times 2} + \frac{s_3^2}{2 \times 2} + \frac{s_2^2}{2} = \frac{s_4^2 + 2s_3^2 + 4s_2^2}{8}, \quad (6.4)$$

and the variance of the whole sample mean is

$$V_{\bar{x}} = \frac{s_4^2}{9 \times 2 \times 2 \times 2} + \frac{s_3^2}{9 \times 2 \times 2} + \frac{s_2^2}{9 \times 2} + \frac{s_1^2}{9}$$

$$= \frac{s_4^2 + 2s_3^2 + 4s_2^2 + 8s_1^2}{72}. \quad (6.5)$$

In words, the variance of a mean at any level in the hierarchy is equal to the mean square within that stage divided by the number of observations that go to make that mean. In particular, the estimated variance of the mean for the whole sample is the between-stations, i.e. within-population, mean square divided by the sample size.

The above formulae also enable us to consider the efficiency of the survey, and in this case to design a more efficient sampling scheme. If for any area we have four stages and know the component of variance for each, then the estimated variance of the mean for any sampling scheme based on those four stages will be

$$V_{\bar{x}} = \frac{\sigma_4^2}{n_1' n_2' n_3' n_4'} + \frac{\sigma_3^2}{n_1' n_2' n_3'} + \frac{\sigma_1^2}{n_1' n_2'} \quad (6.6)$$

where n_1', n_2', n_3', n_4' are the numbers of sub-units to be chosen for each class in the four stages 1, 2, 3, 4, respectively. It is clear that, other things being equal, we should increase the sampling at those stages where the contribution to the variance is the largest. In the case of the Culvers soil this should obviously be at the station stage, since our estimate of σ_1^2 is the largest. The variance estimated from the 72 sampling points was $0 \cdot 004779$, giving a standard error of $0 \cdot 069$, and this is presumably quite adequate when estimating the mean soil pH of an area. If we doubled the number of stations, i.e. let $n_1' = 18$, and did not replicate at the lower stages, i.e. let $n_2' = n_3' = n_4' = 1$, we should have

$$V_{\bar{x}}' = \frac{0 \cdot 0139 + 0 \cdot 005518 + 0 \cdot 02340 + 0 \cdot 02819}{18}$$

$$= 0 \cdot 003945$$

and standard error $0 \cdot 063$. Thus we could reduce the total sample size to a quarter and still improve the precision of our estimate of the mean pH. This comparison is not a strict one because if we increased the number of stations then either they would be closer together, or, if they remained at the same spacing, they would cover a larger area. In the first case σ_1^2 would be likely to be somewhat smaller, and in the second we might expect it to be somewhat larger.

Sampling costs and allocation of resources

In choosing the values of n_1', n_2', n_3', n_4' above, we made the proviso that only the variance components were of concern. In practice this is not always so: the cost of making the observations can also play an important role. To make this clear let us change the context. Suppose that the district being surveyed is not Broome County in New York, but an area of virgin rain forest, and suppose that the stations are a good deal more than one mile apart. The cost simply of reaching a station could then be very substantial, and much more than the cost of replicating observations once there. Similarly, if the survey involves lengthy interviews with farmers or land owners, the cost of interviewing could be considerably larger than the cost of making observations of the soil. In both cases a surveyor might reasonably wish to choose few stations or farms, and attempt to increase the precision of the survey by replication within stations or farms. However, it is by no means obvious how he should apportion his resources to best advantage. The following suggestion is substantially as given by Cochran (1963).

For simplicity we shall consider a situation in which there are two stages only, with n_1 first-stage groups and n_2 second-stage observations in each group. The estimated variance of the mean is

$$V_{\bar{x}} = \frac{s_2^2}{n_1 n_2} + \frac{s_1^2}{n_1}. \tag{6.7}$$

Suppose that we can divide the costs of survey into two parts as follows: c_1 is the average cost per first-stage group, consisting of all expenses that depend solely on the groups and excluding those that result from sub-sampling; c_2 is the average cost per second-stage unit that can be attributed to the sub-sampling alone. Suppose that we wish to sample the soil on a number of farms, which constitute the first-stage groups. Then c_1 would include the costs of selecting farms, travelling to them, interviewing farmers, obtaining permission for access and so on; whereas c_2 would include the costs of selecting the sampling points, reaching them from the farm house, field description, and laboratory analysis.

The cost of survey, C, will then be approximately

$$C = c_1 n_1 + c_2 n_1 n_2. \tag{6.8}$$

Provided we know c_1 and c_2 from prior experience, we can estimate what the total cost of the survey will be for any values of n_1 and n_2. However, the values of n_1 and n_2 depend on the components of variance and on the sampling error that we are prepared to tolerate. Alternatively, if the total budget of the survey is fixed, we shall want to adjust n_1 and n_2 to minimize the sampling error. Thus we may fix either the sampling variance V or the cost of survey C, but in either event we want to choose n_1 and n_2 so as to minimize the product VC in the expression

$$VC = \left\{ \frac{\sigma_1^2}{n_1} + \frac{\sigma_2^2}{n_1 n_2} \right\} (c_1 n_1 + c_2 n_1 n_2)$$

$$= \sigma_1^2 c_1 + \sigma_2^2 c_2 + n_2 \sigma_1^2 + \sigma_2^2 c_1 / n_2. \tag{6.9}$$

In a second form of this equation, n_1 is eliminated and the first two terms are constant. By calculus VC is found to be least when

$$n_2 = \left(\frac{\sigma_2^2 c_1}{\sigma_1^2 c_2} \right)^{1/2}. \tag{6.10}$$

The value of n_2 is determined by using the sampling estimates s_1^2 and s_2^2 in place of σ_1^2 and σ_2^2, and n_1 can then be found by inserting n_2 either in eqn. (6.7) or eqn. (6.8), depending on whether the variance or the cost is fixed.

In practice, n_2 must be integral and at least 1. Cochran gives the following rule for deciding how to round the calculated value of n_2. If the optimal value of n_2 lies between the integers m and $m + 1$ then choose $n_2 = m$ if $n_2^2 < m(m + 1)$, and $n_2 = m + 1$ otherwise.

Let us return now to the example of the Culvers soil, and consider a sampling scheme based on just two levels, stations and sub-stations. We have the following estimates of σ_1^2 and σ_2^2:

$$s_1^2 = 0.02819$$

$$s_2^2 = 0.04283.$$

The latter is the sum of the components at the three lower levels. The optimum value of n_2 is then

$$n_2 = 1.519 \left(\frac{c_1}{c_2} \right)^{1/2}.$$

Applying the above rule, we see that for ratios of c_1/c_2 less than 1·4 we choose $n_2 = 1$, for c_1/c_2 in the range 1·4 to 4·0 we choose $n_2 = 2$, and so on.

The analysis of costs can be extended readily to more than two levels if desired by

$$C = c_1 n_1 + c_2 n_2 n_1 + c_3 n_3 n_2 n_1 + \ldots \tag{6.11}$$

The product VC is minimized when

$$n_2 = \left(\frac{\sigma_2^2 c_1}{\sigma_1^2 c_2}\right)^{1/2}, \quad n_3 = \left(\frac{\sigma_3^2 c_2}{\sigma_2^2 c_3}\right)^{1/2}, \ldots, \tag{6.12}$$

and n_1 is found by substituting in the appropriate equation for variance or cost as before.

We should note again that if we change n_1, the component of variance σ_1^2 will probably change somewhat. This is unlikely to matter much: the analysis is usually worth making even with rough estimates of variances and costs, because a moderately wide range of ratios of both variances and costs yields the same integral value of n_2. Further, there is unlikely to be any serious loss in precision if n_2 is not quite optimal.

Cost of travel

One factor affecting the cost of soil survey is travel. In the earlier discussion it was included in c_1 as part of the cost of the first stage, and by implication directly proportional to the number of first-stage groups. In many situations this is reasonable. However, if a surveyor travels from one first-stage unit to another, the travel costs will be more nearly proportional to $n_1^{1/2}$. The cost of survey is then better expressed as

$$C = c_1 n_1 + c_T n_1^{1/2} + c_2 n_1 n_2 \tag{6.13}$$

where c_T is the average cost of travel to a first-stage group. If the maximum tolerable sampling error is given, then several pairs of values for n_1 and n_2 can be determined using eqn. (6.7) and their costs compared. When the cost is fixed a solution is more tiresome, but Hansen *et al.* (1953) describe how to determine suitable values of n_1 and n_2 and include a table as an aid.

Bulking

In multi-stage sampling the cost per unit, c_w, at the lowest level of sub-division depends very much on what is measured. If it is a character that can be assessed readily from an auger inspection, or a property such as the pH of the topsoil that is easily measured in the laboratory, then c_w will be small. Other chemical and physical properties of the soil are expensive to measure even though collecting the soil material from the field is cheap, so that in sum c_w is large. Examples include moisture characteristics, compression tests, the contents of some chemical elements, particle size analysis, etc. For properties measured on undisturbed soil material the costs of survey are determined as above. However, for properties that are determined on disturbed material costs can be cut, or precision increased by bulking.

The principle of bulking is simple. If n_w cores of soil are taken from some area A and each measured for property X, then the value of X in A is estimated by the sample mean $\bar{x}$, with variance σ_w^2/n_w. If, however, the soil from the n_w cores is thoroughly mixed and carefully sub-sampled for analysis in the laboratory, then X can be determined on the resultant mixture. For simple quantities like total contents of elements, calcium carbonate, particle sizes, and organic matter, the value obtained, say x', will equal the mean $\bar{x}$ apart from laboratory error, and the variance of x' will be σ_w^2/n_w. The latter is often approximately true even when the quantities are not obviously additive, for example available nutrients or pH.

Bulking means that σ_w^2 cannot be estimated from the sample, and implies that only $\bar{x}$ is of interest in area A. If A represents the minimum-sized management unit, say a field, then this is reasonable.

However, if there are many areas like A, representing subdivisions of a region, and we sample a small proportion of them, we can take the mean of the laboratory determinations as the mean for the soil of the region and obtain an estimate of its standard error. We recall that the estimated variance of a sample mean in multi-stage sampling is the mean square at the highest level divided by the total number of observations. If there are just two levels and the primary units are sampled equally, then the variance is

$$V_{\bar{x}} = \frac{1}{n_1 n_2} \frac{\sum_{i=1}^{n_1} n_2(\bar{x}_i - \bar{x})^2}{n_1 - 1}$$

$$= \frac{\sum_{i=1}^{n_1} (\bar{x}_i - \bar{x})^2}{n_1(n_1 - 1)}. \tag{6.14}$$

Thus, we need know only the primary unit means, $\bar{x}_i$, to obtain $V_{\bar{x}}$. This result can usefully be applied when soil is bulked within the primary units. We simply replace the means $\bar{x}_i$ by the values for the bulked soil x_i', so that

$$V_{\bar{x}} = \frac{\sum\limits_{i=1}^{n_i} (x_i' - \bar{x})^2}{n_1(n_1 - 1)}. \tag{6.15}$$

Also, we recall that

$$V_{\bar{x}} = \frac{s_2^2}{n_1 n_2} + \frac{s_1^2}{n_1} = \frac{1}{n_1}\left(\frac{s_2^2}{n_2} + s_1^2\right).$$

By increasing n_2 we can diminish the contribution to the variance made by the first term. Alternatively, we can achieve the same end by bulking. In fact if we bulk sufficient cores, s_2^2/n_2 can be made so small that it may be ignored. The variance of the bulked values about their mean then closely approximates the component of variance for the primary units:

$$\frac{\sum\limits_{i=1}^{n_1} (x_i' - \bar{x})^2}{n - 1} \triangleq s_1^2. \tag{6.16}$$

So by bulking enough cores within, say each field, the component of variance between fields can be estimated economically and with little bias. In the example of the Culvers soil where $s_2^2 = 0.04283$ at 1000 feet spacing and $s_1^2 = 0.02819$ at stations 1 mile apart, bulking twenty cores at each station would lead s_1^2 to be overestimated by about 7·5 per cent. If fifty cores were bulked the bias would be about 3 per cent. In most instances where soil is bulked the cost of collecting soil once on the site is very much smaller than the cost of laboratory procedure, and this degree of bulking is quite feasible. Of course, if an estimate of σ_2^2 is available, for example from a pilot study, then this can be included to improve the estimate of σ_1^2.

In assessing the cost of a sampling scheme that involves bulking care must be taken to assign the costs of laboratory analysis to the correct stage. If the region to be surveyed is divided into primary groups within which individual soil cores are bulked then the cost of laboratory analysis is borne by the primary groups alone. In the terms of the previous section it is embodied in c_1.

Finite population correction

In calculating sampling errors above we proceeded as though we were choosing a small sample from a large population of classes at every stage, and we ignored finite population corrections (f.p.c.). This is not always appropriate in soil survey. In the survey of the Culvers soil, for example, there could be some doubt concerning the number of possible stations at the one-mile spacing. However, if the sampling stages are represented by distinct areas, e.g. districts, farms, and fields, the numbers of divisions in each of the first two stages are finite, and the sampling fraction likely to be appreciable. In these circumstances it is wise to apply finite population corrections. We shall consider the matter here for two stages only.

Suppose that we can divide a survey area into N_1 primary regions (stage 1) of equal area, and we further divide each primary region into N_2 sub-regions. We might, for example divide a $100 \, \text{km}^2$ map sheet into one hundred $1 \, \text{km}^2$ squares and divide each $1 \, \text{km}^2$ square into one hundred $1 \, \text{ha}$ squares. We then randomly choose n_1 primary regions, and within each of those choose n_2 $1 \, \text{ha}$ squares. The f.p.c.s at the two stages are then

$$\text{stage 1} : \frac{N_1 - n_1}{N_1}$$

$$\text{stage 2} : \frac{N_2 - n_2}{N_2}.$$

If in the analysis of variance the mean squares are M_1 and $M_2 = s_2^2$ for stages 1 and 2 respectively, then the stage 1 component of variance is estimated as

$$s_1^2 = \frac{M_1}{n_2} - \frac{N_2 - n_2}{N_2} \frac{s_2^2}{n_2}. \tag{6.17}$$

The estimated variance of the mean for the whole area is

$$V_{\bar{x}} = \frac{N_1 - n_1}{N_1} \frac{s_1^2}{n_1} + \frac{N_2 - n_2}{N_2} \frac{s_2^2}{n_1 n_2}. \tag{6.18}$$

Comparable expressions can be applied if there are more than two stages. Hammond *et al.* (1958) describe several examples of sampling using f.p.c.s in a three-stage scheme in which the first two stages were area subdivisions. Incidentally, a very large proportion of the total variance of several soil properties within large fields was present within areas of a few square metres.

For most soil sampling the f.p.c. of the final stage will be very small. It is likely to be appreciable only for properties that are measured over areas, for example, the proportion of bare soil, or the proportion of the soil surface covered by stones.

We should notice two other extreme cases. If in two-stage sampling $n_1 = N_1$, i.e. if we sample every first-stage group, then the first term in eqn. (6.18) is zero, and the sampling error depends solely on s_2^2. The result is, in fact, stratified sampling with first-stage groups as strata. If $n_2 = N_2$ we should be recording the whole of each chosen primary group, so that we should have simple random sampling.

Unequal sampling

The pilot survey of the Culvers soil was carefully planned so as to lead to a tidy analysis. But soil surveyors do not always have that degree of control over their data. And even if they have, they may wish to vary the sampling from class to class. If some classes cover more ground than others, it is very reasonable that the more extensive classes are better represented in the sample. So either by chance or design sampling can be unequal. This leads to complications in estimation and interpretation. Here we shall consider only the analysis and estimation of variance components in situations where f.p.c. can be ignored.

The analysis of variance of a hierarchy of classes is much the same whether the classes in any one level are sampled equally or not. With n observations there are $n - 1$ d.f. The number of degrees of freedom at any stage in the hierarchy equals the number of classes at that stage less the number of classes at the stage above. The sums of squares are exactly as described on p. 92. However, the numbers of observations m in the classes at any one level are not all the same, and the factors $n_2 n_3 n_4$, $n_3 n_4$, and n_4 in Table 6.2 must be replaced by independently determined values m_i, m_{ij}, and m_{ijk}. Mean squares are calculated as usual. The general scheme is laid out in Table 6.5.

Table 6.5 also differs from Table 6.2 in the coefficients of the variance components. When all groups in each stage are sampled equally the coefficient of each component of variance in the expected mean squares is constant. So, for example, the coefficient of σ_3^2 was n_4 in stages 1, 2, and 3 in Table 6.2. When sampling is not equal the coefficients differ more or less. In Table 6.5 the corresponding coefficients are U_{13}, U_{23}, and U_{33} at stages 1, 2, and 3, and in general these are not equal. Similarly $U_{12} \neq U_{22}$ in general.

TABLE 6.5

Analysis of variance for hierarchical classification with four levels (stages)

Source	Degrees of freedom	Sums of squares	Estimated components in mean squares
Stage 1	$f_1 - 1$	$\sum\limits_{i=1}^{f_1} m_i(\bar{x}_i - \bar{x})^2$	$U_{11}\sigma_1^2 + U_{12}\sigma_2^2 + U_{13}\sigma_3^2 + \sigma_4^2$
Stage 2	$f_2 - f_1$	$\sum\limits_{i=1}^{f_1}\sum\limits_{j=1}^{n_i} m_{ij}(\bar{x}_{ij} - \bar{x}_i)^2$	$U_{22}\sigma_2^2 + U_{23}\sigma_3^2 + \sigma_4^2$
Stage 3	$f_3 - f_2$	$\sum\limits_{i=1}^{f_1}\sum\limits_{j=1}^{n_i}\sum\limits_{k=1}^{n_{ij}} m_{ijk}(\bar{x}_{ijk} - \bar{x}_{ij})^2$	$U_{33}\sigma_3^2 + \sigma_4^2$
Stage 4	$n - f_3$	$\sum\limits_{i=1}^{f_1}\sum\limits_{j=1}^{n_i}\sum\limits_{k=1}^{n_{ij}}\sum\limits_{l=1}^{n_{ijk}} (x_{ijkl} - \bar{x}_{ijk})^2$	σ_4^2
Total	$n - 1$	$\sum\limits_{i=1}^{n_i}\sum\limits_{k=1}^{n_k}\sum\limits_{l=1}^{n_1} (x_{ijkl} - \bar{x})^2$	

f_g is the number of classes at the gth stage

$n_i, n_{ij}, \ldots$ are the numbers of classes at the 2nd, 3rd, $\ldots$ stage in the ith, ijth, $\ldots$ class at the 1st, 2nd, $\ldots$ stages.

$m_i, m_{ij}, \ldots$ are the numbers of observations in the ith, ijth, $\ldots$ class at the 1st, 2nd, $\ldots$ stages.

King and Henderson (1954) describe thoroughly how the coefficients are derived, and Snedecor and Cochran (1967) give a recipe for computing based on a method due to Gower (1962). Both derivation and computing are somewhat lengthy, and readers should refer to the works mentioned for details.

One result of this is that the F ratio of the mean squares cannot be used to test whether $\sigma_1^2 = 0$ or $\sigma_2^2 = 0$. For example, if $U_{23} \neq U_{33}$ then

$$F = \frac{U_{22}s_2^2 + U_{23}s_3^2 + s_4^2}{U_{33}s_3^2 + s_4^2} \neq 1$$

even when $s_2^2 = 0$. Nevertheless, the quantities s_g^2, $g = 1, 2, \ldots$, are unbiased estimates of the corresponding population values. If for table 6.5 the calculated mean squares are M_1, M_2, M_3, M_4 for stages 1 to 4 respectively then

$$s_4^2 = M_4$$
$$s_3^2 = (M_3 - s_4^2)/U_{33}$$
$$s_2^2 = (M_2 - U_{23}s_3^2 - s_4^2)/U_{22}$$
$$s_1^2 = (M_1 - U_{12}s_2^2 - U_{13}s_3^2 - s_4^2)/U_{11}.$$

So although components of variance can be estimated, there are problems associated with unequal sampling and they should not be taken on lightly.

7. Relationships: an introduction to multivariate methods

We would never have learned anything if
we had never thought "This object resembles
this other, and I expect it to manifest the
same properties".

BERTRAND DE JOUVENEL

Chapters 3 to 6 dealt with the description, estimation, and prediction of properties of the soil of an area, taken one at a time. They showed how each could often be done better and survey carried out more economically if the soil were classified. The kind of classification considered was general purpose, often intuitive, with classes recognized on information quite other than actual data on the property of immediate interest. The effectiveness of classification was thus to some extent a matter of good fortune.

Soil can be classified more purposefully by measuring properties of interest and dividing the observations into groups according to the observed values. For single properties it is a simple matter to divide the measurement scale at critical or convenient points to achieve this, a process we called *dissection* in Chapter 5. The process can be extended to situations in which there are two or three properties simultaneously of interest. But as the number of properties increases the number of classes produced by dissecting each scale, even into two, increases exponentially and soon becomes unmanageable. If we wish to classify soil taking into account several or many properties, all of which vary, we have a problem. Traditionally it is the major problem in soil systematics, and it is to this problem that we now turn our attention.

Numerical methods have become feasible in recent years with the advent of computers. They all depend crucially on relationships, either between pairs of individual soil specimens, profiles or sites, or between pairs of different soil characters, or both. This chapter describes these basic relationships and how to measure them as a prelude to the chapters that follow on classification and ordination.

The scatter diagram

We begin with a graphic representation to help our understanding. Suppose that we have measured two soil characters at each of a number of sites, which for present purposes we shall consider to be the population. The population is said to be *bivariate*. We can represent the two characters by perpendicular axes on a graph. The axes define a two-dimensional space that we shall term a *character space*. Any individual can then be located in that space by rectangular coordinates equivalent to its observed values. Table 7.1 contains the values of the clay + silt content and plastic limit of topsoil measured at 40 randomly located sites in west Oxfordshire. The data are displayed in Fig. 7.1.

The graph, called a *scatter diagram*, shows how the 40 sites are distributed in the two dimensions and illustrates the relations between individuals. It also throws light on a quite new aspect – the relation between the characters. We consider these next.

Relations between variables

Examine Fig. 7.1. In general, sites with a large proportion of clay + silt also have large values of plastic limit, while those that have a small

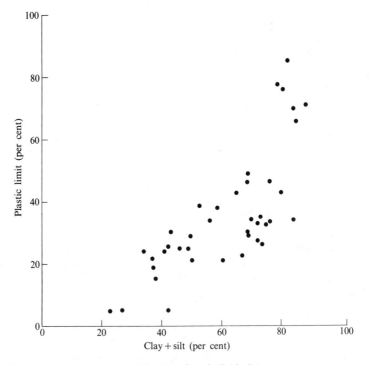

FIG. 7.1. A scatter diagram of the data given in Table 7.1

TABLE 7.1

The clay + silt (material < 0·06 mm diameter) and plastic limit of topsoil at 40 randomly located sites in west Oxfordshire

	Clay + silt (per cent)	Plastic limit (per cent)		Clay + silt (per cent)	Plastic limit (per cent)
1	48·7	25	21	66·6	22
2	49·4	29	22	75·6	46
3	41·0	24	23	78·5	78
4	73·8	26	24	88·9	71
5	84·3	34	25	84·2	70
6	73·0	35	26	69·7	49
7	74·7	33	27	81·7	86
8	58·4	38	28	37·6	22
9	68·2	46	29	23·5	5
10	68·2	30	30	42·3	25
11	72·1	27	31	26·2	5
12	76·5	33	32	36·9	19
13	68·9	30	33	50·6	21
14	72·1	33	34	34·1	24
15	85·6	66	35	70·5	34
16	42·9	5	36	56·4	34
17	80·6	76	37	46·8	25
18	53·8	39	38	65·2	43
19	80·6	43	39	42·9	30
20	60·4	21	40	39·0	16

proportion of clay + silt tend to have small values of the plastic limit. The two sets of measurements depend to some extent on one another; they *co-vary*. We can express the degree of their dependence by a quantity known as the *covariance*. Let the observed values of the two characters X_1 and X_2 on n individuals be $x_{11}x_{12}, x_{21}x_{22}, \ldots, x_{n1}x_{n2}$. Then the variance of X_1 and X_2 are, as before,

$$s_1^2 = \frac{1}{n-1} \sum_{i=1}^{n} (x_{i1} - \bar{x})^2 \qquad (7.1)$$

and

$$s_2^2 = \frac{1}{n-1} \sum_{i=1}^{n} (x_{i2} - \bar{x})^2. \qquad (7.2)$$

In addition the covariance is

$$c = \frac{1}{n-1} \{ \sum_{i=1}^{n} (x_{i1} - \bar{x}_1)(x_{i2} - \bar{x}_2) \} \qquad (7.3)$$

The expression in curly brackets in eqn. (7.3) is known as the *sum of products about the means.* It is clearly analogous to the sum of squares in the expression for the variance of a single variate (eqns. (7.1) and (7.2)).

The covariance c of the percentage of clay + silt and the plastic limit in Table 7.1 is 265·31. The value is difficult to interpret as the measure of relationship because it depends on the two variances and on the scales on which the characters are measured. However, it can be brought to a standard form if it is divided by the geometric mean of the variances, thus

$$r = \frac{c}{(s_1^2 s_2^2)^{1/2}}. \tag{7.4}$$

The c of Table 7.1 becomes

$$r = \frac{265 \cdot 31}{(322 \cdot 62 \times 386 \cdot 05)^{1/2}} = 0 \cdot 752.$$

The quantity r is known as the *product moment correlation coefficient* of the two variates, or usually just their *correlation coefficient*. The correlation of 0·75 between the clay + silt percentage and the plastic limit is moderate, as we shall see.

The correlation coefficient can neither exceed $+1$ nor be less than -1. If r is $+1$ then all the plotted points will lie on a straight line, conventionally rising from left to right (see Fig. 7.2a). If r is -1 then the points will lie on a straight line falling from left to right, as in Fig. 7.2b. In the first case the variates are said to be perfectly positively correlated, while in the second they are perfectly negatively correlated. If r is zero

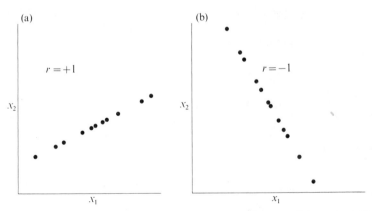

FIG. 7.2. Points that lie on a straight line have a correlation coefficient of $+1$ (a) or -1 (b)

there is no correlation. Perfect correlation is very rare in real populations of material like soil: actual values of r fall between these extremes.

Fig. 7.3 illustrates some intermediate values of r. The variances on the two axes have been made equal, so that if correlation were perfect the points would lie on a line at 45° to the axes, pecked in the figures. It can be seen that r measures the extent to which the points deviate from such a line. The more they deviate, the nearer is r to 0. The more closely they approximate to a straight line, the closer is r to 1 or -1.

Fig. 7.3d shows a configuration for which r is sensibly zero. The two variates do not depend on one another. However, $r = 0$ does not always mean that two variates are independent. The points could, for example, lie on a curve or close to two perpendicular straight lines. When we speak of two variates being uncorrelated strictly we mean only that they are not linearly related. It is always worth drawing a scatter diagram to check this.

If the variances on the two axes of a scatter diagram are not equal, then the angle towards which the configuration tends will not be a 45° bisector. This can be seen in Fig. 7.4 in which the same set of points is plotted with a fixed vertical scale but varying horizontal scale. The correlation coefficient, r, is 0.72. Fig. 7.4a shows the configuration on axes with equal variance. In Fig. 7.4b the horizontal scale has been halved, thereby reducing the variance s_1^2 to a quarter of its original value and the covariance c to a half. The horizontal scale is multiplied by 2·5 in Fig. 7.4c; the variance is multiplied by 6·25 and the covariance by 2·5. Thus by compressing and expanding the scale of measurement the configuration is alternatively compressed and stretched. It is worth noting here that if one or other axis of Fig. 7.3d were compressed the circular configuration of points would be compressed to an ellipse with two distinct principal axes, one almost vertical and the other almost horizontal. This is characteristic of uncorrelated variates.

Actual values of correlation coefficients

Numerous examples of the use of the correlation coefficient can be found in the literature of soil research. In most examples the nature of the investigations has been such that large coefficients could be expected. Published values of correlation coefficients between properties recorded in a routine survey (e.g. McKeague *et al.* 1971; Moore *et al.* 1972; Webster and Butler 1976) lie mainly in the range 0·3 to $-0·3$ and few exceed 0·5 in absolute value. It is likely that when two

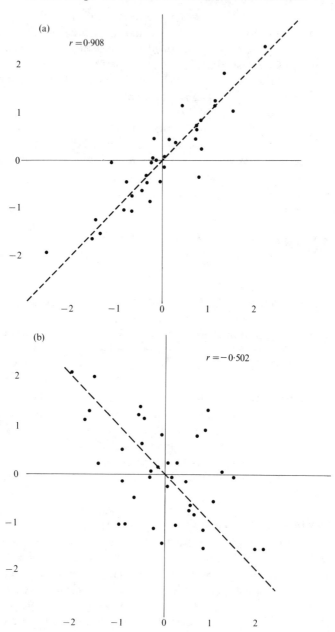

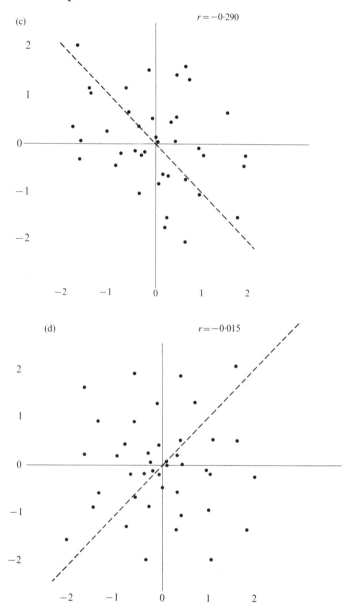

FIG. 7.3. Graphs showing scatter of points for a range of correlation coefficients. The variances are equal on both axes in all four graphs

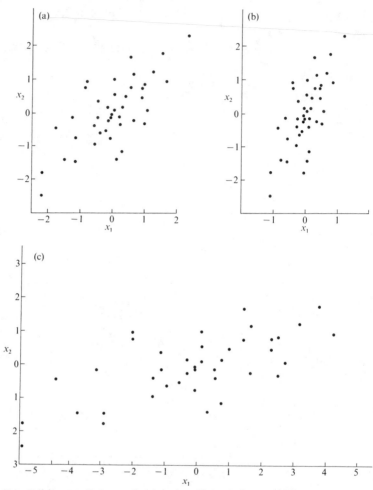

FIG. 7.4. Scatter diagrams showing the effect of change of measurement scale on a configuration of points. The correlation coefficient is 0·72

properties are strongly correlated only one of them is recorded. So neither view of correlation gives an entirely accurate picture of what to expect.

Estimation and significance

When a correlation coefficient is determined on data from a sample, then r is a sampling estimate of the correlation in the parent population, which is usually denoted by ρ. Since r is an estimate it is subject to sampling error, and if it is not equal to zero we might wish to know whether it reflects a real dependence between the variables in the whole population or is a sampling effect. The null hypothesis is that $\rho = 0$, and, assuming normality, can be tested by computing Student's t as

$$t = \frac{r(n-2)^{1/2}}{(1-r^2)^{1/2}} \tag{7.5}$$

where n is the number of individuals. The result is referred to the t table for $n-2$ degrees of freedom. If t exceeds that for the chosen level of probability then the null hypothesis is rejected; the correlation is significant. Inserting $r = 0.752$ and $n = 40$ for the data in Table 7.1 into this expression we have $t = 7.03$, a highly significant result.

Tables of r for several levels of probability and a range of degrees of freedom have been calculated and published (e.g. Fisher and Yates's table VII), and can be consulted directly.

The bivariate normal distribution

We have already seen something of the importance of the normal distribution in both theory and practice for single variables. The bivariate normal distribution, and its extension to situations in which more than two variables are of interest, is equally important in the understanding of 'classical' multivariate methods. We shall therefore explore it in some detail.

We saw that if for a single normally distributed variable we plotted the probability z as ordinate against the values of the variable x as abscissa, we obtained a curve resembling a cross section through a bell. When we have two variables X_1 and X_2 it is helpful to envisage a solid model whose base is defined by the variables on orthogonal axes x_1 and x_2 and the probability z represented vertically. The values of z lie on a curved surface shaped very like a bell (see Fig. 7.5). The equation of the surface is

$$z = \frac{1}{2\pi\sigma_1\sigma_2(1-\rho^2)^{1/2}} \times$$

$$\times \exp\left[-\left\{\frac{(x_1-\mu_1)^2}{\sigma_1^2} - \frac{2\rho(x_1-\mu_1)(x_2-\mu_2)}{\sigma_1\sigma_2} + \frac{(x_2-\mu_2)^2}{\sigma_2^2}\right\}/2(1-\rho^2)\right].$$

$$\tag{7.6}$$

It has five parameters:

$$\mu_1 = \text{the mean of } X_1,$$

$$\mu_2 = \text{the mean of } X_2,$$

$$\sigma_1 = \text{the standard deviation of } X_1,$$

$$\sigma_2 = \text{the standard deviation of } X_2,$$

and

$$\rho = \text{the correlation between } X_1 \text{ and } X_2.$$

The distribution has several interesting properties.

(a)   Its peak lies directly above the means μ_1 and μ_2.

(b)   The two variables X_1 and X_2 are themselves normally distributed, so that projections of the surface parallel to the x_2 and x_1 axes are normal curves with variances σ_1^2 and σ_2^2 on the planes x_1z and x_2z respectively.

(c)   Any vertical section through the surface has a normal distribution.

(d)   Any horizontal section is an ellipse, and is a 'contour' line of equal probability.

(e)   In the univariate case, the expression $(x - \mu)^2/\sigma^2$ in the exponent was distributed as χ^2. So here the expression in square brackets

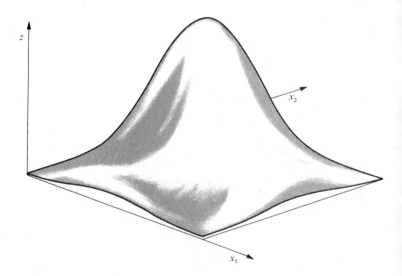

FIG. 7.5. Perspective view of a bivariate normal probability surface

is also distributed as χ^2, this time with two degrees of freedom. As we shall see, this enables us to choose probability contours to enclose any desired proportions of a population. Such contours are analogous to confidence limits in the univariate case. They also show geometrically the connection between correlation and regression, which has applications in many fields of investigation, but which we can touch on only very briefly.

In Fig. 7.6 three concentric ellipses have been drawn to represent the 50 per cent, 90 per cent, and 99 per cent limits of an infinite population which is assumed to be normal and from which the data in Table 7.1 are regarded as a sample. The axes have been moved so that the origin is at the centre of the ellipses.

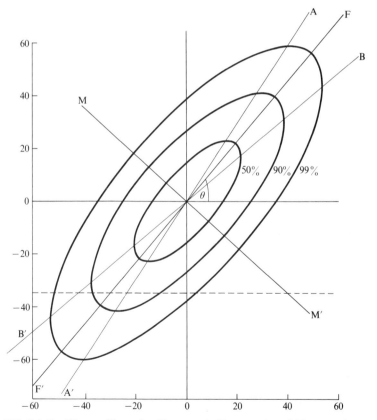

FIG. 7.6. Confidence ellipses for 50 per cent, 90 per cent, and 99 per cent probability for population represented in Fig. 7.1

The major and minor axes of the ellipses, also known as the principal axes, lie on the lines FF' and MM' respectively. The line AA' bisects all horizontal chords to the ellipses, and hence it joins the mean values of x_1 for each value of x_2, $x_{1.2}$. It cuts each ellipse where the tangent to the ellipse is horizontal. It is known as the line of regression of X_1 on X_2. Its equation, assuming the coordinates of the centre are $(0, 0)$, is

$$x_{1'} = b_1 x_2 \qquad (7.7)$$

where

$$b_1 = \rho \frac{\sigma_1}{\sigma_2}.$$

Similarly the line BB' is the regression line linking the mean values of x_2 for every value of x_1, $x_{2.1}$. It cuts the ellipses where their tangents are vertical, and its equation is

$$x_2 = b_2 x_1 \qquad (7.8)$$

where

$$b_2 = \rho \frac{\sigma_2}{\sigma_1}$$

The quantities b_1 and b_2 are known as regression coefficients.

Constructing confidence ellipses

Confidence ellipses aid our understanding of a bivariate population, and we should therefore be able to draw them. We can do so if we first determine the orientation and lengths of their principal axes. Principal axes are considered in detail algebraically in the next chapter. Here we shall anticipate a little, drawing especially on the geometric representation given there.

Orientation. Let the angle between the principal axes and the original axes be θ. In Chapter 8 (p.140) we see that any point with coordinates x_1, x_2 on the original axes can be referred to new axes rotated through an angle θ by two new coordinates y_1, y_2 which are

$$\left. \begin{array}{l} y_1 = x_1 \cos \theta + x_2 \sin \theta \\ y_2 = x_2 \cos \theta - x_1 \sin \theta \end{array} \right\} \qquad (7.9)$$

Now, as mentioned earlier, when the principal axes of a configuration of points coincide with the reference axes, there is no correlation between the variates. Thus, if we rotate the original axes to principal axes we obtain new variates that are uncorrelated. The sum of their products is therefore zero. So, by multiplying eqns. (7.9) for each point, summing and dividing by the number of degrees of freedom, we obtain

$$0 = (s_2^2 - s_1^2) \sin \theta \cos \theta + c (\cos^2\theta - \sin^2\theta)$$

$$= (s_2^2 - s_1^2) \frac{\sin 2\theta}{2} + rs_1s_2 \cos 2\theta \qquad (7.10)$$

where s_1^2, s_2^2, c, and r are the variances of X_1 and X_2 and their covariance and correlation coefficient respectively. The angle θ is then given by

$$\tan 2\theta = \frac{2rs_1s_2}{s_1^2 - s_2^2}. \qquad (7.11)$$

To find the orientation of the principal axes for the configuration shown in Fig. 7.1, we insert the values $s_1^2 = 322 \cdot 63$, $s_2^2 = 386 \cdot 05$, and $r = 0 \cdot 752$ into eqn. (7.11) to give

$$\tan 2\theta = -8 \cdot 362$$

and, taking due care with signs,

$$\theta = 48°24'.$$

Standard deviations. The lengths of the major and minor axes of the confidence ellipses of a bivariate normal distribution are proportional to the standard deviations along them. Let the estimates of these standard deviations from a set of points be u_1 and u_2. Then by squaring eqns. (7.9) for each point, summing, dividing by the degrees of freedom, and finally adding, we obtain

$$u_1^2 + u_2^2 = s_1^2 + s_2^2. \qquad (7.12)$$

Further, from eqn. (7.6) the value of z for the central ordinate, i.e. for $x_1 = \bar{x}_1$ and $x_2 = \bar{x}_2$, is

$$z = \frac{1}{2\pi s_1 s_2 (1 - r^2)^{1/2}} \qquad (7.13)$$

Referred to the principal axes, r is zero and

$$z = \frac{1}{2\pi u_1 u_2}. \qquad (7.14)$$

Since the value of z must be the same whichever way it is calculated,

$$u_1 u_2 = s_1 s_2 (1 - r^2)^{1/2}. \qquad (7.15)$$

Thus we have two eqns. (7.12) and (7.15) in two unknowns that can be solved to find u_1 and u_2.

Inserting the values of s_1, s_2, and r gives

$$u_1^2 + u_2^2 = 322 \cdot 62 + 386 \cdot 05 = 708 \cdot 68$$

$$u_1 u_2 = 17 \cdot 95 \times 19 \cdot 65 \times (1 - 0 \cdot 752^2)^{1/2} = 232 \cdot 50.$$

$$\therefore \quad 2u_1 u_2 = 465 \cdot 0.$$

Adding and subtracting these gives

$$u_1^2 + 2u_1 u_2 + u_2^2 = 1173 \cdot 68$$

and

$$u_1^2 - 2u_1 u_2 + u_2^2 = 243 \cdot 68$$

On taking square roots we obtain

$$u_1 + u_2 = 34 \cdot 26$$

$$u_1 - u_2 = 15 \cdot 60$$

so that

$$u_1 = 24 \cdot 93 \quad \text{and} \quad u_2 = 9 \cdot 33.$$

We now have all the information needed to construct ellipses for any level of confidence. The probability density referred to principal axes is

$$z = \frac{1}{2\pi u_1 u_2} \exp\left[-0 \cdot 5\left\{\frac{y_1^2}{u_1^2} + \frac{y_2^2}{u_2^2}\right\}\right]. \tag{7.16}$$

All terms involving the correlation coefficient disappear since it is zero. The term in square brackets is distributed as χ^2; so by setting first $y_2 = 0$ and then $y_1 = 0$, we can find the values of y_1 and y_2 where the ellipse cuts the major and minor axes. To construct the ellipse containing 90 per cent of the population represented in Fig. 7.1, and hence excluding 10 per cent, χ^2 with two degrees of freedom is 4·605, $(\chi^2)^{1/2} = 2 \cdot 15$; the ends of the major axis are $y_1 = \pm 53 \cdot 60$ and those of the minor axis $y_2 = \pm 20 \cdot 06$.

Confidence ellipses so constructed apply strictly only for distributions that are bivariate normal. Many pairs of soil variables have roughly such a distribution, and for them the ellipses are likely to be good enough approximations. However, since principal axes are defined as that pair of orthogonal axes through the data points for which the co-ordinates are uncorrelated, the angle θ that they make with the original axes of measurement, and the standard deviations along them, u_1 and u_2, hold whatever the distribution. Unlike most univariate statistics, multivariate methods are often exploratory and descriptive in situations where the underlying distributions are quite unknown or immaterial. Transformation to principal axes can then be a valuable means of elucidating structure in a set of data, as we shall see in Chapter 8.

It should also be noted that normal correlation theory is restricted to quantitative variables. Other techniques are available for measuring relations between qualitative characters. They include *rank correlation* for ranked characters and measures of *association* or *contingency* for binary and unordered multistate characters.

Matrix representation

The information contained in the variances and covariance can be expressed as a matrix, **A**, with elements a_{ij}

$$\mathbf{A} = \begin{bmatrix} a_{11} & a_{12} \\ a_{21} & a_{22} \end{bmatrix}$$

The diagonal elements a_{11}, a_{22} are the variances of X_1 and X_2 respectively. The off-diagonal elements a_{12}, a_{21}, which are equal, contain the covariance. If each element is divided by the square root of the product of the diagonal elements in the same row and column, the result is the correlation matrix **R**. Its diagonal elements will clearly all equal 1, and the off-diagonal elements contain the correlation coefficient:

$$\mathbf{R} = \begin{bmatrix} 1 & r \\ r & 1 \end{bmatrix}$$

The original observations will consist of n pairs of measurements, and these too can be arranged in a matrix **X**, conventionally with n rows and 2 columns. If the elements, x_{ij} of this matrix are adjusted so that they are deviations from the variate means, $\bar{x}_j$, then we can form the matrix **S** by

$$\mathbf{S} = \mathbf{X}'\mathbf{X}. \qquad (7.17)$$

This is the matrix of sums of squares and products (of deviations from the means) and is usually found first. Dividing by $n - 1$ gives matrix **A**:

$$\frac{1}{n-1}\mathbf{S} = \mathbf{A}. \qquad (7.18)$$

S is sometimes known as the dispersion matrix; but so is **A**. Therefore, it is safer to avoid ambiguity and refer to them as the sums of squares and products (abbreviated to SSP) matrix and variance–covariance matrix respectively.

Later we shall see how by operating on matrix A or R we can derive the principal axes of ellipses.

Extension to more than two variates

The principles of correlation extend to more than two variables, and in a geometric representation we simply add one new dimension to the character space for each additional variable. For three variables the scatter of individuals occupies a three-dimensional space, and can be displayed by constructing a model or a stereogram. It requires a considerable stretch of the imagination to envisage the associated probability distribution, since this extends into a fourth dimension. However, the probability envelopes, corresponding to the contours of the bivariate case, occupy only three dimensions. For normal distributions they are ellipsoidal, and their size and shape are determined as in the two-dimensional case by the variances on their principal axes. Their orientation is determined by the covariances, of which there are now three, namely c_{12}, c_{13}, and c_{23}. We can again represent the information as a variance–covariance matrix, this time with three rows and three columns:

$$A = \begin{bmatrix} a_{11} & a_{12} & a_{13} \\ a_{21} & a_{22} & a_{23} \\ a_{31} & a_{32} & a_{33} \end{bmatrix}$$

As before, the variances lie on the principal diagonal and the three covariances off the diagonal; and the matrix is symmetric, i.e. $a_{ij} = a_{ji}$ for all i and j.

It requires an even further stretch of the imagination for more than three variables, since the scatter of points must be envisaged in a space of at least four dimensions. Yet all the principles that we have demonstrated for two and three dimensions hold for as many dimensions as we have measured variables. The SSP, the variance–covariance, and correlation matrices all take one more row and one more column for each additional variate. Thus for p variates these matrices are of size $p \times p$. In particular, the probability density for any multivariate normal distribution can be written in general in matrix notation as

$$z = \frac{1}{(2\pi)^{p/2}|\mathbf{A}|^{1/2}} \exp\{-\tfrac{1}{2}(\mathbf{x}-\boldsymbol{\mu})\,\mathbf{A}^{-1}(\mathbf{x}-\boldsymbol{\mu})'\} \qquad (7.19)$$

where $\mathbf{A}$ is now the population variance–covariance matrix and $\boldsymbol{\mu}$ the mean vector.

Matrices of this kind which represent the relationships among variates are sometimes known as *R-matrices*, as distinct from *Q-matrices*, which represent relations among individuals, and which we shall consider next.

Relations between individuals

Normal correlation theory was developed early in this century. Scientists now accept that it provides the most appropriate means of relating two variables, and we can use it with confidence in pedology. Despite the wide interest of systematists in relations between individuals, there is no one measure of relation that is obviously best in all circumstances. Consider the following; they illustrate the kinds of comparison that are the essence of soil systematics.

(a)   Soil I is more acid than soil J.
(b)   The soil at C is stronger than that at D.
(c)   Soil E contains more exchangeable bases than soil F does.
(d)   The soil in the A horizon of profile G is similar to that in the B horizon.
(e)   Profile P is more like Q than R.

It is unlikely that comparison (a) would give rise to any dispute. To compare I and J quantitatively we should simply take the *difference* of their pH values. We might reasonably take a similar view in the second and third instances, and measure the differences in their shear strengths and total exchangeable base content (TEB). However, we might equally reasonably wish to compare them as ratios: the shear strength of soil C is four times that of soil D; the TEB of soil E is twice that of soil F. The latter is often the case, since the difference between the values 2 and 4 meq/100 g soil can be quite as important as that between 30 and 60. And we should note that we have in fact already made this judgement for soil acidity by using the logarithmic pH scale. Measuring the similarity of two horizons is more problematic because there are likely to be several characters to take into account, and comparing profiles adds the factor of pattern, the spatial arrangement of horizons or layers within the profile. So, although we make comparisons of this sort daily, both in ordinary life and in soil survey and research, we need a formal framework if we are to measure them appropriately and consistently; and this we must do to use these comparisons in several of the numerical methods of classification that we shall discuss later.

We shall again use the geometric model to formalize our thinking. We shall represent a single variable as a line, and locate individuals on the line by their values of that variable. The distance separating two individuals is then the measure of their relation. The closer they are, the more alike they are, and vice versa. If individuals are better compared by ratios of their values of the variable, then we shall transform the scale to logarithms first. Notice that this is a matter of choice that rests on pedological judgement.

When there are two variables to be considered simultaneously, we can plot the positions of individuals as in Fig. 7.1, and measure the likeness between any two individuals as the distance between them. Alternatively the distance can be calculated by Pythagoras' theorem. If the coordinates of two points i and j, are x_{i1}, x_{i2} and x_{j1}, x_{j2} then the

distance Δ_{ij} between them is given by

$$\Delta_{ij} = \{(x_{i1} - x_{j1})^2 + (x_{i2} - x_{j2})^2\}^{1/2}. \qquad (7.20)$$

Substituting the values of the first two individuals from Table 7.1,

$$\Delta_{12} = \{(48 \cdot 7 - 49 \cdot 4)^2 + (25 - 29)^2\}^{1/2}$$

$$= 2 \cdot 12.$$

We can extend the geometry to three dimensions without difficulty, but the principles hold for any number of dimensions. If there are p variables then we can postulate a p-dimensional character space, and eqn. (7.20) generalizes to

$$\Delta_{ij} = \left\{ \sum_{k=1}^{p} (x_{ik} - x_{jk})^2 \right\}^{1/2}, \qquad (7.21)$$

The distance Δ is often known as the *Pythagorean distance*, *Euclidean distance*, or *taxonomic distance* between the individuals. It increases with the number of characters involved in the comparison, and so is often divided by $p^{1/2}$ to give an 'average' distance

$$d_{ij} = \left(\frac{\Delta_{ij}^2}{p} \right)^{1/2}, \qquad (7.22)$$

which is actually the square root of the average of the squared distances. Strictly d_{ij} measures the dissimilarity between the individuals i and j.

We can convert d_{ij} to a measure of similarity if we first scale it so that it lies in the range 0 (for identity) to 1 (for maximum dissimilarity) and then take its complement.

$$S_{ij} = 1 - d_{ij}. \tag{7.23}$$

The quantity S_{ij} is known as a *similarity coefficient* or *similarity index*. As defined here it is one of many possible measures of similarity, and we shall consider several other possibilities later.

Standardization

When calculating the relation between two variables we found it convenient to standardize the scales of measurement so that we could more readily interpret the result. When we consider relationships among individuals, standardization is almost essential. Suppose, for example, we wish to assess the relationships between pairs of sampling sites at which we have measured the pH and clay + silt content of the soil. Clay + silt content ranges from perhaps 20 per cent to 90 per cent, as in the data in Table 7.1, while pH for the same sample is unlikely to exceed the range 5·5 to 7·5. If we calculate the Pythagorean distances from such data as they are, the results will depend largely on the differences in clay + silt content, and scarcely at all on pH. To avoid this, the scales are standardized so that they are comparable.

Standardization is usually achieved by dividing each value by the standard deviation of the sample. Every scale then has a standard deviation (and variance) of 1. An equally reasonable alternative is to divide values by the sample range. However, if the sample range happened to be a small proportion of the known range for a variable it might be better to divide by the known range instead. This is equivalent to saying that because the range of a variable is small in the sample now being studied that variable is relatively unimportant. Here again the investigator has a choice that must be based on his experience and judgement.

The similarity matrix

For every pair of individuals i and j, there will be a distance Δ_{ij} separating them in character space, and a corresponding S_{ij}. Like the covariances of the last section these can be arranged in a matrix, sometimes known as a *Q-matrix*. If there are n individuals the matrix will be of size $n \times n$. As an example we can take the first three points in Table 7.1, standardize their values by dividing by the range of silt + clay content and plastic limit respectively, and then calculate the average distances between them. We obtain the dissimilarity matrix:

$$
\mathbf{D} = \begin{bmatrix} 0 & 0\cdot2095 & 0\cdot4958 \\ 0\cdot2095 & 0 & 0\cdot2934 \\ 0\cdot4958 & 0\cdot2934 & 0 \end{bmatrix}
$$

or alternatively the similarity matrix:

$$
\mathbf{S} = \begin{bmatrix} 1\cdot0000 & 0\cdot7905 & 0\cdot5042 \\ 0\cdot7905 & 1\cdot0000 & 0\cdot7066 \\ 0\cdot5042 & 0\cdot7066 & 1\cdot0000 \end{bmatrix}.
$$

Both are symmetric.

Other measures of likeness

Pythagorean distance has been introduced as a measure of relationship between individuals because it derives directly from the geometry of our model and is intuitively appealing. However, it is by no means the only such measure. Many have been proposed, and readers requiring a reasonably full account of them should consult Sneath and Sokal (1973). Here we shall consider just a few measures that have been used in pedology.

We shall see that Pythagorean distance is not necessarily satisfactory if we consider the following situation. Suppose three properties have been measured on five individuals. When standardized their values are:

P_1 0·0   0·0   0·0

P_2 0·0   0·0   1·0

P_3 0·0   1·0   1·0

P_4 1·0   1·0   1·0

P_5 0·0   0·0   0·0

In the geometric representation they occupy positions in a three-dimensional character space with these values as coordinates. The first four individuals occupy different corners of a unit cube, while the fifth coincides with the first. The Pythagorean distances of $P_{1,\ldots,4}$ from P_5 are respectively

$$0, \quad 1\cdot0, \quad 1\cdot41, \quad \text{and} \quad 1\cdot73$$

The last three distances are respectively a side, a diagonal of a face, and a diagonal through the cube. It might be thought that difference in one or relatively few characters makes a disproportionate contribution to the distance and hence to the calculated dissimilarity. We could use the squared distances in this instance, but would encounter similar difficulties with distances to individuals in other positions.

Mean character distance. A reasonable alternative to Pythagorean distance is the sum of the absolute differences in each dimension, $\sum_{k=1}^{p} |x_{ik} - x_{jk}|$, which is known in topology as the *Manhattan* or *city-block metric*. It gives dissimilarities of $P_{1,\ldots,4}$ from P_5 as 0, 1·0, 2·0, and 3·0. When divided by the number of dimensions it becomes

$$d_{ij} = \frac{1}{p} \sum_{k=1}^{p} |x_{ik} - x_{jk}|. \tag{7.24}$$

In this form it is usually known as *mean character distance* (Cain and Harrison 1958), though it had been used much earlier in taxonomic work.

Gower's similarity coefficient. The above two measures assume that the characters on which the comparison is based are continuous variables, though binary characters can be included. In some instances we shall want to include binary and multistate characters. For example we might wish to compare soil profiles on their clay content, pH, presence of coatings, and type of structure simultaneously. Gower (1971) devised a general measure of similarity to accommodate these, given by

$$S_{ij} = \frac{\sum_{k=1}^{p} z_{ijk} \cdot w_{ijk}}{\sum_{k=1}^{p} w_{ijk}}, \tag{7.25}$$

where z_{ijk} is a value for the comparison for the kth character, and w_{ijk} is the weight assigned to it. For continuous variables

$$z_{ijk} = 1 - \frac{|x_{ik} - x_{jk}|}{r_k},$$

where r_k is the range of the character. As mentioned above, r_k can be either the range within the sample being studied or the range known to exist in the population at large. In either case division by r_k standardizes the characters. For qualitative characters $z_{ijk} = 1$ if $x_{ik} = x_{jk}$, and 0 otherwise. The weight w_{ijk} is conventionally set to 1 when a valid comparison can be made between i and j for the character k and to 0 if x_{ik} or x_{jk} or both are unknown or inapplicable.

A point of some subtlety arises with binary characters of the present-or-absent kind for which presence is regarded as important and absence unimportant. For example, the presence of erratic stones in the soil of areas showing no clear evidence of glaciation and the presence of mont-morillonite in areas where the soil clay is dominantly kaolinite might be thought significant, whereas their absence would be of little interest. In these circumstances two soil specimens or profiles may be regarded as alike when both possess the character, and unlike when one possesses the character and the other does not, but no comparison is made when both lack the character. They are accommodated in formula (7.25) by setting $w_{ijk} = 0$ when $x_{ik} = x_{jk} = 0$. Rayner (1966), who first used Gower's coefficient for matching soil horizons, chose to treat the presence of earthworms, manganese concretions, and iron concretions in this way. He treated porosity likewise, scoring it as 1 when men-tioned in the survey record, and 0 otherwise. In doing so, he illustrates another feature of soil survey data. For a surveyor often records only what is present in the soil at a sampling site, little realizing that by ignoring absent characters he could be implying, perhaps justifiably, that they are relatively unimportant in the context of the survey. This leads to uncertainty in the interpretation of the records. Binary characters of this kind should therefore be distinguished from other qualitative characters, and the latter firmly recorded as absent when they are absent.

When all data are quantitative, Gower's coefficient is exactly equivalent to mean character distance. When all are binary and matches between absent characters are ignored, it is the same as that of Jaccard (1908) and Sneath (1957). Furthermore, it can readily be converted to a distance (Gower, 1966) by

$$\Delta_{ij} = \{2(1 - S_{ij})\}^{1/2} \qquad (7.26)$$

Canberra metric. A measure that has no geometric equivalent, but which has been used in several soil studies (Moore and Russell 1967; Campbell *et al.* 1970; Webster and Burrough 1972*a, b*) is the *Canberra metric* developed by Lance and Williams (1967*a*). It is a dissimilarity defined as

$$d_{Cij} = \sum_{k=1}^{p} |x_{ik} - x_{jk}|/(x_{ik} + x_{jk}). \qquad (7.27)$$

It is attractive because it is a measure solely of the individuals being compared and the data need not be standardized beforehand. Differences are measured as proportions of the data values, and hence this metric is appropriate for ratio scales. Qualitative characters can be included as in Gower's general similarity coefficient. However, prior standardization is swift by computer, and proportional differences can be included in any of the coefficients mentioned earlier by transforming the scales to logarithms. Its use is restricted to positive values of characters unless the denominator is replaced by $|x_{ik}| + |x_{jk}|$, as Gower suggested (Sneath and Sokal 1973). Its major weakness is that its validity is in doubt for scales with an arbitrary zero, e.g. colour hue, pH. Its advantages are therefore less than might at first appear.

Generalized distance

In choosing characters for multivariate comparisons and analysis one will omit any character that is necessarily correlated with another already included. For example, the proportion of stones in soil would

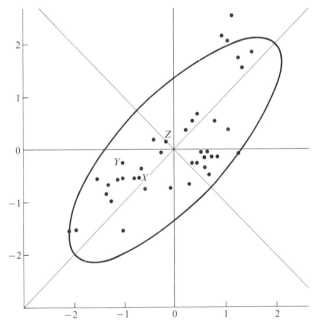

FIG. 7.7. Scatter of points shown in Fig. 7.1 replotted on standardized scales. Correlation coefficient is 0·752

not be included if the percentage of fine earth had already been selected. The two are perfectly correlated (since total soil = fine earth + stones), and to include both would simply be to duplicate data.

However, it often happens that many other characters that an investigator wishes to include are correlated to some extent. If the correlation coefficients are small (in absolute value) they can be disregarded. If they are large, the investigator should consider whether to take them into account when measuring likeness. The situation is illustrated in Fig. 7.7, which shows the scatter of the same forty individuals as Fig. 7.1 but on standardized scales. Consider the relationships between the points X, Y, and Z. X is clearly nearer to Y than it is to Z in the ordinary sense. However, the distance XZ is measured approximately parallel to the long axis of the configuration, whereas XY is approximately at right angles, and so much of the difference between the two distances could be attributed to the correlation. If we were to add a third soil property, such as cation exchange capacity, which, like plastic limit, depends to a large extent on the amount of clay in the

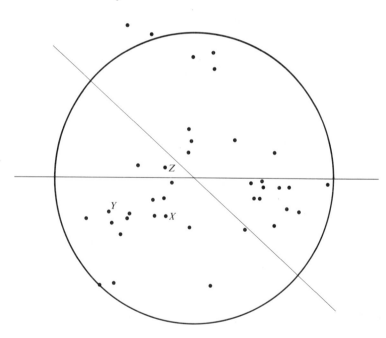

FIG. 7.8. The same points as in Fig. 7.7 plotted on oblique axes cutting at the angle $\cos^{-1} 0 \cdot 752$, i.e. $41°12'$

soil, it is likely that we should still have an obliquely oriented elongated configuration. This elongation could be attributed to the control of two of the properties, plastic limit and cation exchange capacity, by a large component of the third, clay + silt content.

The dominating influence of the last, and correlation effects in general, can be eliminated if we rotate the axes with respect to one another until each pair is inclined at an angle whose cosine is the correlation coefficient between the variates. When this is done, and provided the scales are standardized as here, the distribution is no longer elongated. The ellipse of Fig. 7.7 is transformed into a circle, Fig. 7.8, and the distances XY and XZ become more nearly equal. Distances between individuals in this transformed space can be used as measures of their relationships.

It would be far too laborious in practice to measure the relations between many pairs of points in this way, and impossible if there were more than three variates. But we can calculate the distances in this space from the quadratic form

$$D^2 = (\mathbf{x}_i - \mathbf{x}_j) \mathbf{A}^{-1} (\mathbf{x}_i - \mathbf{x}_j)' \qquad (7.28)$$

where $\mathbf{x}_i$, $\mathbf{x}_j$ are the row vectors of values for the individuals i and j, and $\mathbf{A}$ is the variance–covariance matrix. The quantity D is the *generalized distance* between the two individuals, and takes into account any correlation that there might be between the characters. It is in principle the same as Mahalanobis' generalized distance between groups of individuals that we shall meet later. If there is no correlation, then $\mathbf{A}$ contains the variances of characters in the leading diagonal and zeros elsewhere, so that formula (7.28) simply gives the squared standardized Pythagorean distance.

Correlation coefficient. The product moment correlation coefficient has been much used in some fields of study for comparing individuals (see Sneath and Sokal 1973 for references). It is given by

$$r_{ij} = \frac{\sum\limits_{k=1}^{p} (x_{ik} - \bar{x}_i)(x_{jk} - \bar{x}_j)}{\left\{ \sum\limits_{k=1}^{p} (x_{ik} - \bar{x}_i)^2 \sum\limits_{k=1}^{p} (x_{jk} - \bar{x}_j)^2 \right\}^{1/2}}. \qquad (7.29)$$

The characters must be standardized and be centred so that their means are zero if results are to be sensible. When this is done, r_{ij} approximates to the cosine of the angle subtended by i and j at the origin. The smaller is this angle, the more alike are the individuals judged to be.

The correlation coefficient calculated for pairs of individuals needs to be viewed with caution. The population of points $x_{1k}, x_{2k}, k = 1, \ldots, p$, is unlikely to be even approximately bivariate normal. So statistical theory has no place in interpreting a value of r_{ij}. The size of r_{ij} does not depend primarily on the size of the original measurements, only on their angular relations. Any two individuals, however, far apart, would be judged very similar if they happened to lie in much the same direction from the origin. A user should therefore be sure that he wants this angular measure before he chooses it. When many characters are included in a comparison, r_{ij} is often found to give results comparable to those obtained using a distance measure. But this is no justification for its use (see Sneath and Sokal 1973, and Eades 1965 for further discussion of this point).

The correlation coefficient was used in exploratory studies on the comparison of soil profiles by Moore and Russell (1967), and Cuanalo and Webster (1970). However, it is now generally regarded as inappropriate and is not recommended.

Character weighting

A problem that arises in multivariate comparisons that does not occur in univariate studies is how to choose characters and their relative weights. So far we have assumed that we know the values of all characters on the individuals we wish to compare, and though we introduced the idea of standardization to bring characters to comparable scales, we avoided the matter of the weights to be assigned to the different characters. With one exception we have considered only formulae that assign weight to characters equally. This principle, usually attributed to the eighteenth century French botanist Michel Adanson, seems inappropriate to some pedologists; others point out that the inclusion of some characters and the omission of others in an analysis is in effect differential weighting.

Characters need not be given equal weight for mathematical reasons. Gower's formula, eqn. (7.25), for calcualting similarities leaves its user free to choose whatever weights w_{ijk} he considers reasonable, and similar adjustments can be made to other formulae. But differential weighting does raise serious logical difficulties. How should such weights be chosen? If the aim is simply to express relationships in existing data, whether as similarities between individuals, or in summary form as a classification or ordination (see later) then there is no obvious case for assigning more weight to some characters than to others. If we are to collect data by which to assess relationships then the logical starting point is to record those characters that are obvious and those that are known to be important. Characters known to be unimportant should be excluded; otherwise they blur the picture. However, the relative importance of characters can be judged only in relation to purpose, and it is only when we know what purpose we aim to serve that we can choose differential weights rationally. If we lack this information then there is no reasonable alternative, *a priori* at least, to giving equal weight to the characters for which we have or can easily obtain data.

Concomitant variables

A more subtle problem arises when the soil properties in which we are interested are influenced by one or more others that are themselves of no interest. For example, the water content or suction of the soil at the time of sampling is transient, and we should be unlikely to want to use it when comparing two profiles for general purposes. Yet if consistence, strength, and colour are used for comparing profiles, then any variation in water content or suction will be embodied in our comparison. In this situation water content is a *concomitant* variable. Provided this is recognized, its effects can be eliminated by standard regression methods as in the analysis of covariance. Marriott (1974) discusses the matter at some length and shows how to adjust the main data accordingly.

Special problems of comparing soil profiles

The above measures take no account of any relation between different parts of the individuals being compared. They further assume that if an individual has several parts, their properties can be matched to those of corresponding parts of other individuals. This correspondence between parts of two or more individuals is known in biology as *homology*. In pedology it is a question of recognizing corresponding horizons or levels in the soil profile.

The measures that we have discussed so far can be applied to soil profiles for which we have information at several levels provided we can recognize corresponding levels in all the profiles under study in a particular exercise. If we have recognized, say, four horizons, then we compare each property of the first horizon in one profile with the same property of the first horizon of the second profile, and repeat for each horizon in turn. Recognition of horizons involves the subjective judgement of the pedologist, of course. To avoid this, profiles can be described at several fixed depths. In both cases each property in each level is treated as an independent variate. Despite the comments of Lance and Williams (1967c), this is theoretically sound, and the generalized distance can be computed as the measure of dissimilarity to remove effects of correlation between levels if desired.

Nevertheless, the treatment depends on the levels being comparable. Rayner (1966) devised a means for comparing profiles that avoids this assumption, as follows. Each horizon in each profile is initially considered as an individual, and similarity coefficients are computed between all pairs of horizons. The similarity between two profiles, say P_1 and P_2, is then computed from the similarity coefficients between their horizons. The first horizon of P_1 is compared with each horizon of P_2 in turn. The most similar horizon in P_2 is chosen as the best match. The second horizon in P_1 is then compared with each horizon in P_2, starting with the best match found for horizon 1 and proceeding downwards. The third horizon of P_1 is compared with the horizons in P_2, starting with the best match for horizon 2, to find the best match for it, and so on until all horizons in P_1 have been matched with ones of P_2. The roles of P_1 and P_2 are reversed and procedure repeated. Matching need not be symmetrical: the best match between a horizon of P_1 among those in P_2 is not necessarily the best match when the roles are reversed, as Rayner shows. Having found which pairs of horizons match, the similarity between P_1 and P_2 is finally computed as the average of the similarities between the matched horizons.

Rayner's method is attractive. Not only does it allow soil at different depths or in different horizons to be compared, it also allows similarities between profiles with different numbers of horizons to be calculated automatically. It takes account of the order in which horizons occur down the profile; so that if, for example, one profile was turned upside down, substantially different similarities with other profiles would result. Whether the advantages of the method over the simpler techniques justify the increased computing is uncertain.

Williams and Rayner (1977) included in a study of clay soils a comparison of a similarity matrix calculated in this fashion with ones derived by the simpler techniques described earlier. They found little difference in the patterns of relationships. Further comparative study is needed to assess the actual advantages of the method over the simpler ones, and to identify situations that justify the substantially increased computing that the method entails.

Two other methods for measuring the similarities between soil profiles have been tried. The first (Moore *et al* 1972) computes for each profile the relation between depth and each soil property as a polynomial function. The coefficients of the function are then treated as variates from which the similarities are calculated. The second, due to Dale *et al.* (1970), and based on transition matrices, classifies the horizons or levels first and then considers the order in which they occur in the profile. The more closely the order of horizons in one profile matches those in another, the more similar are the profiles judged to be. The method has been explored by Moore *et al.* (1972) and by Norris and Dale (1971) but seems to have few advantages in practice.

Although we have condemned prior weighting of characters when matching soil specimens or profiles, a reasonable case can be made for assigning more weight to characters of the topsoil than to those in the deep subsoil, at least in a biological context, and especially when

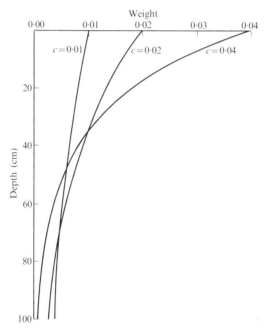

FIG. 7.9. Graphs showing how the weight changes with depth down a profile when using Russell and Moore's weighting function

the soil has been described at equal intervals down the profile. Russell and Moore (1968) considered this situation, and proposed that the weight w given to each level should decline exponentially with increasing depth according to the formula

$$w = c \exp(-cx) \tag{7.30}$$

where x is the depth and c is a parameter set by the user. When a profile has been described by layers bounded by upper and lower limits x_1 and x_2, the expression on the right-hand side of eqn. (7.30) can be integrated between x_1 and x_2 to give the weight for each layer as

$$w = \int_{x_1}^{x_2} c \exp(-cx) \, dx. \tag{7.31}$$

Russell and Moore found from their experience that a value of $c = 0 \cdot 02$ (and depth expressed in centimetres) fairly reflected the change in biological activity down a profile, but suggested that other values of c in the range $0 \cdot 01$ to $0 \cdot 04$ might be tried. The way in which comparisons are biased in favour of the upper parts of profiles is shown in Fig. 7.9. Notice that this is no different in principle from comparing profiles horizon by horizon and treating thin horizons near the surface on an equal footing with thicker ones beneath.

8. Ordination

'What is the use of a book,' thought Alice,
'without pictures or conversations?'

LEWIS CARROLL,
Alice in Wonderland

When just one soil property has been measured on a set of individual specimens, profiles, or sampling sites, we can represent the measured values by their positions on a single scale or line. The relation between any pair of individuals can be represented by the distance between them and relations among several individuals can be appreciated simultaneously from their relative positions on the line. If we wish we can classify the individuals by simple dissection of the line (Chapter 5). Relations are slightly more difficult to assess if we have two properties, but a scatter diagram shows the similarities between individuals and among groups of individuals. When there are many properties of interest we can measure the relation between any pair of individuals by calculating their similarity or dissimilarity (Chapter 7). But though we may postulate the scatter of individuals in a multidimensional space, it is almost impossible to envisage their positions in it and the relations among more than two individuals simultaneously. The traditional means of overcoming this difficulty has been to classify the individuals, and in Chapter 7 we introduced the idea of multivariate relationships as a prelude to numerical classification. However, classification is not the only way of expressing such relations, and for continuously variable material like soil it is by no means the most satisfactory way.

An alternative is to arrange the individuals along one or a few new axes chosen so as to preserve as much as possible of the original information. The arrangement can then be displayed graphically as histograms or scatter diagrams, or in three dimensions by constructing models or stereograms. This reduction of an arrangement in many dimensions to one in a few dimensions has become known in ecology as *ordination.* The term was apparently introduced by Goodall (1954) as a translation of the German *Ordnung*, and is the one we shall use.

Several ordination methods have been proposed, some specially suited to qualitative data (see later, p.154). Hole and Hironaka (1960) first attempted ordination of soil using a method devised by Bray and

Curtis (1957) for ecological work. Since then, however, most ordination studies, not only in pedology but in other branches of science also, have used vector methods. It is to these that we now turn our attention, and especially to principal-component analysis, which has proved to be one of the most valuable means of exploring relationships among soil profiles.

Principal components

Consider again Fig. 7.1. Forty points are scattered in two dimensions representing the two soil characters silt + clay content and plastic limit. The variances on these axes are 322·6 and 386·0 respectively. The two characters are correlated to the extent that $r = 0·752$, and the configuration of points is elongated, rising from left to right. In Chapter 7 we found the principal axes of this configuration, and calculated the variances on these axes as 621·5 for the long one and 87·1 for the short. The proportion of the total variance accounted for by the longer principal axis is thus considerably larger than that represented by either of the original axes. If we were prepared to forego the remainder, we could represent our data in only one dimension by projecting the points orthogonally on to the longer principal axis. This is the basis of ordination by principal components. Of course, when only two characters have been measured we need not lose information in this way in order to see all the relationships. But the principle of the method extends to many dimensions and is then of considerable practical value. In general, the analysis finds the principal axes of a multidimensional configuration and determines the coordinates of each individual in the population relative to these. This is equivalent to rotating the configuration to new axes such that: the sum of the squares of the perpendicular distances from the first axis to the points representing the individuals is least; a second axis is chosen at right angles to the first to minimize the sum of the squares of the perpendicular distances from the points to it; third and subsequent axes all perpendicular to one another are chosen similarly. We can then display the relations among individuals on the plane defined by the first two principal axes, or a model of the first three, and these displays will be more informative than those on any other set of two or three axes. However, it is sometimes helpful to project the scatter on to other pairs of low-order axes.

The good sense of component analysis for ordination depends on the variances of the original variates being approximately equal. Otherwise the orientation of the principal axes will be controlled largely by

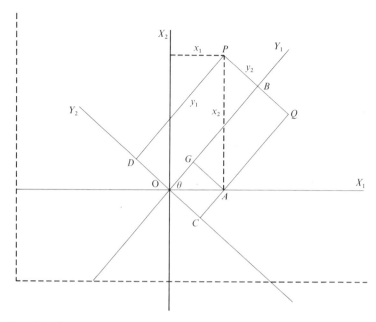

FIG. 8.1. The geometry of axis rotation

those characters with the largest variances. Variates can be standardized to make their variances equal, and this should be done as a matter of course when they are measured on different scales.

Rotation and projection are important both in ordination and as the means of understanding several other multivariate methods, and we shall therefore consider them in careful detail.

Fig. 8.1 illustrates the transformation that we require. One of the points P of Fig. 7.1 is located at x_1, x_2 on axes OX_1 and OX_2. The origin has been moved to the centre O of the configuration to make the transformation as clear as possible. The principal axes make an angle θ, which we shall ultimately wish to determine, with the original axes, and having found θ we shall require the values of y_1 and y_2. By simple geometry we can see that the line OB is made up of two parts, namely

(1) OG, which is the projection of OA on OY_1 of length $x_1 \cos \theta$, and

(2) GB, the projection of AP on OY_1, of length $x_2 \sin \theta$, or alternatively $x_2 \cos (90^\circ - \theta)$.

Similarly the line OD consists of

(1) $CD = PQ$, the projection of PA on the perpendicular from P on to OY_1, of length $x_2 \cos \theta$

less

(2) OC, the projection of OA on OY_2 and of length $x_1 \sin \theta$.

Thus the coordinates of P relative to the principal axes are

$$\left.\begin{aligned} y_1 &= x_1 \cos \theta + x_2 \sin \theta \\ y_2 &= -x_1 \sin \theta + x_2 \cos \theta. \end{aligned}\right\} \tag{8.1}$$

Eqns. (8.1) constitute a linear transformation, which we can write in matrix form:

$$\mathbf{y} = \mathbf{xC'}$$

where $\mathbf{x}$ and $\mathbf{y}$ are row vectors $\mathbf{x} = [x_1 x_2]$, and $\mathbf{y} = [y_1 y_2]$ for the individual, and

$$\mathbf{C} = \begin{bmatrix} c_{11} & c_{12} \\ c_{21} & c_{22} \end{bmatrix} = \begin{bmatrix} \cos \theta & \sin \theta \\ -\sin \theta & \cos \theta \end{bmatrix}.$$

Since $\sin \theta = \cos (90° - \theta)$ the elements of $\mathbf{C}$ are the cosines of the angles between the new axes and the old.

We should notice that

$$\begin{aligned} \mathbf{CC'} &= \begin{bmatrix} \cos \theta & \sin \theta \\ -\sin \theta & \cos \theta \end{bmatrix} \begin{bmatrix} \cos \theta & -\sin \theta \\ \sin \theta & \cos \theta \end{bmatrix} \\ &= \begin{bmatrix} \cos^2\theta + \sin^2\theta & -\cos \theta \sin \theta + \sin \theta \cos \theta \\ -\sin \theta \cos \theta + \cos \theta \sin \theta & \cos^2\theta + \sin_2\theta \end{bmatrix} \\ &= \begin{bmatrix} 1 & 0 \\ 0 & 1 \end{bmatrix} = \mathbf{I}. \end{aligned} \tag{8.3}$$

So, by post-multiplying the matrix of direction cosines by its transpose, we obtain the identity matrix. Notice also that if we pre-multiply eqn. (8.3) by $\mathbf{C}^{-1}$ it becomes

$$\mathbf{C'} = \mathbf{C}^{-1}.$$

Thus, the transpose of $\mathbf{C}$ equals its inverse.

If we could determine the angle θ we should be able to find the co-ordinates $y_1 y_2$, of any point $x_1 x_2$. But we know that the new variables will be uncorrelated, so that their variance–covariance matrix will be a diagonal matrix with zeros off the diagonal. By convention we represent the variances on the principal axes by λ_1 and λ_2, and the new variance–covariance matrix can be written

$$\frac{1}{n-1}\mathbf{Y}'\mathbf{Y} = \begin{bmatrix} \lambda_1 & 0 \\ 0 & \lambda_2 \end{bmatrix} = \boldsymbol{\Lambda} \tag{8.5}$$

Since $\mathbf{Y} = \mathbf{XC}'$, we have

$$\frac{1}{n-1}\mathbf{Y}'\mathbf{Y} = \frac{1}{n-1}\mathbf{CX}'\mathbf{XC}',$$

and since $\dfrac{1}{n-1}\mathbf{X}'\mathbf{X} = \mathbf{A}$, the variance–covariance matrix (Chapter 7) is

$$\boldsymbol{\Lambda} = \mathbf{CAC}'. \tag{8.6}$$

Post-multiplying by $\mathbf{C}$ we have

$$\boldsymbol{\Lambda}\mathbf{C} = \mathbf{CA},$$

which on multiplying out gives

$$\begin{bmatrix} c_{11}\lambda_1 & c_{12}\lambda_1 \\ c_{21}\lambda_2 & c_{22}\lambda_2 \end{bmatrix} = \begin{bmatrix} c_{11}a_{11} + c_{12}a_{21} & c_{11}a_{12} + c_{12}a_{22} \\ c_{21}a_{11} + c_{22}a_{12} & c_{21}a_{12} + c_{22}a_{22} \end{bmatrix}$$

and on rearrangement

$$\begin{bmatrix} c_{11}(a_{11}-\lambda_1) + c_{12}a_{21} & c_{11}a_{12} + c_{12}(a_{22}-\lambda_1) \\ c_{21}(a_{11}-\lambda_2) + c_{22}a_{21} & c_{21}a_{12} + c_{22}(a_{22}-\lambda_2) \end{bmatrix} = \mathbf{O} \tag{8.7}$$

where $\mathbf{O}$ is the 2×2 matrix with all elements zero. If we assume that the c_{ij} are unknowns, we can equate the elements of the first rows of eqn. 8.7 to give two simultaneous equations

$$\left. \begin{aligned} c_{11}(a_{11}-\lambda_1) + c_{12}a_{21} &= 0 \\ c_{11}a_{12} + c_{12}(a_{22}-\lambda_1) &= 0 \end{aligned} \right\}. \tag{8.8}$$

Similarly for the second rows

$$\left. \begin{aligned} c_{21}(a_{11}-\lambda_2) + c_{22}a_{21} &= 0 \\ c_{21}a_{12} + c_{22}(a_{22}-\lambda_2) &= 0 \end{aligned} \right\}. \tag{8.9}$$

One solution of these would be $c_{11} = 0$ and $c_{12} = 0$, but in that event all values of y_1 would be zero also, and this is clearly not the solution we require. Now it is a fact that if a system of homogeneous equations such as that above is to have other than this trivial solution, then the determinant of the coefficients of the equations must be zero. Thus

$$\begin{vmatrix} a_{11} - \lambda_1 & a_{21} \\ a_{12} & a_{22} - \lambda_1 \end{vmatrix} = 0. \tag{8.10}$$

Similarly

$$\begin{vmatrix} a_{11} - \lambda_2 & a_{21} \\ a_{12} & a_{22} - \lambda_2 \end{vmatrix} = 0, \tag{8.11}$$

and in general

$$\begin{vmatrix} a_{11} - \lambda & a_{21} \\ a_{12} & a_{22} - \lambda \end{vmatrix} = 0. \tag{8.12}$$

On multiplying the determinant out we obtain a quadratic in λ,

$$\lambda^2 - (a_{11} + a_{22})\lambda + a_{11}a_{22} - a_{12}a_{21} = 0 \tag{8.13}$$

which, since it is a quadratic, has two roots λ_1 and λ_2. These are known as *latent roots*, *characteristic roots*, or *eigenvalues* of the variance–covariance matrix $\mathbf{A}$. They are found by solving the determinantal equation, generally written

$$|\mathbf{A} - \lambda I| = 0. \tag{8.14}$$

The associated vectors $\mathbf{c}_1$ and $\mathbf{c}_2$ are known as *latent vectors* or *eigenvectors*. It is worth noting that in a quadratic of the form $x^2 - bx + q = 0$, b is the sum of the roots and q the product. Eqn. 8.13 gives

$$\lambda_1 + \lambda_2 = a_{11} + a_{22} \tag{8.15}$$

and

$$\lambda_1 \lambda_2 = a_{11}a_{22} - a_{12}a_{21}. \tag{8.16}$$

In words, the sum of the roots equals the sum of the variances of the original variates, and their product equals the product of the variances minus the square of the covariance, i.e. the determinant of $\mathbf{A}$, the same result as we found by a different route in Chapter 7.

If now we recall eqn. (8.7) and the simultaneous eqns. (8.8) and (8.9) derived from it we have, for example, on rearranging

$$c_{12} = \frac{(a_{11} - \lambda_1)}{a_{21}} c_{11}. \tag{8.17}$$

Since $c_{11}^2 + c_{12}^2 = 1$ we can solve for c_{11} and c_{12}.

Let us again illustrate the procedure using the data on particle size and plastic limit given in Table 7.1. The variance–covariance matrix is

$$\begin{bmatrix} 322\cdot63 & 265\cdot31 \\ 265\cdot31 & 386\cdot05 \end{bmatrix}$$

and hence we need to solve

$$\begin{vmatrix} 322\cdot63 - \lambda & 265\cdot31 \\ 265\cdot31 & 386\cdot05 - \lambda \end{vmatrix} = 0$$

Therefore

$$\lambda^2 - (322\cdot63 + 386\cdot05)\lambda + 322\cdot63 \times 386\cdot05 - 265\cdot31^2 = 0$$

and thus

$$\lambda_1 = 621\cdot53 \quad \text{and} \quad \lambda_2 = 87\cdot14.$$

If we now substitute these values in eqn. (8.17),

$$c_{12} = -\frac{(322\cdot63 - 621\cdot53)}{265\cdot31}c_{11}$$

$$= 1\cdot127\,c_{11}.$$

But since $c_{11}^2 + c_{12}^2 = 1$, we have

$$c_{11}^2 + (1\cdot127\,c_{11})^2 = 1$$

hence

$$2\cdot270\,c_{11}^2 = 1.$$

Therefore $c_{11} = 0\cdot6638$ and $c_{12} = 0\cdot7479$, and since $c_{11} = \cos\theta$ we have $\theta = 48°24'$ as before.

Having determined the elements of **C** in this way, we can calculate the coordinates for any point given its value on the original axes of measurement from eqn. (8.2).

We have pursued the analysis for two variates in detail. The principles are quite general, however and we can always proceed by solving the determinantal equation

$$|\mathbf{A} - \lambda I| = 0.$$

If there are p variates there will be p roots. It is also worth remembering the following properties that are associated with a rigid rotation to principal axes:

(a)
$$\sum_{i=1}^{p} \lambda_i = \sum_{i=1}^{p} s_i^2, \qquad (8.18)$$

(b)
$$\prod_{i=1}^{p} \lambda_i = |A|, \qquad (8.19)$$

(c)
$$c_i A = \lambda_i c_i, \qquad (8.20)$$

and
$$c_i c_i' = 1, \qquad (8.21)$$

where c_i is a row vector $[c_{i1} \quad c_{i2}, \ldots, c_{ip}]$ of C and $i = 1, 2, \ldots, p$. Two further points need mention. If any variate is linearly dependent on one or more others, then the matrix A is positive semi-definite (psd) and at least one root will be zero: the individuals are then distributed in fewer than p dimensions. Secondly, if any two roots are equal, then the distribution in the corresponding plane is circular, and though we may place orthogonal axes in that plane their orientation is quite arbitrary. There are thus many vectors that can be associated with these roots.

In practice, where principal-component analysis is desired there are often many variates, and hence large matrices. It would be very laborious indeed to find their latent roots except by computer, and few analyses would be attempted without one. Most scientific computer centres now have library programs for finding latent roots and vectors.

For ordination it is then desirable to rank the roots from largest to smallest and to accumulate the sum of the roots as each is considered in turn. Since the sum of all the roots equals the sum of the p original variances, we can see what percentage of the total variance the first $k (k < p)$ roots account for. It is usually hoped that the first few roots will represent a large portion of the total variance. In most soil studies to date the hope has been realized: four or five roots out of a total of between twenty and forty have commonly accounted for about 70 per cent of the variance of standardized variates. The coordinates of the individuals, often known as their component scores, are computed for the first few dimensions and the population scatter displayed to advantage by plotting their positions on planes defined by these axes in turn. The other dimensions can usually be ignored. A display on axes 1 and 2 is the most informative, of course.

It is worth amplifying the earlier remarks on measurement scales. The results of a principal-component analysis depend on the scales on which the original observations are recorded. Using again the illustration of clay + silt content and pH, components calculated from such data are likely to be largely determined by clay content, since this is likely to have a much larger variance than pH. As in the calculation of similarities between individuals, we can avoid this effect by standardizing the scales so that all have a standard deviation of 1. The variance—covariance matrix thereby becomes the correlation matrix, and in ordination studies involving properties measured on different scales components are calculated on this matrix.

It is also worth noting that the procedure is not restricted to normally distributed populations. It is simply a convenient transformation to new axes to obtain informative displays in few dimensions and economy in the number of variates for use in further analyses.

Interpretation of latent vectors

Although a component analysis is often carried out to display relationships between individuals, those relationships can often be understood better if some meaning can be attached to the component axes. The matrix of latent vectors contains the information for this interpretation. An element c_{kj} with a value near 1 means that the axis representing the jth original variate is closely aligned to the kth component axis, and hence makes a large contribution to that component. Conversely if c_{kj} is near 0 the two axes are nearly at right angles, and the contribution of variate j to component k is small. A projection of the vectors on to a plane can sometimes be helpful, see for example Fig. 8.3.

Examples

Two examples will illustrate how component analysis can be used to display and interpret relationships in multivariate soil populations.

The first is from a study reported by Cuanalo and Webster (1970) on data collected in a survey of soil in west Oxfordshire by Beckett and Webster (1965*b*). Sites had been chosen by randomly sampling seventeen physiographically distinct types of land. A number of morphological and physical properties of the soil had been measured at 13 cm and 38 cm depths at each site. Here fifteen properties at each of the two depths for 85 sites are analyzed. The variates used are listed in Table 8.1. The variates were standardized to unit variance and the population centred at the origin. The six largest latent roots of its variance—covariance matrix, which on standardized variates is also the

TABLE 8.1

Latent vectors of correlation matrix from west Oxfordshire soil study

Variates		Vectors for topsoil (13 cm)				Vectors for subsoil (38 cm)		
		1	2	3		1	2	3
Colour hue (Munsell)	1	-0.1573	0.0197	0.0310	16	-0.2024	-0.0430	-0.0970
Colour value (Munsell)	2	-0.0003	0.1968	0.2295	17	-0.1643	-0.0377	0.2001
Colour chroma (Munsell)	3	0.2371	0.0225	0.0018	18	0.1726	0.0975	-0.0699
Chroma of mottles (Munsell)	4	0.0173	-0.0580	0.1785	19	0.0236	-0.0316	0.1006
Mottle abundance	5	-0.1062	-0.0718	-0.0417	20	-0.1280	0.0423	0.3094
Clay + silt	6	-0.2347	0.2509	0.0532	21	-0.2536	0.1437	0.1496
Fine sand	7	0.1605	-0.3557	0.0448	22	0.1352	-0.3701	0.0164
Stone content	8	0.1703	0.1750	-0.1070	23	0.2066	0.1597	-0.1009
Plastic limit	9	-0.2171	0.2457	-0.0886	24	-0.2118	0.1753	-0.0550
Liquid limit	10	-0.2088	0.2725	-0.0881	25	-0.2359	0.2038	-0.0224
pH	11	-0.0049	-0.0728	-0.5226	26	0.0117	0.1074	-0.5261
Soil strength in summer	12	0.2248	0.2113	0.2365	27	0.2430	0.2345	-0.0032
Soil strength in winter	13	0.2434	0.1538	0.1351	28	0.2312	0.2277	-0.0604
Matric suction in summer (pF_1)†	14	0.1746	0.2676	0.1793	29	0.1815	0.2248	0.1243
Matrix suction in winter (pF_1)	15	0.1508	0.0857	-0.0630	30	0.2405	0.0679	0.0716

† $pF_1 = \log_{10}$ (cm water + 50)

TABLE 8.2

Latent roots of correlation matrix for 30 variates in west Oxfordshire soil study

Order	Root	Percentage of known variance	Cumulative percentage
1	9·6951	32·32	32·32
2	4·8334	16·11	48·43
3	2·3423	7·81	56·24
4	1·7764	5·92	62·16
5	1·6684	5·56	67·72
6	1·3037	4·35	72·06

correlation matrix, are given in Table 8.2. The first is much the largest, and the first two, out of thirty, account for nearly half the variance in the sample. Projection of the population scatter on to the plane defined by the first two principal axes gives much the most informative single display of relations in the whole space, and Fig. 8.2 illustrates the relationships among the 85 sampling sites in this way.

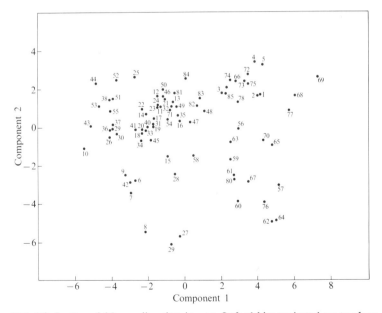

FIG. 8.2. Scatter of 85 sampling sites in west Oxfordshire projected on to plane of the first two principal components

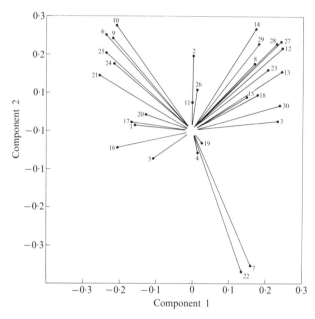

FIG. 8.3. Graph of vectors showing the contribution the variates listed in table 8.1 make to the first two principal components

In the original interpretation the first principal axis, the horizontal one, was thought to represent gleying, while the second, shown vertically, was thought to represent texture. A more careful examination of the latent vectors shows that interpretation is not so simple (Fig. 8.3.). Bright colour (large chroma) and high matrix suction undoubtedly contribute strongly to component 1, but so does clay + silt content (in the opposite sense). Fine sand content contributes strongly to component 2. Atterberg limits and several other properties contribute strongly to both components. The vector diagram suggests that if an interpretation is required, then further rotation would help, and this is discussed later (p.151).

A second example is taken from work of Kyuma and Kawaguchi (1973) in which they rank sites for paddy rice according to the 'chemical potential' of the soil to produce the crop. They analysed laboratory measurements of 23 mainly chemical properties of soil from some 40 rice-growing sites in South-east Asia. The latent roots and vectors are given in Table 8.3. The first component accounts for 36 per cent of the variance, and the first four for over three quarters.

TABLE 8.3

First four latent roots and vectors for correlation matrix for
23 chemical properties of 41 paddy soils

		Roots			
		1	2	3	4
	Root	8·252	3·903	3·069	2·129
	Percentage of variance	35·9	16·9	13·4	9·2
	Cumulative %	35·9	52·8	66·2	75·4

	Variates	Vectors			
		1	2	3	4
1	pH	0·126	−0·223	−0·324	−0·079
2	Electrical Conductivity	0·285	−0·188	−0·080	0·105
3	Total C	0·144	0·389	0·100	0·039
4	Total N	0·149	0·385	0·140	−0·003
5	NH_3-N	0·097	0·186	0·205	0·153
6	Bray-P	0·101	0·165	−0·231	0·450
7	Exchangeable Ca	0·250	0·038	−0·097	−0·355
8	Exchangeable Mg	0·308	−0·115	−0·112	−0·161
9	Exchangeable Na	0·275	−0·184	−0·085	0·187
10	Exchangeable K	0·288	−0·114	−0·045	0·001
11	Free Fe	0·045	−0·243	0·371	0·145
12	Free Mn	0·189	−0·236	0·200	0·257
13	Silt	0·044	−0·029	0·477	−0·077
14	Moisture	0·272	0·228	0·105	−0·072
15	Kaolin	−0·237	−0·117	0·080	0·237
16	Illite	−0·057	−0·184	0·254	−0·044
17	Cation exchange capacity	0·303	0·128	−0·014	−0·231
18	Available Si	0·262	−0·157	−0·092	−0·101
19	Total P	0·164	0·334	0·146	0·196
20	0·2 N HCl-P	0·134	0·180	−0·182	0·436
21	0·2 N HCl-K	0·305	−0·116	−0·036	0·067
22	Reducible Mn	0·144	−0·279	0·198	0·287
23	Sand	−0·180	0·012	−0·376	0·184

Large contributions to the first component derive from exchangeable cations, cation exchange capacity, electrical conductivity, and available silicon. Kyuma and Kawaguchi concentrate on the first component, presumably because it accounts for so much of the variance, and also because it seems to represent chemical characteristics that are desirable in a paddy soil. They find that morphologically similar soils possess similar values of the first component; young marine sediments have the largest values; sandy, kaolinitic ones have the smallest values; soils on clayey marine alluvium and swamp deposits have above average values; brown soils on more weathered materials have values somewhat below

TABLE 8.4

*Correlation coefficients between the first four principal components
and the soil properties measured in South-east Asia*

Soil properties	Principal components			
	1	2	3	4
pH	0·36	−0·44	−0·57	−0·01
Electrical conductivity	0·82	−0·37	−0·14	0·15
Total C	0·41	0·77	0·18	0·06
Total N	0·43	0·76	0·25	0·00
NH₃-N	0·28	0·37	0·36	0·22
Bray P	0·29	0·33	−0·40	0·66
Exchangeable Ca	0·72	0·07	−0·17	−0·52
Exchangeable Mg	0·89	−0·23	−0·20	−0·23
Exchangeable Na	0·79	−0·36	−0·15	0·27
Exchangeable K	0·83	−0·22	−0·08	0·00
Free Fe	0·13	−0·48	0·65	0·21
Free Mn	0·54	−0·47	0·35	0·37
Silt	0·13	−0·06	0·84	−0·11
Moisture	0·78	0·45	0·18	−0·11
Kaolin	−0·68	−0·23	0·14	0·35
Illite	−0·16	−0·36	0·45	−0·06
Cation exchange capacity	0·87	0·25	−0·03	−0·34
Available Si	0·75	−0·31	−0·16	−0·15
Total P	0·47	0·66	0·26	0·29
0·2 N HCl-P	0·38	0·36	−0·32	0·64
0·2 N HCl-K	0·88	−0·23	−0·06	0·10
Reducible Mn	0·41	−0·55	0·35	0·42
Sand	−0·52	0·02	−0·66	0·27

average. Kyuma (1973*a*, *b*) later refines the concept of chemical potential, and combines it with other soil properties to predict rice yield.
However, he introduces a further aid to the interpretation of principal
components by calculating the correlation coefficients between the
components and the original variates. As we should expect, these
(Table 8.4) show that the properties that make the largest contribution
to the first component are also quite strongly correlated with it; r is
in the range 0·8–0·9, a useful result for interpretation. The correlation
coefficients are in general less (in absolute value) for the higher-order
components.

Rotation of principal components

The ease with which principal components can be interpreted in any
physical sense is largely fortuitous. Principal components are mathematical constructs, and do not necessarily have any physical meaning.

We saw in the example from Oxfordshire that although we obtained an informative two-dimensional display of the relationships between sampling sites, we could not easily express the axes of variation in physical terms.

There have been numerous attempts, especially in psychology, to obtain meaningful variates from combinations of others using methods that are known collectively as 'factor analysis'. Some of the methods allow the user to specify which original variates are to be combined to derive a specific factor, and it seems that much of the popularity of factor analysis derives from this: the scientists can embody his experience, or prejudice, in the analysis. They therefore impose structure on the data, and this is undesirable for ordination in which the aim is to reveal structure. Readers who wish to pursue the topic should consult one of the standard texts, e.g. Harman (1967), and Lawley and Maxwell (1971). They should also read Blackith and Reyment's (1971) criticism of factor analysis and several of the references given there.

There are, however, several methods whereby meaningful factors can be obtained with relatively little control from the investigator. These are simply analytic rotations of the principal components. We shall consider only one of these, the Varimax rotation, developed by Kaiser (1958) and probably the most widely used in other sciences. The principle of the method is intuitively simple. The first few principal components are chosen on the assumption that they adequately represent the scatter in the data. This is, of course, a subjective decision, but it is the only one the investigator needs to make in the Varimax method. The distribution of points is projected into the space defined by these components, and the configuration then rotated rigidly to new axes so that, as far as possible, each original axis of measurement is closely aligned to one of the new factor axes and at right angles to all others; thus each original variate contributes strongly to one of the factors and little to the others. The factor axes remain orthogonal, and in their new positions are said to have a 'simpler' structure; that is, they are simpler to interpret.

Kaiser defined the simplicity of a factor i as the variance of its squared loadings, say V_i. Thus if we have a $k \times p$ matrix $\mathbf{M}$ of loadings, then

$$V_i = \frac{1}{p} \sum_{j=1}^{p} \left\{ m_{ij}^2 - \frac{1}{p} \sum_{j=1}^{p} m_{ij}^2 \right\}^2 \qquad (8.22)$$

Then for the whole matrix

$$V = \sum_{i=1}^{k} V_i. \tag{8.23}$$

Kaiser's original technique was to maximize V.

Formula (8.22) gives equal weight to all variates regardless of the proportion of their variances retained in the principal components. This seemed less than satisfactory, and Kaiser considered that a better measure would be obtained by dividing the squared elements of **M** by their corresponding *communalities*. The communality of a variate, h^2, is a measure of the proportion of its variance that is represented by k principal components, and for the jth variate is calculated as

$$h_j^2 = \sum_{i=1}^{k} m_{ij}^2. \tag{8.24}$$

The Varimax criterion calculated is thus

$$V' = \sum_{i=1}^{k} \left[\frac{1}{p} \sum_{j=1}^{p} \left\{ \frac{m_{ij}^2}{h_j^2} - \frac{1}{p} \sum_{j=1}^{p} \frac{m_{ij}^2}{h_j^2} \right\}^2 \right]. \tag{8.25}$$

The values of m_{ij} are modified, subject to the condition that they retain the relationships in the original configuration, and V' increased by iteration until a maximum is found. The values of m_{ij} that achieve this define the required rotation. Readers can find the details in Kaiser (1958), and a useful program for the calculation is given by Cooley and Lohnes (1971).

The technique has been applied to the Oxfordshire data as an illustration. In this instance the first two components have been rotated, and the results are shown in Fig. 8.4 and 8.5. By confining the rotation to the first two dimensions the relationships of the individuals to one another in the plane are exactly retained. Thus Fig. 8.4 is still the most informative two-dimensional display. Similarly the angular relationships among the vectors remain, Fig. 8.5. However, it is clear that there has been a clockwise rotation through approximately 40°, and this enables meaning to be given to the new axes. The first axis, the horizontal one, now strongly represents colour chroma, average matrix suction, and strength of the soil – all properties associated with the water regime of the soil. The driest, strongest, and brightest-coloured soil profiles are on the right; the wettest, weakest, and dullest are on the left. The second axis has strong contributions from particle size and plastic and liquid limits, properties embodied in the texture of the soil. The heaviest

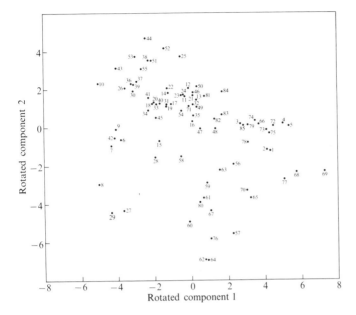

FIG. 8.4. Scatter of 85 sampling sites rotated in the plane of the first two principal components by Varimax criterion

textured profiles are at the top, the lightest at the bottom. It is worth noting that there are very few profiles falling immediately to the left of centre with negative values of the second factor. In our interpretation there are very few moderately wet, light-textured profiles. If the soil is light then it is likely to be dry or very wet, whereas heavier textured soil shows almost the full range in wetness.

Principal coordinates

Principal-component analysis, as we have seen, adheres strictly to the geometry of the original Euclidean model. And though we may eventually project the scatter from many dimensions into few, the distances between plotted points, and hence the relationships that they represent, are approximations to the Euclidean distances as defined in Chapter 7. We have also seen that Euclidean distance is not always the most appropriate measure of the likeness between two individuals, and that if our data are not metric we might be unable to calculate it anyway. Several methods have been proposed to display relationships among individuals on metric scales in few dimensions from data that are all or mainly

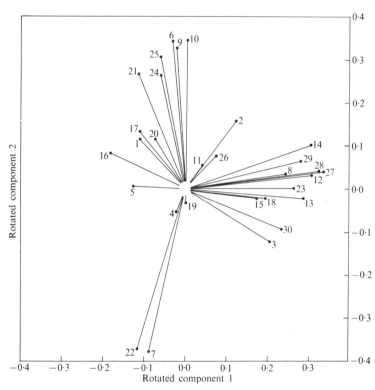

FIG. 8.5. Rotation of vectors by Varimax method. The variates are listed in table 8.1

qualitative. These include Kruskal's (1964) *multidimensional scaling*, and *correspondence analysis* (Benzécri, 1973), or *reciprocal averaging* as it is termed by Hill (1973, 1974). However, Gower (1966) has shown that provided a suitable measure is used for calculating similarities or dissimilarities between individuals their coordinates can be found relative to principal axes. He calls the method *principal-coordinate analysis*. It has been used to elucidate structure in several soil populations by Rayner (1966, 1969), Campbell *et al.* (1970), and Webster and Butler (1976).

Principal coordinates are calculated from a matrix of 'distances' between individuals. So the first step in the analysis is to calculate a distance d_{ij} between every pair of individuals i and j. We may use one of the measures described in Chapter 7. Alternatively, if we have measured likeness using one of the similarity indexes S, we can scale it in the range 0 (for maximum possible dissimilarity) to 1 (for identity) and take

$$d_{ij} = \{2(1 - S_{ij})\}^{1/2}. \tag{8.26}$$

From the distances between individuals we form the $n \times n$ matrix $\mathbf{Q}$, with elements $q_{ij} = -\tfrac{1}{2}d_{ij}^2$. The matrix $\mathbf{Q}$ is now adjusted by subtracting from each element the corresponding row and column means and adding the general mean. Thus, we form $\mathbf{F}$ with elements

$$f_{ij} = q_{ij} - \bar{q}_i - \bar{q}_j + \bar{\bar{q}} \tag{8.27}$$

The latent roots and vectors of $\mathbf{F}$ are found, and the vectors arranged as columns in a $n \times n$ matrix $\mathbf{C}$. The rows then represent coordinates of the points, thus

$$\mathbf{C} = \overbrace{\begin{bmatrix} c_{11} & c_{12} & \cdots & c_{1n} \\ c_{21} & c_{22} & \cdots & c_{2n} \\ \cdot & \cdot & \cdots & \cdot \\ \cdot & \cdot & \cdots & \cdot \\ \cdot & \cdot & & \cdot \\ c_{n1} & c_{n2} & & c_{nn} \end{bmatrix}}^{\substack{\text{vectors} \\ 1 \quad 2 \ \ldots \ n}} \left.\begin{array}{l} 1 \\ 2 \\ \cdot \\ \cdot \\ \cdot \\ n \end{array}\right\} \text{points} \tag{8.28}$$

The vectors are now normalized so that the sums of squares of their elements equal their corresponding latent roots. This transforms the matrix $\mathbf{C}$ into a new matrix, say $\mathbf{G}$, with elements

$$g_{ik} = \left\{ c_{ik}^2 \lambda_k \Big/ \sum_{i=1}^{n} c_{ik}^2 \right\}^{1/2}. \tag{8.29}$$

That is,

$$\mathbf{G}'\mathbf{G} = \mathbf{\Lambda}, \quad \text{and} \quad \mathbf{G}\mathbf{G}' = \mathbf{F}.$$

Gower shows that when this transformation is made, and starting from the matrix $\mathbf{Q}$ as defined above, the square of the distance between any two points i and j, whose coordinates are the ith and jth rows of $\mathbf{G}$, equals d_{ij}^2. The latent vectors scaled in this way represent exactly the distances between individuals and define their positions relative to principal axes. The matrix $\mathbf{F}$ must be psd, i.e. it must have no negative roots, otherwise the individuals cannot be represented in Euclidean space. Many kinds of similarity matrix are psd and can therefore be analyzed in this way (Gower 1966). Note that the positions of n points can always be represented in $n-1$ dimensions, so that $\mathbf{F}$ always has at least one zero root.

As in principal-component analysis, it is usual to find that a few roots are much larger than the others, so that a good representation can be obtained in a few dimensions. Since we transformed the vectors so that $\sum_{i=1}^{n} g_{ik}^2 = \lambda_k$, contributions to the distances between points from vectors corresponding to small roots must themselves be small, and can often be ignored.

When the starting matrix $\mathbf{Q}$ consists of Pythagorean distances calculated as in eqn. (7.24), Gower's method gives results identical with those of principal-component analysis. This is true not only for fully quantitative variates but also for binary characters (scored 0 or 1) for which principal-component analysis is often thought to be invalid. However, its attraction is that it can be used when Pythagorean distance is inappropriate or impossible to calculate because the data are wholly or partly qualitative.

Although principal-coordinate analysis is more versatile than classical component analysis, the latter is preferable from two standpoints. First, component values are linearly related to the values of the soil properties: the elements of the latent vectors can be considered as the contributions made by the original variates to the new components, and often enable the new axes to be interpreted in a pedologically meaningful way. Principal-coordinate analysis does not allow this. Secondly, if there are many individuals and few variates, component analysis is much the more efficient ordination method. By suitable use of backing store an almost unlimited number of individuals can be included in a component analysis. In a principal-coordinate analysis the $n \times n$ matrix of similarities or distances, or its $n(n+1)/2$ lower triangle at least, has to be held in core, and core size therefore imposes a ceiling on the number of individuals that can be handled in a single analysis. This is between 300 and 400 for the bigger computers. However, coordinates relative to principal axes can be found for additional points as described below.

Additional individuals

When we have carried out an ordination we may wish to add new individuals to the scatter diagrams, i.e. we may wish to calculate their coordinates relative to the principal axes already found. After a component analysis there is no difficulty: we simply compute for a new point i_{n+1},

$$y_{n+1} = x_{n+1}C'.$$ (8.30)

When principal axes have been found from the matrix of distances or similarities the task is less easy, but Gower (1968) has again provided a solution.

We proceed by first calculating the distances between the new $(n+1)$th individual, and all the initial individuals, $i = 1, 2, \ldots, n$. Let us denote these distances by $d_{n+1,i}$. We also require the distances between the original individuals and the centroid of the configuration, d_i. These are contained as their squares in the diagonal of the matrix F. This follows from $GG' = F$ and the fact that in forming F from Q we transferred the centroid of the n points to the origin. So

$$d_i^2 = f_{ii} = \bar{\bar{q}} - 2q_i.$$ (8.31)

We now compute a row vector e with elements

$$e_i = d_i^2 - d_{n+1,i}^2.$$ (8.32)

The coordinates of point i_{n+1} relative to the principal axes are then given by

$$g'_{n+1} = \tfrac{1}{2} \Lambda^{-1} G' e'.$$ (8.33)

Missing values

A tiresome problem, not only in principal-component and -coordinate analysis but in almost all kinds of multivariate analysis, occurs when values of variables are missing for some individuals. Component analysis cannot proceed without a complete data matrix, so when data are missing a necessary preliminary is to replace them by suitable values. In the absence of better information, the best value to insert for a variate is the mean of that variate. If other information is available then a better estimate may be inserted. In either case, provided there are only few missing values, estimating them in this way is unlikely to affect the outcome appreciably or to mislead.

Many of the formulae for calculating similarities between individuals can be adapted to deal with missing values without inserting estimates. Similarities are brought to a common scale by dividing the sum of similarities, distances or whatever for single characters by the number of characters involved in each comparison of individuals. If we take mean character distance between individuals i and j as an example, we have

$$d_{ij} = \frac{1}{p_{ij}} \sum_{i=1}^{k} |x_{ik} - x_{jk}|/r_k \tag{8.34}$$

where p_{ij} is the number of attributes for which $|x_{ik} - x_{jk}|$ can be calculated. If either x_{ik} or x_{jk} is missing or inapplicable then there is one less element in the sum $\Sigma|x_{ik} - x_{jk}|$ and p_{ij} is diminished by 1. This seems to give principal-coordinate analysis a further advantage over component analysis.

In fact this is something of a delusion. If there are few missing values then the result is again little altered by whichever method we choose to deal with the problem. If there are many, then it is likely that the similarity or distance matrix will have some negative roots, and real coordinates in Euclidean space cannot then be found. Furthermore, as Anderson (1971) points out, since the method represents similarity for the missing variates by the similarity for those that are present, it is unlikely to be satisfactory when characters are not strongly related. It is sounder to estimate the similarity for a missing variate by the average of all similarities for that variate; and this is equivalent to replacing missing values by the mean for the variates concerned, as before.

9. Numerical classification: hierarchical systems

A fool sees not the same tree
that a wise man sees.
        WILLIAM BLAKE
    Marriage of Heaven and Hell

Chapter 1 introduced the idea of replacing classification by measurement to describe soil precisely and consistently. Quantitative measurement was regarded as superior to qualitative classification. Chapters 7 and 8 described how we could use measurements to relate individual soil specimens, profiles and sampling sites to one another, and to see order among them. Nevertheless it is often helpful to classify soil even when data are quantitative. A classification gives a simple picture of the data. It is convenient to be able to talk about one or more groups of soil using names, rather than lists of characters and their values. A classification might enable expensive measurements to be made more economically than otherwise. Land must be divided into parcels (classes), any one of which can be treated uniformly for planning and management. But equally, when quantitative data are available the soil scientist will want to take full advantage of them to classify the soil in definable and repeatable ways.

We saw in Chapter 5 how we could classify soil in a simple numerical way from measured values. We saw that we could divide the measured range of a property of interest at certain critical or convenient points. We called the process *dissection.* If two or three properties were judged to be important then we could divide all of their scales to produce a classification still with manageably few groups. However, when many soil characters are relevant, simultaneous dissection of every scale is clearly not feasible: far too many groups result. If we are to classify soil populations taking into account many characters then we must find some alternative.

Dissection as described has another potential disadvantage: it takes no account of any discontinuities in the soil population. If the frequency distribution of a variable has several peaks it might be thought that the most sensible or 'natural' place to divide the range would be through the troughs between the peaks. So unless there are critical values at which a scale should be divided, some means is needed for discovering suitable dividing points. When extended to several dimensions it is easier to think of those individuals in the more densely occupied parts of the character space as constituting *clusters*, and we may very reasonably wish to isolate them in our classification.

The concept of 'natural' classification has a second facet. The term is often used to mean a classification in which the individuals in any one group are generally similar to one another. It applies especially to populations possessing many characters of interest, so that members of a natural group should be similar in many respects, and that grouping should be useful for many purposes (see Gilmour 1937).

These twin threads of division at the gaps and classes that are generally useful have strongly influenced the search for mathematical solutions to the problem of classifying multivariate populations. There have been other influences. Many of the problems have been in biology with its long tradition of hierarchical classification and a genetic theory to account for hierarchical arrangements of organisms. So it has been thought that a classification derived mathematically should also be hierarchical, hopefully recognizing species, genera, families, etc. Some workers have expressly sought to identify genetic links between members of a population in this way, and been more or less successful. There have been mathematical and computational considerations: the attraction of elegant algorithms by which classification might be created, and the need to obtain results without monopolizing the computer for too long or having jobs terminated by the operators. These too have tended to favour a hierarchical approach to classification. So we find that most attempts to classify individuals mathematically or numerically have sought to create classes within which the members are generally alike and substantially different from the members of other classes, and to arrange them in hierarchies.

A hierarchical classification is one in which individuals belong to small groups, the small groups belong to larger groups, and so on. It may also be thought of as a division of character space in which the whole space is divided into large compartments, which are divided into smaller compartments, and these in turn are divided into yet smaller compartments. Division or grouping is usually made at a few distinct levels of generalization, known as *categories*. In general, classes in any one category are disjoint, since any appreciable overlap of classes is incompatible with a hierarchy. The methods for creating hierarchies numerically are themselves either agglomerative, putting individuals together into larger and larger groups, or divisive, creating smaller and smaller groups from a single population. However, they do not usually proceed through distinct categories.

Methods for creating classification are often known by the general name of *cluster analysis*. They are intended to identify clusters in the population. The name is misleading, however, because most methods will create classes whether there are clusters in any true sense or not. The hierarchical methods also arrange the individuals and classes hierarchically, again irrespective of whether the population possesses hierarchical structure. So these methods cannot be expected to perform well on populations that are poorly structured, as most soil populations seem to be. Nevertheless, they are the best-developed means of numerical classification, and the agglomerative procedures have become popular in soil science. This chapter therefore describes the general agglomerative strategy and details of particular forms of it, and then discusses it critically. We shall look briefly at divisive schemes, but leave non-hierarchical methods until Chapter 11.

Hierarchical agglomerative grouping

The starting point for most agglomerative methods is a set of similarities (or dissimilarities) between individuals. A measure is chosen to represent the relations between individuals and its value calculated between all pairs to form a matrix (see Chapter 7). In practice, the measure is usually expressed as similarity and scaled so that identity is represented by the value 1, and maximum dissimilarity by zero. This matrix contains all the information needed.

To make matters as clear as possible, however, we shall assume that our starting matrix is a dissimilarity matrix and its values are the Euclidean distances between individuals.

The values in the matrix are scanned to find the smallest, which is, of course, the distance between the closest pair of individuals. These individuals are fused to form a group. From here on there are several possible courses of action, and we have to choose. The simplest of these is the single-linkage method, and for this reason it is described first.

Single-linkage grouping

This was the first method for creating a hierarchy from a similarity matrix, and was made widely known largely through the work of Sneath (1957). Rayner (1966) and Moore and Russell (1967) used it in their early work on soil classification. In ecology it is also known as the *nearest-neighbour* strategy (Lance and Williams 1967b).

TABLE 9.1
*Values of the first two principal
components of nine sites*

Site	Components	
	1	2
6	−2·630	−2·809
14	−2·089	0·726
34	−2·396	−0·661
45	−1·861	−0·729
47	0·367	0·266
57	5·200	−3·023
59	2·481	−1·728
63	2·594	−0·807
70	4·354	−0·732

After fusion of the closest pair of individuals, grouping proceeds as follows. The matrix of distances is re-scanned and the second shortest distance found. If this is between a member of the first group and a third individual then the latter joins the group. If it is between two other individuals, they are fused to form a second group. The process is repeated a third and further times, and fusion decided as above. Now, however, if the two individuals in question are in two different groups,

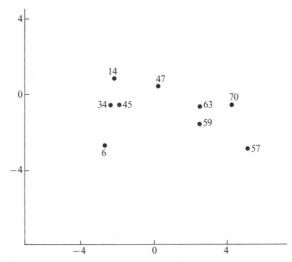

FIG. 9.1. Scatter of nine points in a plane. Their coordinates are given in Table 9.1

the two groups are fused. The process continues until all individuals are contained in a single group.

To illustrate the procedure nine sites have been chosen from the survey of west Oxfordshire for which principal components were calculated in Chapter 8. Their values are given in Table 9.1. Fig. 9.1 shows their relative positions in the plane of the first two principal components as before. The values of these two components only are used here as data from which to construct a hierarchy.

The first fusion is between sites 34 and 45, separated by 0·54 units of distance. The next fusion is of sites 59 and 63 at a distance 0·93, and the third occurs to join site 14 and 34, which already belongs in the group with site 45. Other fusions take place in sequence (the relevant inter-point distances are shown in Fig. 9.9, discussed on p.178), and the final one occurs when site 47 joins site 63.

The result can be shown as a tree or *dendrogram*, Fig. 9.2. The vertical scale represents distance in character space, and the horizontal lines joining the vertical stems of the tree are placed at positions corresponding to the distances at which fusion occurs. The horizontal dimension has no scale, and the order in which individuals are placed is to some extent arbitrary. Any part of the tree can be rotated about the stem immediately below without changing its structure, as in a mobile.

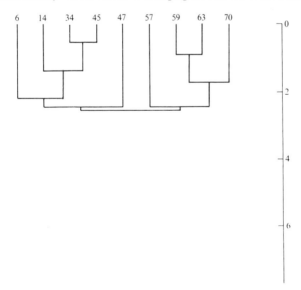

FIG. 9.2. Single linkage dendrogram for the nine points in Fig. 9.1

A classification with some desired number of classes can readily be obtained from the tree by drawing a horizontal line through it to cut just that number of vertical stems. For example, two classes can be obtained by drawing a line at value 2·45, while a line at 2·0 gives five classes.

A feature of the single-linkage strategy is that fusion is always decided on the distances between pairs of individuals only. The distance between a group and another individual is thus the distance between the individual and the nearest member of the group. The distance between groups is similarly the distance between their nearest members. The dispositions of the groups as a whole are not taken into account, and this is undoubtedly a weakness of the method.

A closely related feature is that as a group grows, it becomes increasingly likely that it has neighbouring individuals that will soon fuse with it. There is therefore a strong tendency for successive additions of individuals to existing groups rather than the formation and then fusion of groups of roughly equal size. The process is known as 'chaining', and its effect is illustrated for soil by Moore and Russell (1967). Chaining can result from chain-like structure in the population. With soil it is more often an artifact, and at worst can lead to a

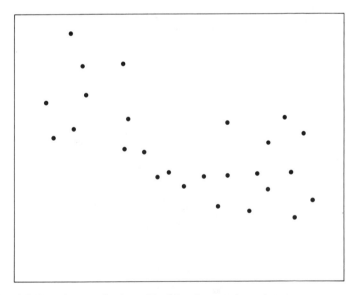

FIG. 9.3. Two clusters of points with chain of connecting points

grouping that quite fails to recognize obvious clusters. The extreme is shown in Fig. 9.3 where two clusters are connected by a few close individuals. Single-linkage agglomeration applied to this situation will begin among the connecting individuals and proceed by successively adding individuals or small groups from the two main clusters.

There is thus serious risk that a hierarchy formed by single linkage will misrepresent relationships among individuals, and that a classification derived by cutting it will be poor. To overcome this Wishart (1969a) modified the technique so that fusion occurred only when several near-neighbouring individuals were identified. The number of neighbours and the radius within which they are judged to be near can be set to identify true clusters and to avoid chaining through the connections. Wishart calls the method *mode analysis*, and it is an option is the fairly widely available CLUSTAN program (Wishart 1969b).

Single linkage is simple, it will recognize gaps in a distribution, and in the form of mode analysis will identify clusters. Despite this the strategy has lost favour to other strategies, some of which we consider now.

Centroid method

Perhaps the most attractive fusion strategy from a geometric point of view is Gower's (1967b) centroid method. In it a newly formed group becomes, in effect, a synthetic individual whose position in the Euclidean character space is defined by the centroid of the group. Distances between this centroid and other individuals are then calculated and substituted for the distances from the pair it represents. All distances are re-examined and the procedure repeated, as described for single linkage.

The situation at fusion is illustrated in Fig. 9.4. Here a group at A containing n_A individuals is about to fuse with a group at B containing n_B individuals to form a new group that will contain $n_A + n_B$ individuals. This group will be placed at its centroid, C, on the line AB such that the ratio $AC:CB = n_B:n_A$. Distances to other individuals, the one at E for example, are then calculated as follows

$$d_{CE} = \left\{ \frac{n_A}{n_A + n_B} d_{AE}^2 + \frac{n_B}{n_A + n_B} d_{BE}^2 - \frac{n_A n_B}{(n_A + n_B)^2} d_{AB}^2 \right\}^{1/2} .(9.1)$$

The reader might like to verify this for himself.

When we use the strategy to group the population displayed in Fig. 9.2, the first two fusions are of sites 34 and 45, and 59 and 63. The third fusion adds site 14 to the group 34 + 45, and as it happens the distance between site 14 and the centroid of 34 + 45 is 1·42. Fusion proceeds until finally the group comprising sites 6, 14, 34, 45, and 47 joins the one consisting of 57, 59, 63, and 70. Fig. 9.5 shows the result.

The first three fusions by this method are identical with those achieved using single linkage. The fourth also joins sites 70 to group

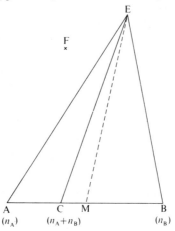

FIG. 9.4. Geometric relationships of centroid strategy (see text for explanation)

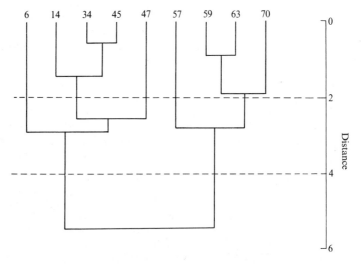

FIG. 9.5. Dendrogram resulting from centroid fusion of nine points in Fig. 9.1

59 + 63. The next fusion of site 47 to the group 14 + 34 + 45 is different, however, and we consider what has happened in this left-hand group. When site 34 joined 45, the synthetic individual representing them took up a position mid-way between them. Site 14 joined them, and the centroid of the three then lay somewhat above this mid-point, where it was nearer to site 47 than to site 6. The group was joined by site 47, and the centroid moved to the right. At each stage it moved further from individual 6. This action is known as *drift*, and can have important consequences. Nevertheless the centroid method seems to separate the two main groups more clearly than single linkage does: compare Figs. 9.5 and 9.2.

Let us now apply the strategy to a more realistic situation: 40 individuals on each of which 30 properties have been measured are to be classified. The individuals have been chosen at random from the 85 analysed earlier (Chapter 8), and their distribution in the plane of the first two principal components is shown in Fig. 9.6. The matrix of distances between individuals is calculated, then examined, and fusion proceeds as before. The result is presented in Fig. 9.7. The general structure of relationships evident in the scatter diagram can be seen in the dendrogram. However, the reader will remember that when the scatter of individuals in a character space of many dimensions is projected, the distances between individuals in the chosen plane represent only approximations to their true relations. The precise order of agglomeration cannot therefore be determined from a scatter diagram, and the early fusions often provide information about relationships that are obscured in the projection on principal axes. We should note that the last few fusions in this example are of individuals and small groups. The dendrogram cannot be cut to give a tidy classification with few groups, as we might have wished.

The centroid strategy takes account of the positions of all members of each group in determining fusion. However, despite this and its exact geometric representation it is still not entirely satisfactory.

Weighted centroid method

In some instances it happens that a pair of groups that are to be fused contain disparate numbers of individuals, so that in eqn. (9.1) n_A and n_B are very different. If n_A is very much larger than n_B, for example, then the distance from the new group to the group at E is heavily weighted towards the distance AE (Fig. 9.4). If the groups at A and B are well-defined clusters, one of which just happens to be poorly

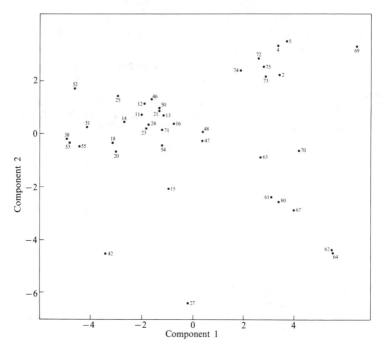

FIG. 9.6. Scatter diagram of 40 soil profiles in west Oxfordshire projected on to plane of first two principal components

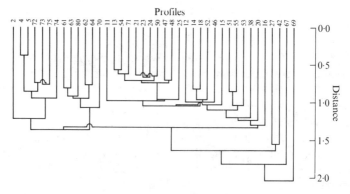

FIG. 9.7. Dendogram from centroid fusion of 40 west Oxfordshire profiles

represented in our sample, we should not want the bias that would be present in the group that they form. We should almost certainly prefer groups to have equal weight regardless of the number of individuals they contain. If so then we should place the new group at M, the mid point on AB, and distance to E becomes

$$d_{EM} = \{\tfrac{1}{2}d_{AE}^2 + \tfrac{1}{2}d_{BE}^2 - \tfrac{1}{4}d_{AB}^2\}^{1/2}. \qquad (9.2)$$

The terms 'weighted' and 'unweighted' in the context need explanation. Normally we should regard formula (9.1) as weighted and formula (9.2) as unweighted. However, the terms were used by Sokal and Michener (1958) in the reverse sense. Their attention was focused on the original individuals, so that by unweighted they meant that all individuals had equal weight. Thus in Fig. 9.4, C is the unweighted centroid of all the individuals constituting the new group comprising the groups at A and B. In eqn. (9.2), if the groups at A and B are of different size, then the original individuals in them do not have equal weight in determining the centroid, and so in this sense the formula is weighted. This usage has become conventional in numerical classification, and we shall adhere to it to avoid confusion. Weighted centroid agglomeration is also known as *median grouping* (Lance and Williams 1967a).

Group-average method

In general, as agglomeration proceeds successive fusions take place between individuals and between groups that are further and further apart. However, in the centroid method fusion occasionally creates a group whose centroid is nearer to another group or individual than the distance between its constituent members. Suppose in Fig. 9.4 that the group or individuals centred at E were displaced to a point F, approximately on the perpendicular through C. The distance AB is only a little less than either AF or BF, and when fusion takes place and the new group is centred at F, FC is shorter than AB. Such an event is known as a *reversal*, and several are apparent in Fig. 9.7. The process is no longer monotonic: the order in which fusions take place is not the same as the order of the similarity values at fusion.

Intuitively reversals seem undesirable, and they can be avoided by using the group-average method developed earlier by Sokal and Michener (1958). In this method when two individuals or groups join, the distances or similarities between the new group and every other are computed as the *average* distance or similarity between all the members of the new group and those of the others. This destroys the nice geometry of the centroid method, and average distances are usually a little larger than distances between centroids. However, the differences between the two are usually small, and the group-average method ensures that agglomeration proceeds monotonically.

As with the centroid method, either individuals or groups can be given equal weight, as desired.

Complete linkage grouping

This method, also called the *furthest-neighbour* strategy (Lance and Williams 1967b), is the exact antithesis of single-linkage grouping. When an individual is considered for admission to an existing group, the criterion applied is the distance between it and the furthest member of the group. Similarly the distance between two groups is regarded as the distance between their most distant members.

Fusion again depends on distances between pairs of individuals. However, as a group grows so its distance from its neighbours, as measured by the above criterion, increases. The result is that groups tend to be hyperspherical and, at some stage in the procedure, to be of roughly equal extent in character space.

The procedure was compared with others by Moore and Russell (1967), but has not otherwise been used in pedology.

Combinatorial representation

Lance and Williams (1966, 1967b) have shown that all the above methods for creating hierarchies are variants of a single linear system. To understand this, consider again Fig. 9.4 and its meaning. Two groups at A and B with n_A and n_B members respectively fuse to form a group with $n_A + n_B$ members, notionally at some point, say K, in the vicinity of C and M. We consider the relation between this new group and another group at E. Before fusion the distances or dissimilarities d_{AB}, d_{AE}, d_{BE}, and group sizes n_A and n_B are all known and can be used to calculate the value of d_{EK} from the equation:

$$d_{EK} = \alpha_A d_{AE} + \alpha_B d_{BE} + \beta d_{AB} + \gamma |d_{AE} - d_{BE}|. \qquad (9.3)$$

Lance and Williams call this relation *combinatorial*, and proceed to derive the values of the parameters α_A, α_B, β, and γ for each strategy. Lance and Williams also point out that when $\gamma = 0$ agglomeration will proceed monotonically provided that

$$\alpha_A + \alpha_B + \beta \geqslant 1.$$

The parameters for each of the strategies so far considered are as follows.

(i) *Unweighted centroid.* Here, provided dissimilarity is defined as the square of the distance between groups, we can readily see from eqn. (9.1) that

$$\alpha_A = \frac{n_A}{n_A + n_B}, \quad \alpha_B = \frac{n_B}{n_A + n_B},$$

$$\beta = -\frac{n_A n_B}{(n_A + n_B)^2} = -\alpha_A \alpha_B,$$

and $\gamma = 0$.

(ii) *Weighted centroid.* Dissimilarity is again squared distance, and the parameters are very simply

$$\alpha_A = \tfrac{1}{2}, \quad \alpha_B = \tfrac{1}{2}, \quad \beta = -\tfrac{1}{4}, \quad \text{and} \quad \gamma = 0.$$

(iii) *Unweighted group average.* This is combinatorial for all measures of dissimilarity.

Assume that the group at E contains n_E individuals, and that the dissimilarity between the jth individual in it and the ith individual in the group at A is represented by $1 - S_{ij}$. Then the average dissimilarity between the two groups at E and A is

$$d_{AE} = \frac{1}{n_A} \frac{1}{n_E} \sum_{i=1}^{n_A} \sum_{j=1}^{n_E} (1 - S_{ij}). \tag{9.4}$$

Likewise

$$d_{BE} = \frac{1}{n_B} \frac{1}{n_E} \sum_{i=1}^{n_B} \sum_{j=1}^{n_E} (1 - S_{ij}). \tag{9.5}$$

The average dissimilarity d_{EK} that we require is

$$d_{EK} = \frac{1}{n_E} \frac{1}{n_A + n_B} \sum_{i=1}^{n_B + n_A} \sum_{j=1}^{n_E} (1 - S_{ij})$$

$$= \frac{n_A}{n_A + n_B} d_{AE} + \frac{n_B}{n_A + n_B} d_{BE}. \tag{9.6}$$

The parameters for the combinatorial equation are thus

$$\alpha_A = \frac{n_A}{n_A + n_B}, \quad \alpha_B = \frac{n_B}{n_A + n_B},$$

$$\beta = 0, \quad \gamma = 0$$

It can now be seen that when dissimilarities are given as distances, the group average distance d_{EK} will be greater than the corresponding centroid distance by

$$\beta d_{AB}^2.$$

(iv) *Weighted group average.* The parameters for this are even more simply

$$\alpha_A = \alpha_B = \tfrac{1}{2}, \quad \beta = 0, \quad \gamma = 0.$$

(v) *Single linkage.* Here the dissimilarity d_{EK} is equal to the smallest of d_{AE} and d_{BE}. The parameters that give this are

$$\alpha_A = \tfrac{1}{2}, \quad \alpha_B = \tfrac{1}{2}, \quad \beta = 0, \quad \gamma = -\tfrac{1}{2}.$$

(vi) *Complete linkage.* We here wish to identify d_{EK} with the largest of d_{AE} and d_{BE}, and the parameters are

$$\alpha_A = \alpha_B = \tfrac{1}{2}, \quad \beta = 0, \quad \gamma = +\tfrac{1}{2}.$$

The advantages of a combinatorial strategy are considerable. For once the matrix of similarities or distances between individuals has been calculated, the original data are no longer needed, and the space that they occupy in the computer can be released for other purposes. The combinatorial equation can be used to calculate all new similarities as grouping proceeds, though in some instances it is not quite the most efficient way.

Flexible grouping strategy

In a procedure such as complete-linkage agglomeration the distances between groups effectively increase as the groups grow. It appears as though the space around them dilates. The larger a group becomes the less likely it is to fuse with a single individual or small group, and the latter will tend to join together in preference. Therefore, groups tend to be of roughly equal size. The converse is true with single linkage, and we have already noted its tendency to chain. The centroid methods retain the geometric relationships, and the group-average methods also appear to conserve the space. Nevertheless chaining can still occur, and when the aim is to produce a classification with few groups this can be a nuisance. The complete linkage method thus has a potential advantage over the other methods. The tendency is strong, and a strategy with only moderate space dilation might be preferred.

To achieve this Lance and Williams (1966) proposed their *flexible strategy.* It is combinatorial, obeying eqn. (9.3) with the following constraints:

$$\alpha_A + \alpha_B + \beta = 1,$$

$$\alpha_A = \alpha_B,$$

$$\beta < 1,$$

$$\gamma = 0.$$

The strategy is flexible in that the user can adjust β and so vary the degree of space distortion around the growing groups. Values of β near 1 produce very strong space-contraction and chaining. As β is decreased this effect is less marked, until at some small negative value (Lance and Williams are unable to define it precisely) space is conserved. Thereafter, decreasing β causes space dilation and increasingly distinct groups in the dendrogram. Lance and Williams (1967*b*) illustrate these effects by dendrograms in their paper. They recommend $\beta = -0.25$ for general use. This is slightly space-dilating. When $\beta = 0$ the result is the weighted-group average strategy. Note also that since $\alpha_A + \alpha_B + \beta = 1$, agglomeration is monotonic.

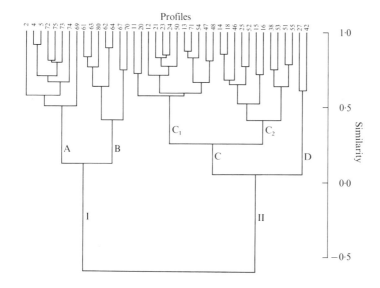

FIG. 9.8. Dendrogram for 40 soil profiles in west Oxfordshire obtained using the flexible strategy with $\beta = -0.25$ and the mean character distance as similarity coefficient

The flexible strategy is conceptually attractive, but there is the risk that β will be so chosen that it obscures information on the structure of a population that would be revealed in a space-conserving strategy. The strategy has been used with $\beta = -0.25$ by soil scientists in Australia (Moore and Russell 1967; Campbell *et al.* 1970; Moore *et al.* 1972) where this option is standard in several large classification programs. Fig. 9.8 illustrates the use of the strategy on the same forty sites as in Fig. 9.7 with β set to -0.25, and using the mean character distance as the dissimilarity coefficient. The evident advantages are (a) all individuals are fused early; (b) chaining, which was to some extent present in Fig. 9.7, no longer occurs; (c) the structure evident in the scatter diagram (Fig. 9.6) still seems well represented; and (d) a classification into few groups can easily be made by drawing a horizontal line through the lower part of the tree.

We have already given meaning to the axes of the scatter diagram. As it happens, in this instance we can also give meaningful conventional names to several branches of the tree. At the two-group level, I contains entirely brown earths, while II consists of gleys and gleyed brown earths. At the four-group level A consists of medium-textured brown earths, and B of brown sandy soil; C consists of medium and heavy textured gleys and gleyed soil, and D consists of sandy gleys. Further subdivision of C gives C_1, a group of moderately gleyed profiles, and C_2 gleys of heavy texture.

Ward's method

This technique, due to Ward (1963), enjoys some popularity and has been used in several soil studies. It aims to minimize the 'error sum of squares', that is, the sum of the squares of the distances between individuals and their group centroids, Σd^2. Its starting point is a matrix of distances between individuals. At each stage the fusion that takes place is the one that causes the least increase in Σd^2. As Wishart (1969a) points out, for the fusion of two groups A and B with n_A and n_B members respectively, this increase is equivalent to

$$\frac{n_A - n_B}{n_A + n_B} d^2_{AB}$$

where d_{AB} is the distance between the group centroids. The method clearly favours the fusion of individuals and small groups, and is strongly space dilating.

At first sight Ward's method appears the same as optimizing a non-hierarchical classification using the SS_w criterion, described in Chapter 11. But this is not so. The method is strictly hierarchical: once two individuals or groups are joined they remain so, however inappropriate this might be at coarser levels of classification. The quantity Σd^2 might be near its minimum at some stage in the hierarchy, but cannot be so at every stage.

Other hierarchical methods

A number of other agglomerative methods have been devised for hierarchical classification. None have any obvious advantages over those we have discussed for classifying soil, but readers who wish to study the subject further should see the much more comprehensive account by Sneath and Sokal (1973) and follow the many references they give.

A feature of agglomerative classification that can be a serious limitation is that the $\binom{n}{2}$ similarity (or dissimilarity) coefficients must usually be held in the core of the computer. The process is likely to be prohibitively time-consuming otherwise. This imposes a ceiling on the number of individuals that can be classified in a single run, usually between 300 and 400 on large computers. Faced with this situation, a possible alternative is to use a divisive strategy. *Association analysis*, developed by Williams and Lambert (1959), is the best known of these and has been valuable in ecological classification. The starting point is a set of binary data, the presence or absence of each of p attributes for each of n individuals. In ecology the individuals to be classified are usually quadrats, or 'stands', and the attributes are species. If the properties of interest are continuous variables, as they mostly are for soil, then each scale is divided into two parts, one of which is assigned the value 0 and the other 1, and can be considered to represent absence and presence of the attribute. For each attribute the association between it and every other attribute is measured in turn, and the values combined to give a measure of the degree to which this attribute is associated with others. The measure used is the familiar χ^2. For each comparison between attributes, say i and j, a 2×2 table is formed.

	0	j	Totals
0	n_A	n_B	$n_A + n_B$
i	n_C	n_D	$n_C + n_D$
Totals	$n_A + n_C$	$n_B + n_D$	$n_A + n_B + n_C + n_D$

The values n_A, n_B, n_C, and n_D are the numbers of individuals that lack both i and j, lack i and possess j, lack j and possess i, and possess both i and j respectively. χ^2_{ij} is then computed as

$$\chi^2_{ij} = \frac{(n_A n_D - n_B n_C)^2 (n_A + n_B + n_C + n_D)}{(n_A + n_B)(n_C + n_D)(n_A + n_C)(n_B + n_D)}$$

For each attribute i, χ^2 is summed over the remaining $p - 1$ attributes: $\sum_{j=1}^{p} \chi^2_{ij}$, $i \neq j$. The attributes for which $\Sigma \chi^2$ is largest is chosen, and the population divided into two groups, one containing those individuals that possess the attribute and the other containing those that do not. These groups are sub-divided similarly using the attribute with the second-largest value of $\Sigma \chi^2$, and the process is repeated. Division ends either when a pre-determined number of groups has been created or a critical value of $\Sigma \chi^2$ is reached.

We notice immediately a disadvantage of the method for fully quantitative data. It provides no means of deciding at which values to divide the measurement scales. It cannot be expected to find gaps in a continuously variable population such as soil, unless the scales have first been divided at minima in their frequency distributions.

Minimum spanning tree

In the above account of the more frequently used agglomerative methods, we have seen that these methods not only provide means of classification, but often give the investigator insight into the structure of a population. In the early stages of fusion they show which pairs of individuals are most similar. When several methods are used in conjunction with an ordination analysis, other relationships between individuals and groups can become evident. A technique that can help to clarify relationships among individuals is to form the *minimum spanning tree*.

When we have a set of n individuals distributed in character space we can join them together by a network of $n - 1$ links such that every indiviudal is connected to every other individual through the network and there are no closed loops. The result is a tree spanning all the individuals. That tree in which the total length of the network is least is the minimum spanning tree (MST).

Topologically the MST is the exact equivalent of the dendrogram formed by single-link grouping (Gower and Ross 1969). It has two important advantages over the dendrogram, however. The first is that

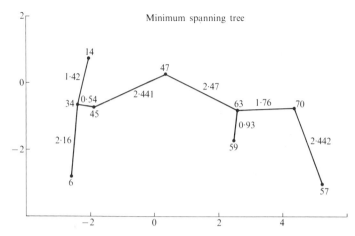

FIG. 9.9. Minimum spanning tree fitted to scatter of nine points in plane (see Fig. 9.1). The lengths of each link are given

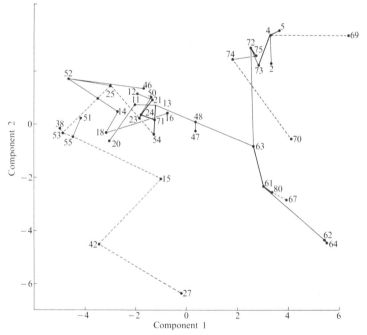

FIG. 9.10. Minimum spanning tree fitted to scatter of 40 west Oxfordshire profiles. The shortest links are drawn bold, the longest are drawn with dashed lines

the MST can be derived more efficiently than the corresponding dendrogram. Ross (1969) presents algorithms for its computation and printing, and for deriving a single-linkage dendrogram from it. The second advantage of the MST is that all its nodes occur at positions occupied by individuals. The MST therefore reveals not only which pair or pairs of individuals are most alike, but also which pairs of individuals in different branches of the tree are most similar. The tree can be drawn to show these relationships, and one of the most informative ways of doing this is to superimpose the MST on the corresponding scatter diagram. Fig. 9.9 illustrates the MST for the nine points of Fig. 9.1 in this fashion. With few points distributed in two dimensions the MST is especially clear. In this instance the only link that might be in doubt is that between individuals 6 and 34, which is only very slightly shorter than that between 6 and 45.

In Fig. 9.10 the MST for the forty sites for which dendrograms have been computed is superimposed on their scatter in the plane of their first two principal components (Fig. 9.6). In this graph the computed lengths of the links are indicated by different kinds of line. The shortest links are shown bold, and the longest links by dashed lines. The remainder are of intermediate length. The distances in a two-dimensional projection are more or less different from the true distances in the whole space. By drawing the MST on the principal-component projection, some of the distortion resulting from that projection is revealed. In this instance individuals 38 and 53, and 53 and 55 (far left) are shown to be considerably further apart than appears in the projection. So are individuals 67 and 80 (lower right). Individual 70 (right) is most similar to individual 74 and not 63; and individual 52 (far left) is more similar to 14 and 46 than would have been thought otherwise. The MST is thus a useful way of exploring the distribution of individuals in character space and complements ordination analysis.

If a dendrogram is required to represent single link grouping then it is readily obtained from the MST. Individuals joined by the shortest link are fused first, followed by those with the next shortest, and so on. Conversely, groups can be derived by dividing the tree though its longest link, followed by division through the link next to length, and so on.

Regional classification

When soil descriptions are made as part of the survey of an area there is an additional feature of the data, namely the geographic location of each sample point. Should this affect classification, and if so in what circumstances and how?

There are undoubtedly situations where the classification of soil should be independent of its location. But equally where soil maps are made to delineate different types of soil for purposes of land management, the larger the parcels and the smoother their boundaries, the more freedom the planner has and the easier is management likely to be. Soil surveyors recognize this. They try to create classes so that individual parcels are reasonably large and compact. They recognize that many soil boundaries are very diffuse, that the precise positions of such boundaries are immaterial, and they are prepared to turn a blind eye to minor occurrences of one kind of soil within parcels of other but similar kinds. Provided sampling points are sufficiently closely spaced, the same can be achieved numerically.

Several geographers (e.g. Berry 1966; Ahmad 1966; Spence 1968) have treated the spatial coordinates of data points as an additional pair of variates to calculate similarities between individuals, and then carried out agglomeration on the resultant matrix. They have obtained regions that are fairly compact, with few fragmentary outliers and inliers. The coordinates need to be weighted heavily to have appreciable effect. Constraints can be added to ensure that each class is a single continuous tract of land. Such classes are obviously desirable for some planning and administrative purposes. However, the same kind of soil can occur in widely separated areas and regional classification should allow this.

Webster and Burrough (1972b) proposed a technique which would smooth local irregularities and eliminate small fragmentary parcels while at the same time recognizing widely separated but otherwise similar parcels of soil in the same class. This is done by varying the contribution made to the similarity index by location according to the distance between pairs of sites.

Consider two individual sampling points i and j a distance u_{ij} apart on the ground, and for which a dissimilarity d_{ij} has been calculated and scaled to lie in the range 0 to 1. By extension of Gower's general similarity coefficient we could modify d_{ij} to take account of u_{ij} by

$$d'_{ij} = \frac{d_{ij} + w \cdot u_{ij}/u_{\max}}{1 + w} \qquad (9.7)$$

where $u_{\max}$ is the separation between the most distant pair of points on the ground, i.e. the range of u, and w is the weight assigned to distance. The dissimilarity increases linearly with distance and, as Webster and Burrough show, this is unsatisfactory.

However, the contribution made by distance can be varied inversely as the square (or other power) of that distance, thus:

$$w'_{ij} = \frac{w}{u^2_{ij}} \qquad (9.8)$$

and

$$d'_{ij} = \frac{d_{ij} + w'_{ij}/u_{\max}}{1 + w'_{ij}}. \qquad (9.9)$$

For close points u_{ij} is small, w'_{ij} is large, and d_{ij} can be diminished appreciably to d'_{ij}. As u_{ij} is increased w'_{ij} decreases rapidly initially, until at medium and large distances it has almost no effect on d_{ij}.

Burrough and Webster devised a second solution that modifies the dissimilarity between two individuals as an exponential function of separating distance. The formula is

$$d'_{ij} = d_{ij}\{1 - \exp(-u_{ij}/w)\}. \qquad (9.10)$$

Again the effect on the dissimilarity is powerful when u_{ij} is small; there is an initial rapid decline in effect as u_{ij} is increased, and little effect at medium and large distances.

It will be evident that if formulae (9.8) or (9.10) are used as stated, then w must be expressed in suitable units (a) to ensure that w'_{ij} or u_{ij}/w are dimensionless, and (b) to take account of the units in which the distance u is measured. In the examples used to illustrate the use of these measures sampling was carried out on a square grid, and all distances were standardized (and hence made dimensionless) by dividing them by the grid interval. For irregular sampling a suitable divisor would be the average distance between neighbouring points (for their definition and means of identifying them, see p.227). The value of w should be of order 1, but can be varied so that the area over which smoothing effectively occurs can be increased or decreased as desired. Agglomeration then takes place on the matrix of modified dissimilarities.

Webster and Burrough applied these modifications in two areas in south central England. The data for one of them, an area on the terrace of the River Thames at Kelmscot in Oxfordshire, have been reworked and the results presented in Figs. 9.11 to 9.15. The area, 1400 m × 600 m, is part of a large flat tract of gravel. The soil varies in thickness from about 30 cm to over 1 m, it is mainly brown calcareous and medium textured, but in the south west (lower left in the figures) is heavier and somewhat gleyed. The area was sampled at 100 m intervals on a square grid, and the following properties measured at each grid node:

1st horizon (plough layer, *c.* 20 m thick): hue, value, chroma, degree of mottling, sand, silt and clay contents, available Mg, P, and K, organic

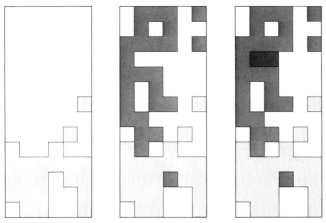

FIG. 9.11. Maps of the Kelmscot area showing sampling points classified into two, three, and four groups without regard to geographic location. This and the next four figures were obtained using the flexible strategy with $\beta = -0.25$ and mean character distance

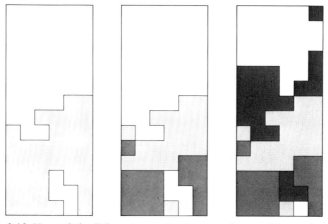

FIG. 9.12. Maps of the Kelmscot area showing two, three, and four soil classes, derived using inverse square weighting for distance (formula (9.9)) and $w = 2$

matter, cation exchange capacity, structure (size and degree of development), and consistence;

2nd horizon (> 20 cm): hue, value, chroma, degree of mottling, sand and clay contents; and for the whole profile, depth to mottling.

Using these data dissimilarities between sampling points were calculated using mean character distance as coefficient, and grouping

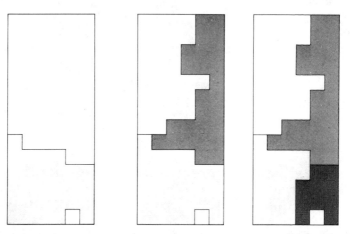

FIG. 9.13. Maps of the Kelmscot area for two, three, and four classes derived using inverse square weighting for distance (formula (9.9)) and $w = 4$

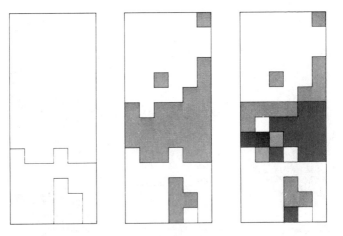

FIG. 9.14. The Kelmscot area divided into two, three, and four classes, varying the contribution from distance exponentially (formula (9.10)) and $w = 1.5$

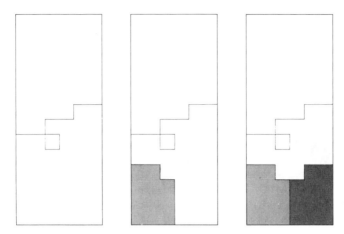

FIG. 9.15. The Kelmscot area divided into two, three, and four classes, varying the contribution from distance exponentially (formula (9.10)) and $w = 3$

performed using the flexible strategy with $\beta = -0.25$. Fig. 9.11 shows the classification that results without any regional consideration, i.e. $w = 0$, for two, three, and four groups. There is appreciable fragmentation. Figs. 9.12 and 9.13 show how regional smoothing consolidates the groups on the map using inverse square weighting (eqn. (9.9)) first with $w = 2$ and then more so for $w = 4$. Figs. 9.14 and 9.15 show the same kind of effect for exponential weighting (eqn. (9.10)) with w set to 1·5 and then 3.

Critical appraisal of hierarchical systems

We have now looked at the mechanism of hierarchical classification. We saw that strict adherence to the geometric model was not always satisfactory, and we saw how to obviate some of its shortcomings. We shall now consider the hierarchical strategies more generally.

We should first ask what they achieve. For association analysis the answer is clear: all members of any class will be identical with respect to the attributes chosen for division. If the attributes are derived from continuous variables by dividing their scales, then the individuals will not necessarily be identical, but will be similar with respect to these. The classes will be separated by planes dividing the character space perpendicular to the axes of the discriminating variables. When the attributes are chosen by the potential user of a classification to achieve some specific purpose the result is unexceptionable. However, when, as is usual, the aim is to derive more generally useful classes the result can be less happy. Some individuals are likely to be assigned to groups of others to which they bear little overall resemblance, simply because they happen to possess or lack, as the case may be, one or more of the discriminating attributes. Groups can be very heterogeneous with respect to attributes not used for division. And if the population is clustered there is a risk that one or more clusters will be split (see Gower 1967*b* for an illustration). This is clearly unsatisfactory, and is the main reason why divisive numerical methods have not been used for classifying soil, and little used in most other fields. They suffer the same disadvantage as several modern systems of soil classification, though in the latter case misuse of Aristotelian logic is to blame (Webster 1968).

The agglomerative methods do not suffer this defect since classes are formed by fusing individuals on their overall similarity. Each class contains individuals that are generally similar, and is therefore 'natural' in the sense of Gilmour (1937). However, in a group so derived the individuals comprising it, though generally similar, might possess no attribute in common. Or, if the characters are continuous variables, groups can overlap on all the original dimensions. Planes parallel to the original axes will not separate them, and divisions between them in character space need not even be straight.

The concept of a group in which individuals share many attributes, yet for which no attribute is either sufficient or necessary to confer class membership, was first clearly stated by Beckner (1959). Sokal and Sneath (1963) coined the term *polythetic* to describe such a group. Polythetic classes are not confined to formal taxonomy; they are indeed the norm in everyday life and language, as a little careful reflection should make apparent. The antithesis of a polythetic group is one which Sokal and Sneath call *monothetic*. It is one in which the possession of one or more attributes is both sufficient and necessary for class membership. Agglomeration will almost always produce polythetic groups, though some groups will be fully polythetic as above while others are only partially polythetic; that is, groups in which every member possesses one or more attributes. Association analysis and similar divisive schemes are monothetic. Polythetic division is possible, and a theoretically attractive method was proposed by Edwards and Cavalli-Sforza (1965), described briefly on p.211. Unfortunately the time taken to compute it is prohibitive for more than about twenty individuals.

In comparison with monothetic classes, polythetic groups have two disadvantages: (a) though they might be generally useful, they cannot be expected to be the most suitable for any particular purpose, and indeed might not be useful for any desired purpose (see Webster and Butler 1976 for an example); and (b) it can be very difficult to create keys for their later identification and allocation of new members.

We have seen some of the undesirable properties of hierarchical agglomeration, the effects of unequal group size and the tendency to chain, and how we can avoid them. We associated chaining with single-linkage grouping. However, we also saw (Chapter 7) how strict adherence to Euclidean geometry appears to exaggerate the difference between individuals that differ in one or a few properties. The effects extend into the agglomeration process and increase the tendency to chain in the centroid and group-average techniques (Moore and Russell 1967; Cuanalo and Webster 1970). The same effect is present in Fig. 9.7.

There is a further potential defect. When individuals are clustered in character space, i.e. several portions of the space are more densely occupied than their surroundings, small differences in similarities produced by calculating them in different ways will not appreciably alter the course of fusion. Suppose, for example, three individuals P, Q, R constitute a cluster. By one method P might first fuse with Q and then with R, whereas by another it might fuse with R first and then with Q. Such differences are of little consequence, and all the methods discussed are likely to isolate clusters. Similarly, if characters are measured by different techniques, or on different sub-samples by the same techniques, and the same similarity coefficient and fusion strategy applied, then the results will be much the same if the population is clustered. However, when individuals are more evenly spread, small changes in the calculated similarity values can have pronounced effects. The individual R, for example, might find that because of a small change in similarity it is no longer nearest to the group $P + Q$, but to some other individual or group F and G. This can be especially serious if two similarities are exactly equal. Which fusion should take precedence? None of the strategies provides the answer, and only with single linkage does it not matter. The particular groupings that occur at any stage of agglomeration are irrevocable and direct its later course, and there can be appreciable drift in the apparent positions of the groups. With this sort of population different procedures are likely to give different results, and a single analysis can lead to erroneous conclusions. Likewise, if the data describe a sample from a larger population that lacks clusters, then sampling error is likely to have a major effect on the analysis.

The only safe course is to perform analysis by several methods and compare results. If the study is based on a sample then several samples should be analysed. If the results are much the same then the population is almost certainly clustered, and those from any one method and sample will suffice. If the results are appreciably different then this too gives useful information about the structure of the population. The data do not have a hierarchical structure, and a dendrogram is a poor way of expressing relationships. It will usually be worth drawing one or more scatter diagrams, after a principal-component analysis or similar ordination procedure, to illustrate a classification. They will help explain the results. If the groups of the classification do not occupy reasonably compact regions of one or other diagram then the classification is unlikely to be useful.

Few soil populations studied so far have been clustered, and none have been shown to possess hierarchical structure. Such populations can be divided in many equally reasonable ways, and it is unlikely to matter which of these is chosen. This being so, the user who wants foremost to obtain a classification from his data will want one in which the groups are distinct and of roughly equal size. The flexible strategy with a negative value of β is the best hierarchical method for this purpose. The user would do better still, however, to choose one of the non-hierarchical methods described in Chapter 11.

Finally, it is worth comparing agglomerative hierarchical analysis with ordination by component or coordinate analysis (PCO). As we have seen the distances between individuals in a PCO projection are only approximations to the true distances between them. In particular, pairs that appear close can be far apart in the whole space, and therefore need to be treated with special caution. In an agglomerative analysis, on the other hand, individuals that fuse early are necessarily near one another: the technique is most reliable for identifying close neighbours. Thus hierarchical agglomeration and ordination are complementary ways of exploring relationships among individuals spread in multidimensional space. It is best to regard use of both sets of techniques as voyages of discovery rather than scheduled sailings with assured destinations.

10. Analysis of dispersion

The difference, sir? — There you place me
in a difficulty . . . that difference is
best postponed to some other occasion.
                    CHARLES DICKENS
                    Our Mutual Friend

In Chapter 5 we studied analysis of variance. If we had a soil population
that we classified, we saw that we could divide the total variance of that
population or a sample from it into a within-class variance and a
between-class variance. The within-class variance measured the average
dispersion within classes, and more generally the utility of the classification. The between-class variance measured the difference between
or among class means, and when expressed as a ratio of the total
variance showed the effectiveness of the classification. Chapter 7
showed how to express the joint dispersion of several variates by a
matrix of their sums of squares and products (the SSP matrix) or of
their variances and covariances. We envisaged the population scattered
in a multidimensional character space with the variance—covariance
matrix defining an ellipsoid within which some predictable proportion
of the population was likely to occur. We shall now bring these two
sets of ideas and techniques together in the multivariate analysis of
variance or, more succinctly, *analysis of dispersion.*
    When there are two or more groups of individuals and we have
measured several characters on every member of them, we can calculate
a separate variance—covariance matrix for each group. The groups may
be envisaged as ellipsoids in character space, one for each group. The
ellipsoids will overlap more or less, depending on the probability
chosen and the differences between the groups. Fig. 10.1 illustrates a
likely situation for two variates. The three ellipses represent equal
probability contours for three groups, whose centroids are at A, B, and
C. As in the univariate case we shall now want to ask questions about
this situation:

    (a)   How different are the groups?
    (b)   How do we describe their dispersion on average?
    (c)   Can we compare this dispersion with the total spread, and so
            obtain a measure of the effect of classification?

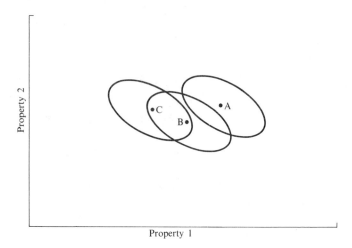

FIG. 10.1. Ellipses representing probability contours of three groups of equal dispersion with centres at A, B, and C

A preliminary answer to the first question is simple. Whereas for a single variate we could compare means, in the multivariate case we represent each group by a vector of means, say m_k for the kth group. If there are j variates then

$$m_k = \begin{bmatrix} m_{1k} \\ m_{2k} \\ \cdot \\ \cdot \\ \cdot \\ m_{jk} \end{bmatrix}$$

This vector defines the position of the centroid of the ellipsoid.

A simple measure of difference between two groups is the distance between their centroids, which can be represented by the vector of differences between their mean vectors, say

$$d = m_1 - m_2. \tag{10.1}$$

This takes no account of the degree to which the ellipsoids overlap, and we shall return to this later.

The second question involves the idea of average dispersion, and will be clear if we look again at Fig. 10.1. Any two of the ellipses as drawn can be slid, without rotation, and superimposed on the third. Thus, apart from their positions they are identical, and any one could represent the dispersion within any of the groups. In a real situation they will not fit exactly on top of one another, but provided they are reasonably similar, each can be regarded as an estimation of within-group dispersion in general, and by combining them we can get a better estimate. We therefore calculate a pooled within-groups variance—covariance matrix from the sums of squares and products of the deviations of the individual values from their respective group means.

If a group k contains n_k individuals on which we have measured p variates, we can represent the data as a $n_k \times p$ matrix, $\mathbf{X}_k$. Its SSP matrix $\mathbf{W}_k$ will be of order p with elements

$$w_{kij} = \sum_{a=1}^{n_k} (x_{ai} - \bar{x}_i)(x_{aj} - \bar{x}_j) \tag{10.2}$$

where $\bar{x}_i, \bar{x}_j$ are the means for variates i and j respectively for that group; i.e. $\mathbf{W}_k$ contains the sums of squares and products of deviations about the group means. The SSP matrix $\mathbf{W}$ for all groups, of which there are say g, is simply the sum of the SSP matrices for the individual groups, i.e.

$$\mathbf{W} = \sum_{k=1}^{g} \mathbf{W}_k. \tag{10.3}$$

It has $\sum_{k=1}^{g} (n_k - 1)$ degrees of freedom, so by dividing $\mathbf{W}$ by this value, we obtain the within-groups variance—covariance matrix, $\mathbf{V}$:

$$\mathbf{V} = \frac{1}{\sum_{k=1}^{g} (n_k - 1)} \mathbf{W}. \tag{10.4}$$

This answers our second question, and we are ready to tackle the third.

The dispersion in the whole set of data can be represented by the matrix of sums of squares and products of deviations about the general mean. Let this be $\mathbf{T}$. We can obtain the total variance—covariance matrix $\mathbf{A}$ from it by

$$\mathbf{A} = \frac{1}{n-1} \mathbf{T} \tag{10.5}$$

where $n = \sum_{k=1}^{g} n_k$, i.e. the total number of individuals. We can also calculate a between-groups SSP matrix $\mathbf{B}$ analogous to the between-groups sum of squares in analysis of variance. Like $\mathbf{W}$ and $\mathbf{T}$, it is of order p, and its elements are

$$b_{ij} = \sum_{k=1}^{g} n_k(\bar{x}_{ki} - \bar{\bar{x}}_i)(\bar{x}_{kj} - \bar{\bar{x}}_j) \qquad (10.6)$$

where $\bar{\bar{x}}_i$, $\bar{\bar{x}}_j$ are the general means of the ith and jth variates. **B** and **W** sum to **T**.

In the analysis of variance we calculated mean squares and compared them, both to assess the effectiveness of classification and to provide a test of significance. As it happens, in multivariate analysis comparisons are made from the SSP matrices. We compute the ratio of the determinant of the within-groups SSP matrix to that of the total SSP matrix:

$$L = \frac{|\mathbf{W}|}{|\mathbf{T}|} \qquad (10.7)$$

This ratio is Wilks' Criterion (Wilks 1932). It can vary between 1 and 0, and is like the relative variance that we introduced for the univariate case, except that the relative variance was the ratio of two mean squares, not the sums of squares. If L is 1 then **W** and **T** are the same; there are no differences between the groups, i.e. $|\mathbf{B}| = 0$, and classification achieves nothing. For a given set of data **T** is constant and L depends only on **W**. The less the dispersion within the groups, i.e. the more compact they are, the smaller is $|\mathbf{W}|$ and hence L. If the population has been classified in several different ways L can be used to compare them and to identify the best in the sense of the one in which the classes are most compact.

When the individuals for which we have data constitute a sample from a larger population, L is an estimate of a population parameter Λ. The sampling distribution of L was worked out by Wilks, and we can therefore test L for significance. We calculate $n \log_e L$, which is distributed approximately as χ^2, with $p(g-1)$ degrees of freedom. A somewhat more accurate test can be performed if n is replaced by $n - 1 - (p + g)/2$ in the above formula.

It is worth noting that L does not depend on the measurement scale. In fact any linear transformation of the data will give the same result.

However, there are other snags to watch for. The data matrix must not be over defined; there must be more individuals than variates ($n > p$), otherwise **T** and **W** will be singular and hence have zero determinants. In fact, n must be greater than $p + g$ for **W** to be non-singular and the outcome sensible. Equally, any property that is invariant within classes will give $|\mathbf{W}| = 0$ and should be avoided. Finally **T** and **W**

will be singular if there is any exact linear relation between any pair
of variates or if any variate is an exact linear function of several others.

Homogeneity of Dispersions

In the last section we proceeded with our analysis on the understanding that the variance–covariance matrices for the groups were
equal or nearly so. We introduced the idea of sliding the ellipses of
Fig. 10.1 so that they were superimposed. Now it is quite possible to
draw two or more ellipses that cannot be superimposed by sliding them
to new positions. Fig. 10.2 illustrates the possibilities. Take ellipse A
as reference. Ellipse B is much bigger than A; there is much more dispersion in group B than in group A. Ellipse C is much narrower than A;
the correlation in this group is much stronger. Ellipse D is the same
size and shape as A, but has a different orientation; it represents a
correlation of different sign. Other ellipses could be drawn that differ
from A in more than one of these respects. If any of these situations
occurs in a set of data under study we should want to know, and to
consider whether a general comparison among the group mean vectors
can be meaningful.

Inequality among the group dispersions can be tested by the formula

$$c = - \log_e \prod_{k=1}^{g} \left\{ \frac{|V_k|}{|V|} \right\}^{(n_k - 1)} \tag{10.8}$$

where V_k is the variance–covariance matrix for the kth group and V
the pooled within-groups variance–covariance matrix as before. The

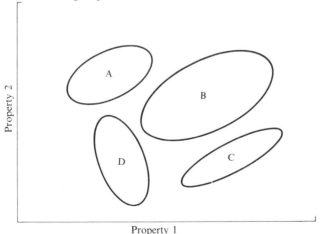

Property 1

FIG. 10.2. Ellipses representing probability contours of four groups with different
dispersions

quantity c is distributed as χ^2 with $p(p+1)(g-1)/2$ degrees of freedom. To simplify computing the formula is converted to

$$c = -\sum_{k=1}^{g}(n_k-1)\log_e\frac{|V_k|}{|V|}. \qquad (10.9)$$

It might seem desirable to make this test before comparing group means, but it does not necessarily give practical guidance. If the sample were large and the result non-significant, then we might proceed to further analysis with confidence. If not, we should be in a dilemma. Are the dispersions so different that further analysis would be invalid? And can we be sure that departure from normality is not the cause of the result? Like Bartlett's test (see Chapter 5) this test is more sensitive to such departure than tests based on Wilks' Criterion. Experience suggests that analysis of dispersion and discriminatory analysis (see Chapter 11) are fairly robust and that we may reasonably proceed unless differences among the sample dispersions are very large.

Mahalanobis distance

We now return to the matter of differences between groups that we left earlier. Our preliminary measure of the difference between two groups was the difference between their mean vectors. This took no account of the variation within the groups. Yet we tend to attach less

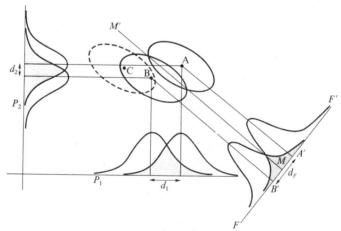

FIG. 10.3. Elliptical probability contours for three groups. Graphs of normal distribution of original variates for groups A and B are represented on axes P_1 and P_2, and of discriminant function on axis FF'

importance to a given difference when variation within groups is large than we do when it is small. This was so, for example, in the case of a single variate. If d is the difference between means and σ the standard deviation then we tend to judge a difference between two groups in terms of the ratio d/σ. The idea extends to the multivariate situation.

Fig. 10.3 represents the same three groups as Fig. 10.1, though this time graphs of the normal distribution have been added for the variates on their axes P_1 and P_2. If the difference between the groups A and B on axis 1 is d_1, and the within-group standard deviation for that variate is σ_1, assumed to be the same for both groups, then we can measure the difference between the two groups as d_1/σ_1 for that variate. Similarly the difference for variate 2 is d_2/σ_2. The separation between the groups on axis 2 is small, and the overlap in their distributions (shown shaded) is large; d_2/σ_2 is consequently small. The separation on axis 1 is larger, and d_1/σ_1 larger than d_2/σ_2. The overlap of their distributions is less. However, on neither axis is the separation as measured by d/σ as large as it could be, and there is in fact a maximum value of d/σ that can be illustrated as follows. A line MM' is drawn through the points of intersection of the ellipses. A second line FF' is drawn perpendicular to MM'. The centroids of A and B are projected parallel to MM' on to FF', and graphs of their distributions drawn also on FF'. A line such as FF' is often known as a discriminant axis. The separation d_F on FF' divided by the standard deviation of these distributions σ_F is a unique measure of the differences between the groups. It can be represented in matrix notation very simply as the quadratic form.

$$D^2 = \mathbf{d}'\mathbf{V}^{-1}\mathbf{d} \qquad (10.10)$$

where $\mathbf{d}$ is the vector of differences between the means of the two groups and $\mathbf{V}$ the pooled within-groups variance–covariance matrix as before. This measure of difference between two multivariate groups or populations is due to Mahalanobis (1927), and values of its square root D are known as *Mahalanobis distances*. The meaning of 'distance' in this sense will be made clear later.

Addition of a third property extends the geometry into three dimensions, so that the ellipses become ellipsoids which intersect on a plane. We can add further dimensions if we wish, and the principles of the method hold. In general MM' is a hyperplane with a discriminant axis FF' normal to it. There is always a single value of D, representing the difference between the two groups and equivalent to the maximum value of d/σ, that can be found analytically.

We should notice the importance of correlation between properties within groups. If there were no such correlation then the ellipses would be circles, and the standard deviations on all projections would be equal (provided that the original variates had first been standardized). In that event the maximum separation between groups could be measured along the lines joining their centroids, and the Mahalanobis distance would be equal to the Pythagorean distance divided by the within-group standard deviation. When there is correlation this is not so, as can be seen clearly in Fig. 10.3.

A second effect of correlation can be seen if we consider a third group in Fig. 10.3 with its centroid at C. The distance separating C from B is about the same as that between B and A: B is equally far from A and C. However, when measured in terms of d/σ the difference between A and B is much larger than that between B and C and on these grounds we consider B to be more like C than it is A. Intuitively this makes sense.

Two groups can be compared using either Mahalanobis D^2 or Wilks' criterion, L. The two statistics, though not exactly equivalent, are closely related. In general the larger is D^2 the smaller is L, and vice versa. When D^2 is used for a comparison based on sample data it estimates Δ_M^2, the squared Mahalanobis distance between two populations. Its significance can be tested by calculating

$$U = \frac{n_1 n_2 (n_1 + n_2 - p - 1)}{p(n_1 + n_2)(n_1 + n_2 - 2)} D^2 \qquad (10.11)$$

which is distributed as the F ratio with p and $(n_1 + n_2 - p - 1)$ degrees of freedom, and where n_1 is the number of individuals in the first group, n_2 is the number of individuals in the second group, and p is the number of variates.

The quantity $(n_1 n_2/(n_1 + n_2))D^2$ is Hotelling's T^2, developed quite independently by Hotelling (1931). Finally, if there is only one variate, U reduces to Student's t.

Geometric representation of Mahalanobis distance: canonical variates

We saw in Chapter 7 how we could represent the generalized distance between points in a population in which two variates were correlated by rotating the axes and standardizing the variates so that the elliptical distribution became circular. The generalized distance could then be displayed in the transformed space, and measured if necessary. Provided the dispersions within the groups are approximately equal, we can carry out a similar transformation to represent Mahalanobis distances between groups. In this case we rotate the axes and standardize the within-group variances so that the ellipses representing the distributions within the groups become circles. The distances we seek are then the distances between the group centroids in this space. The axes of the space are known as *canonical axes*. They have their origin at the centroid of the whole distribution. If the groups contain equal numbers of individuals then the directions of the axes are such that the sum of the squares of the distances of the group centroids to the first axis is a minimum; the second lies at right angles to the first and is chosen to minimize the sum of the squares of the distances of the group centroids to it; and so on. The procedure is analogous to that of finding the axes in the principal-component analysis. If the groups are not of equal size, then the directions will be approximately as above, though they will still be at right angles to one another. If there are only two groups then one canonical axis exactly represents the distance between their centroids and is equivalent to the line FF' in Fig. 10.3. If there are three groups then, unless the three centroids are collinear, there will be two canonical axes. In general, if there are k groups and p variates the transformed space will have either $k-1$ or p dimensions, whichever is the smaller.

The values of canonical variates for group centroids (mean canonical points) and for individuals are determined in a way similar to that for finding principal components. In this case we have to find the latent roots and vectors of the matrix $W^{-1}B$.

The latent roots $\lambda_1, \lambda_2, \ldots, \lambda_i$, are defined by the determinantal equation

$$|W^{-1}B - \lambda I| = 0. \tag{10.12}$$

The equation

$$(W^{-1}B - \lambda_i I)c_i = 0 \tag{10.13}$$

gives the ith canonical vector. It is equivalent to

$$(B - \lambda_i W)c_i = 0, \tag{10.14}$$

from which form it is usually solved. The equations are similar to those in principal-component analysis. The obvious difference is that $W^{-1}B$ has replaced the total variance–covariance matrix. The canonical vectors define the relations between the original variates and the canonical axes. By multiplying the two we obtain the canonical variates needed for plotting. Thus if the centroid of a group is represented by its mean vector $\mathbf{m}$, its position on the ith canonical axis is

$$z_i = \mathbf{m}'\mathbf{c}_i. \tag{10.15}$$

Canonical variate values of individuals can be found likewise.

When there are two or three groups the relations between group centroids can be represented exactly on a plane graph. When there are more than three groups a display in two dimensions is only an approximation to these. Nevertheless, projection on to the plane of the first two canonical axes is the best display and will sometimes be found to account for a large proportion of the variation among groups.

As pointed out earlier, the probability contours for the groups on the plane of canonical axes are circular. The variances are standardized to unity. Therefore, it is a simple matter to add contours for any desired probability. These have radius $(\chi^2)^{1/2}$ with two degrees of freedrom. In some instances it is helpful to display confidence regions for group centroids. For the kth group this has a radius of $(\chi^2/n_k)^{1/2}$, where n_k is the size of the group.

It is interesting to note that when the groups are of equal size the same projection of group centroids can be found by a principal-coordinate analysis of the matrix of Mahalanobis D between the groups (Gower 1966).

Numerical illustration

Chapter 9 illustrated a method of devising a regional soil classification using data from the Kelmscot district in west Oxfordshire. We shall use the same data here. The data were gathered originally to see how increasing field effort or increasing scale of mapping affected the quality of a soil classification map. Three maps of the Kelmscot area had been made, notionally for publication at 1:63 360, 1:40 000 and 1:25 000. The first and last divided the area into three soil series:

   (1)   Badsey: shallow, medium textured, brown calcareous soil over limestone gravel;

   (2)   Carswell; deep, more or less grey mottled soil of heavy texture;

   (3)   Kelmscot; soil intermediate in character between Badsey and Carswell.

The second map was made largely by air-photo interpretation, but with the same three groups of soil in mind. After the maps had been made the area was sampled at the intersections of a 100 m grid and the soil properties measured at each. The data were then divided into the groups of each soil map in turn and used to compare the three classifications. The results for the 1:63 360 map classification were as follows

$$|T| = 2 \cdot 385 \times 10^{36}$$

$$|W| = 1 \cdot 120 \times 10^{36}$$

$$L = \frac{|W|}{|T|} = 0 \cdot 4697.$$

There were 84 test sites (n), three groups (g), and 21 variates (p). Thus chi square is given by

$$\chi^2 = -\{n - 1 - (p + g)/2\}\log_e L$$

$$= -71 \times \log_e 0 \cdot 469 = 53 \cdot 7$$

with $p(g - 1) = 42$ degrees of freedom.

The probability of achieving this by chance is slightly over $0 \cdot 1$, and we should usually regard this evidence as insufficient to establish that the three classes differ with respect to the properties measured in this area. Note that the sampling was quite independent of the boundary drawing, the situation is probabilistic, and a significance test appropriate.

We obtain the values for the other classifications similarly, and the results for all three can be compared in Table 10.1. They show how by increasing effort and attention to detail when drawing the soil boundaries a better soil map is made, using 'better' in the sense of less variation within the mapping units. For the 1:40 000 and 1:25 000 scale maps the differences among the groups are highly significant.

Table 10.2 gives the Mahalanobis distances between the groups for

TABLE 10.1

Sample estimates of $|W|$, L, χ^2, and probability of null hypothesis being true for three map classifications of the Kelmscot area

	Map scale		
	1:63 360	1:40 000	1:25 000
$|W|$	$1 \cdot 120 \times 10^{36}$	$7 \cdot 184 \times 10^{35}$	$4 \cdot 203 \times 10^{35}$
L	0·4696	0·3011	0·1761
χ^2	53·66	85·22	123·32
approx. P	$> 0 \cdot 1$	$< 0 \cdot 001$	$< 0 \cdot 001$

$|T| = 2 \cdot 385 \times 10^{36}$ and $p(g - 1) = 42$, the number of degrees of freedom, are constant.

TABLE 10.2

Mahalanobis distances between groups for three map classifications, F ratios, degrees of freedom and approximate probabilities on null hypothesis

Map	Group comparison	Mahalanobis distance	F ratio	Degrees of freedom in denominator	Approx. probability
1:63 360	1, 2	2·65	1·55	40	0·15
	1, 3	1·27	0·87	54	v. large
	2, 3	2·85	0·65	8	v. large
1:40 000	1, 2	3·84	1·45	8	0·2
	1, 3	1·07	0·52	50	v. large
	2, 3	3·77	4·56	44	<0.001
1:25 000	1, 2	4·95	3·47	14	0·01
	1, 3	2·65	4·09	52	<0·001
	2, 3	3·39	2·91	36	<0·01

Number of degrees of freedom in numerator = 21 in all comparison.

TABLE 10.3

Latent roots of the matrix $\mathbf{W^{-1}B}$ for three map classifications

	Order	Root	Percentage of Trace
1:63 360	1	0·630	67·3
	2	0·307	32·7
1:40 000	1	1·792	90·4
	2	0·189	9·6
1:25 000	1	2·346	77·1
	2	0·697	22·9

each classification. On average, the Mahalanobis distances increase as the map scale increases. None are significant for the 1:63 360 map. The Mahalanobis distance between groups 2 and 3 is significant in the 1:40 000 map, and though the distance between groups 1 and 2 is larger there are too few degrees of freedom to be reasonably sure that this difference is real. In the 1:25 000 map all the differences are significant.

The effects of each classification are perhaps the best grasped from Figs. 10.4 to 10.6, in which the group distributions are displayed on canonical axes. Since there are only three groups, the group centroids are represented exactly. Distances between them can be measured and

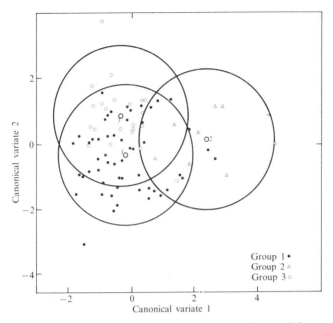

FIG. 10.4. Scatter of Kelmscot sampling sites on plane of canonical axes for 1:63 360 soil map. Group centroids are labelled 1, 2, and 3, and 90 per cent confidence circles are drawn around them

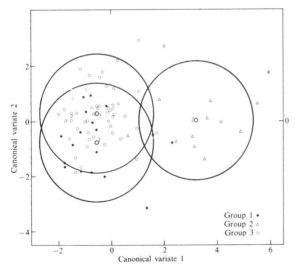

FIG. 10.5. Scatter of Kelmscot sampling sites on plane of canonical axes for 1:40 000 soil map. Labels 1, 2, and 3 show group centroids. Circles limit 90 per cent confidence regions

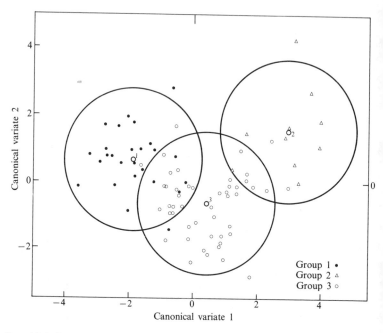

FIG. 10.6. Scatter of Kelmscot sampling sites on plane of canonical axes for 1:25 000 soil map. Group centroids are labelled 1, 2, and 3. Circles limit 90 per cent confidence regions

will be found to equal the Mahalanobis distances given in Table 10.2. The points representing the individual sampling sites are projections. The circles have radius 2·15, equal to $(\chi^2)^{1/2}$ with two degrees of freedom at the 90 per cent confidence level. Thus they show for each group a circle within which 90 per cent of the individuals will on average lie. In Fig. 10.4 for the 1:63 360 map there is considerable overlap of these circles: the groups are not well separated. In Fig. 10.5 for the 1:40 000 map, group 2 is well separated from groups 1 and 3, but the latter are scarcely separated at all. Fig. 10.6 for the 1:25 000 map shows less overlap among the groups, and groups 1 and 2 are especially well separated. The analysis used to derive the canonical variates is summarized in Table 10.3. The canonical vectors for pre-standardized variates are shown for the 1:25 000 map classification in Fig. 11.3.

11. Allocation and optimal classification

Le mieux est l'ennemi du bien.
                    VOLTAIRE
        Dictionnaire philosophique

Allocation, that is the identification of the group to which an individual belongs or the assignment of an individual to the class that it best fits, is a matter of everyday life. It is crucial to success in many tasks and especially in the use of language. Communication would be hopelessly inefficient if we could not allocate the individual and the particular to general groups of object or action. Similarly agricultural and pastoral people must be able to identify the soil at particular places with more general classes so that they can talk about their soil and learn from the experience of other people elsewhere. Allocation or identification by the layman, and by many scientists in their specialities, is largely intuitive. But because it is intuitive, it is not necessarily consistent. Different people can assign things differently, and any one person might judge matters differently on different occasions. One has only to attend a meeting of pedologists to realize that this is just as true in soil science as it is in everyday life.

Pedologists, quite naturally, have wished to avoid such inconsistency. They have sought criteria that would enable individual occurrences of soil to be assigned unequivocally to the correct or most appropriate group. The criteria have usually been the presence or absence of simple attributes such as calcium carbonate, or critical values of variables, e.g. 35 per cent of clay, and 8 per cent of organic matter. Assignment often involves several decisions, which are made in some prescribed order, as in a key. Using soil characters in this way is equivalent to attempting to identify planes through character space that (a) separate the classes of soil in question, and (b) are orthogonal to the character axes. Unfortunately the commonly recognized classes of soil are not usually separated in this way. Their properties are interdependent and they themselves are polythetic – they overlap in almost every dimension. So planes orthogonal to the soil property axes do not distinguish between the classes. Using simple criteria in these circumstances inevitably leads to some wrong identifications and some inappropriate allocation. Some pedologists have attempted to overcome this difficulty by changing the classification — redefining classes so that simple criteria can be used for identification. They have not notably succeeded, and in any case, they have dodged the central issue, which is to allocate individual soil specimens, profiles, or sites to existing classes.

So in order to discriminate between known classes of soil we need divisions through the character space that are oblique to the character axes, and might need to be curved. One of the most promising means of achieving this is by the classical procedure known as *multiple discriminant analysis*, which was developed by Fisher (1936) and Rao (1948, 1952).

Discriminant analysis is being used increasingly for identifying items from automatically recorded data (see, for example, Bracewell and Robertson 1973). In soil survey the technique has been applied experimentally more or less successfully to spectral measurements of soil and crops obtained using airborne sensors. There have also been several experiments to assess its value for identifying soil types from laboratory data (e.g. Oertal 1961; Little *et al.* (1968). Further, studies by Norris and Loveday (1971) and Webster and Burrough (1974) show that discriminant analysis has considerable potential in routine field survey.

Principle of multiple discriminant analysis

The principle is an extension of those discussed in the last chapter. Consider again Fig. 10.3. The ellipses with centres at A and B represent two groups of individuals on each of which we have measured two properties. Suppose now we have another individual on which we have measured the same two properties and we wish to allocate it to one of the two existing groups. Which group is the most appropriate? We saw that the line MM' divided the groups best, and that by projecting the distributions of the groups on to the line FF', perpendicular to MM', we were able to see the difference between the groups to best advantage. In a like manner we can decide the most appropriate allocation of a new individual by projecting its position orthogonally on to FF'. The point M on that line is the cutting value. If our new individual when projected lies above and to the right of M, then it is assigned to the class whose centre is at A; if it lies below and to the left of M, then it is assigned to the class with its centre at B. For this reason FF' is sometimes known as a discriminant axis — it is an axis that allows best discrimination between individuals of the two groups. Notice that in this example both of the original soil properties would be relatively poor discriminators if used independently: there is no horizontal or vertical line that separates the groups as well as the line MM' does. The principle extends to as many properties as we wish; MM' is in general a hyperplane in one dimension less than the number of properties, but there is always an axis, such as FF' orthogonal to MM', that will provide the best discrimination between the groups.

If, however, there are more than two groups this simple solution will not serve, for we need to consider simultaneously the possibility of allocation to every group. Rao (1952), in his solution of this problem, considers the discriminant space to be divided into regions, each of which is associated with one of the groups. Any one region is that part of the space defined by the canonical axes that is nearer to its associated group centroid than it is to any other centroid. Discriminant functions are calculated for an individual and serve to identify the region in which that individual falls. However, distances in the discriminant space are in fact Mahalanobis distances, and it seems more natural to express relations in these terms. Thus if we calculate the Mahalanobis distance between a new individual and each group centroid, we can allocate the individual to that group whose centroid is nearest. The two procedures are exactly equivalent.

To identify by discriminant analysis the class of soil to which a new profile or sampling site belongs, we need first representative individual profiles or sites from each class, preferably chosen at random, and the relevant properties measured on each individual. This information is used to calculate the discriminant functions and the weights to be assigned to the different soil properties, or the transformation of the character space and the group centroids, depending on the way the technique is viewed. In either event it can be regarded as 'calibrating' information. It is sometimes known as a 'training set', since the computer 'learns' to recognize members of each group from it. The other information needed consists of measurements of the same properties on each new individual to be allocated. Mean vectors $\mathbf{m}_j$ for each group, j, $j = 1, 2, \ldots, k$, and the pooled within-group variance–covariance matrix $\mathbf{V}$ are computed from the training set. The Mahalanobis distances between an individual i and each group centroid can then be calculated from

$$D_{ij}^2 = (\mathbf{x}_i - \mathbf{m}_j)' \mathbf{V}^{-1} (\mathbf{x}_i - \mathbf{m}_j), \qquad (11.1)$$

where $\mathbf{x}_i$ is the vector of observed values for the individual. The new individual is allocated to that group for which D_{ij}^2 is least.

Character weights and correlation

The technique raises two matters of some importance. The first concerns the relative weights that become assigned to characters for discrimination. We saw in Chapter 7 that when calculating the similarities between individuals, whether for their own sake or as a preliminary to ordination or classification, we should treat all the properties in our analysis as of equal importance, and hence give them equal weight. There seemed no logical alternative unless we had some special purpose in mind. Our task in discriminant analysis is quite different. When we wish to allocate an individual to the correct or most appropriate class we shall clearly wish to give greatest weight to those characters that discriminate best between classes. And we shall wish to avoid using information shared between several correlated characters more than once.

We illustrate the point by considering two groups a and b on which we have measured two properties. Initially we suppose that the properties are uncorrelated within the groups and that the within-group variances are equal: thus their distributions may be represented by

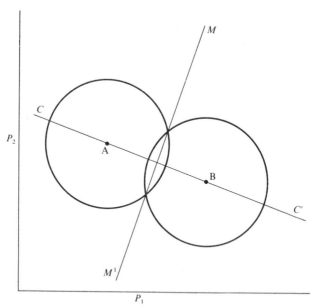

FIG. 11.1. Two classes with centres at A and B with intersecting circular confidence contours

circles of equal probability, as in Fig. 11.1, with centres at A and B respectively. The line MM' best separates the groups, and lies at right angles to the line CC' through A and B, which is a discriminant axis. It is clear that in choosing MM' we give more weight to property P_1 than we do to property P_2. In an extreme situation A and B might have equal value on the P_2 scale and MM' would then be vertical; P_2 would then have no discriminating power and P_1 could be used alone. If MM' makes an angle of $45°$ with the horizontal then P_1 and P_2 have equal weight.

The second feature of this situation is that when we wish to identify the most appropriate group for a new individual we can calculate the Pythagorean distance between it and each group centre, and allocate the individual to the group for which this distance is least. All points above and to the left of MM' are nearer to A than they are to B; all points below and to the right of MM' are nearer to B. In this case the Pythagorean and Mahalanobis distances are the same.

However, when there is correlation between the characters the Mahalanobis distances are not the same as the Pythagorean distances. The situation that arises if we then disregard correlation is illustrated in Fig. 11.2. Allocation based on Pythagorean distances is equivalent to choosing CC' through the group centres as discriminant axis, and the perpendicular QQ' through the mid-point of AB as separator between the groups. However, the best separator in these circumstances, as we have seen, is the line MM' through the points of intersection, and the best discriminant axis is some line at right angles to it, say FF' in Fig. 10.3. Thus, if we use Pythagorean distances for allocation instead of Mahalanobis distances, we shall assign any new individuals in the hachured area to group b (centred at B) whereas they properly belong in group a (with centre at A), and any new individuals in the stippled area to group a instead of b. If we recall the transformation to canonical variates the situation will be clear. For in that transformation the probability contours are transformed into circles. Then a point on a contour at, say, X becomes the same distance from A as any other point, Y, on that contour, and, provided it lies above and to the left of MM', will be further from B.

Finally we knit together the ideas of canonical variates and discriminant analysis. When there are only two groups there is only one discriminant axis, and this is identical with the one canonical axis. If there are more than two groups, canonical axes will not in general coincide with any of the discriminators between pairs of groups.

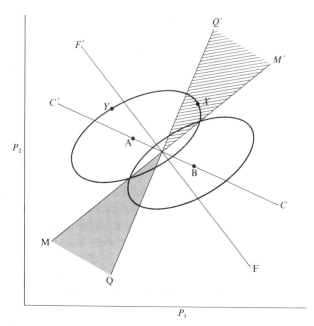

FIG. 11.2. Two classes within which variates P_1 and P_2 are correlated. Ellipses are confidence contours

However, the first canonical axis is the best single discriminator among all the groups. If we have two or three groups, or only two variates, then we can see from a graph of canonical variates to which group centroid a new individual is nearest in the Mahalanobis sense, and hence to which group it is most likely to belong. Further, the canonical vectors contain the coefficients by which the original data values are multiplied to obtain canonical variates. If we have only two groups then there is only one vector, and provided we first standardize the original variates, the coefficients in the vector represent the relative weights (and hence importance) to be attached to each original variate for the purpose of discrimination. If there are more than two groups then the order of importance is less easy to discern, though the magnitude of the coefficients is still a good guide, and a vector diagram is likely to be helpful. Fig. 11.3 shows the canonical vectors for the 1:25 000 map classification whose scatter on canonical axes is illustrated in Fig. 10.6. When we wish to allocate a new individual to this classification the length of the vectors indicate the relative importance we

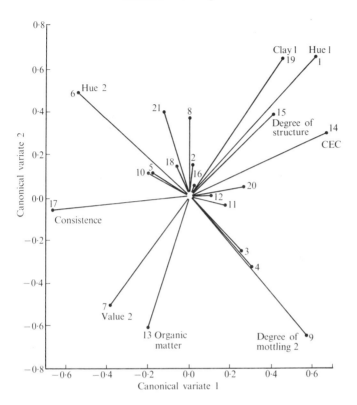

FIG. 11.3. Vector diagram of contributions made by original soil properties to canonical variates for 1:25 000 map classification of figure 10.6. Only the largest contributions are named

should attach to the original variates in arriving at our decision. In this example, the colour hue, clay content, degree of mottling, consistence, and organic matter are more important than the other properties.

Suspending judgement

So far we have assumed that any new individual would necessarily be assigned to one or other of the existing groups. This is not always sensible. If the new individual lies a long way from every group then obviously we should want to know, and would probably not wish to allocate it to an existing group: we should probably regard it as representing a class that we had not encountered hitherto. Now the

Mahalanobis D_{ij}^2 between an individual i and the centroid of a group j is distributed approximately as χ^2 with p degrees of freedom (where p is the number of variates). So for any one potential allocation we can determine the confidence with which the individual may be allocated simply by consulting a table of χ^2. If D_{ij}^2 is large we shall have little confidence. If D_{ij}^2 is small for one value of j and large for all others then we shall have high confidence in allocating the individual to group j. If D_{ij}^2 is small for two values of j then we may consider the individual as belonging to both groups, or allocate it to the nearest in the Mahalanobis sense, depending on our point of view.

A more subtle problem arises when some of the information about an individual needed for its unequivocal identification is lacking. For example, we might have recorded the morphology of a new soil profile in the field, but not have the laboratory measurements of the kind used to create the classification initially and that are necessary for correct identification. We might have only the spectral 'signature' of a crop from an airborne sensor, and want to know what the crop is. Or we might wish to bring a new block of land into cultivation, but are undecided whether it should be used in one way rather than another. In this case we have no measures of its performance, and the best we can do is to match it to the kinds of land that are already being used in the two ways. We are now concerned not only with good or bad allocation but with right or wrong identification. In the first example, we could decide unequivocally to which class the individual properly belonged by making laboratory determinations. In the second, there is a specific crop whose identity we could verify by going into the field. In the third example there is a best use of the new land even though it would be very troublesome to discover it. Before, we did not need to concern ourselves with borderline cases of allocation. If an individual fell neatly between two groups it was largely immaterial to which group we assigned it. Now the situation is different; there is a strong chance that we shall make a wrong decision when we have a borderline case. In these circumstances we might reasonably suspend judgement until we have obtained more information. In the space defined by the available information our new individual falls in a sort of no-man's land. Thus, although the individual were closer to, say, group A than group B, if the probability of its belonging to group B exceeded say 20 per cent we might decide not to make judgement without further evidence — at least some laboratory measurement, further sampling, or field trials respectively in the examples above.

Unequal groups

A further aspect of the allocation problem arises if the groups occur with unequal frequencies. In these circumstances we can minimize the risk of wrong identification by considering their relative frequencies or probabilities of occurrence. In Fig. 10.3 our cutting point for discrimination was the mid-point, M, between the projections of A and B. If the group represented by A was more likely to occur than that represented by B, then we could reduce the risk of misidentification by moving the cutting point down and to the left in the direction of B. The best position depends on the expected frequencies or probabilities of occurrence. Let these be q_A and q_B. Then we move the cutting point to K such that

$$MK = \frac{\log_e q_A - \log_e q_B}{A'B'}. \tag{11.2}$$

In practice, we allocate an individual i to the group j to which it is nearest in the Mahalanobis sense. If we know the probabilities of occurrence beforehand we can modify the Mahalanobis distances that we calculate by

$$G_{ij} = D_{ij}^2 - 2\log_e q_j \tag{11.3}$$

and allocate the individual to the group for which G_{ij} is least. It will be evident that since a probability q_j is always less than 1 and its logarithm is negative, the smaller q_j is the larger is the increment to D_{ij}^2.

A somewhat different situation arises if the dispersions of the groups are unequal. Mahalanobis distances between individuals and group centroids can still be calculated, but using separate variance–covariance matrices for each group, thus:

$$D_{ij}^2 = (x_i - m_j)'V_j^{-1}(x_i - m_j) \tag{11.4}$$

where V_j is the variance–covariance matrix for the jth group.

Generally speaking, this refinement is justified only when each group is represented by a large sample: with small samples V_j is subject to large error. Several other points need mention. Whereas with equal V_j the partitions between groups were planar, with unequal V_j they are curved. If some groups are more dispersed than others there will be a tendency for individuals to be assigned preferentially to those groups with the larger spreads. If some groups are much more dispersed than others, their influence could completely swamp that of the more tightly packed groups, and the technique is not then inappropriate.

Improving and optimizing classifications

The reader should by now be thoroughly familiar with the idea that in general the less dispersed are the individuals within their classes, the better is the classification. If we want a classification for general purposes we shall want to choose the one in which the classes are most compact. If we want a classification for a specific purpose and one that be identified with a particular soil property, we usually prefer that classification for which the within-class variance of the property is least. Allocation by discriminant analysis is a further facet of the same concept, and the groups that result from adding new individuals in this way are likely to be more compact in the discriminant space than any that could have been obtained by allocating the individuals differently.

With this in mind Webster and Burrough (1974) proposed a method for soil classification that exploited the human talent to recognize useful classes and create classifications intuitively. For each intuitively-recognized class of soil, several profiles are chosen as a representative sample. The sample contains only those profiles that seem unequivocally to belong to that class, and are therefore easy to recognize. The sample may be thought of as a 'core'. The centroids of the cores and the pooled variance–covariance matrix within the cores are calculated. Every other profile is then allocated to the core to whose centroid it is nearest in the Mahalanobis sense. If it is thought that some of the initial representatives were ill chosen, then the Mahalanobis distances between them and the group centroids can be calculated. They can then be reallocated if desired to improve the classification. Provided that the individuals initially chosen to represent the classes we have in mind do truly represent them the final classification will approximate to the most compact arrangement from that starting point. The method promises a particularly happy combination of man and machine, allowing each to do what they do best: the man to use his experience and intuition to choose the broad classes, the machine to handle large quantities of data and make routine decisions. All the hard decisions, the borderline issues that take a disproportionate amount of human's time and attention, can be made by the computer.

The above approach does need someone with sufficient experience and flair to choose a reasonable set of cores. If we have little idea how a population should be classified it is unlikely to be useful, and we need an alternative. We could use one of the hierarchical techniques described in Chapter 9 to form a dendrogram, and cut the dendrogram to give some desired number of classes. Such a procedure is very unlikely to produce the most compact classes, except in the early stages of fusion. Other means are needed for creating classifications that are optimal in this sense.

Optimal classification

Edwards and Cavalli-Sforza (1965) proposed a polythetic method of hierarchical classification that divided first the whole population into two classes, and subsequently each class into two, until all classes consisted of single individuals. They regarded the best partition as the one for which the sum of the squares SS_w of the distances between individuals and their class centroids was least. To find the best split at any stage they divided the individuals in two groups in every possible way and computed SS_w for each. The procedure can be extended in principle to any number of groups at a single stage. It need not be hierarchical. Unfortunately it is practicable only for small numbers of individuals, for the computing time required increases as a function of $n!$ where n is the population size. For populations larger than about 20 this solution usually takes too long.

However, it is possible to cut the computing load very considerably if we will be satisfied with local optima. Several authors (Rubin 1967; Friedman and Rubin 1967; Demirmen 1969; Marriott 1971) have shown how this can be done. The procedure, sometimes known as *dynamic clustering*, is as follows. The population of individuals is divided into the desired number of groups in some convenient way, for example, by cutting an agglomeratively formed hierarchy, or by intuitive judgement of what is reasonable, or even by random partition. A test criterion is chosen and is calculated for this classification. The criterion can be SS_w, calculated on standardized characters, or Wilks' criterion L, or equivalently $|W|$, or some other measure of the compactness of groups or of the separation between them. We consider which measure to use later. Any individual that lies further from its class centroid than from some other is then transferred to the group whose centroid is nearest, and the criterion recalculated. The change is regarded as an improvement and retained if the criterion is diminished, and not otherwise. The procedure is repeated until no further improvement seems possible.

The result of the above procedure is an optimum classification; but it is likely to be only a local and not a global optimum. And even if it is a global optimum, there is no ready means of knowing that this is so. The techniques can be elaborated to try to improve a classification by overcoming any local optima. One procedure is to transfer individuals to neighbouring groups even though they are not nearer to those group centroids. Gower and Ross (1974) do this in the GENSTAT system, and also switch the procedure from simple transfers to exchanges of individuals between groups. When that ceases to produce an improvement they switch back again, and so on. An alternative is to start again from different randomly generated classifications, and retain the classification with the best optimum. This can be very time-consuming if it is repeated often, but according to Rubin works well. Rubin describes a swifter alternative whereby a local optimum is overcome by transferring a substantial number of individuals from one group into one or more other groups, and then allowing optimization to proceed as before. Rubin's experience suggests that with refinements of this kind a true optimum will often be found, and will usually be found if the data are at all clustered.

The procedure can be repeated for other numbers of groups. If a population is clustered an investigator will usually wish to identify the clusters as classes, in which case there is also an optimal number of classes. Marriott (1971) suggests how this number can be determined, and which of several optimum classifications is best. Using Wilks' criterion L as the measure of goodness, optimal classifications are found with different numbers of groups g, for $g = 2, 3, \ldots, k$. The quantity $g^2 L$ is plotted against g. For a homogeneous population $g^2 L$ is expected to fall fairly steadily from a value of 1 when $g = 1$. If for some value of g there is a sharp decline below the trend, then this strongly indicates that g clusters are present in the population and have been identified.

Test criteria

Which test criterion should we use; L (or $|\mathbf{W}|$) or $SS_{\mathbf{w}}$, or some other such as the trace of the matrix $\mathbf{W}^{-1}\mathbf{B}$, as suggested by Friedman and Rubin (1967)? If there is little or no correlation between the variates within the initial groups, or we do not care to preserve any correlation that there might be, then we should choose $SS_{\mathbf{w}}$: it will involve least computing. If we are creating a classification from an unclustered population, then again our main concern is likely to be that the variances within the final groups are small on average. We should not usually want to create correlation within groups, nor to preserve any that happened to arise from an initial random partition. So again we should choose $SS_{\mathbf{w}}$ as test criterion. The original variates must have been standardized to make the test sensible. If we wish to preserve any within-group correlation present in the initial classification, or to isolate elongated clusters that might be present in the population, then we should attempt to minimize L, which is equivalent to minimizing $|W|$ since T is constant. This takes account of the covariances in addition to the variances within the groups. An alternative criterion to L is Trace $W^{-1}B$, which is a measure of the separation between group centroids. It represents the sum of the Mahalanobis D^2, weighted by the group sizes, between the group centroids and the centroid of the whole population. Rao (1952) termed it the generalization of D^2 to more than two groups. If an unweighted criterion is preferred, then unweighted forms of W and B can be used, so that Trace $W^{-1}B$ then represents the sum of the unweighted Mahalanobis distances between the groups and the grand centroid. Clearly the best classification in this sense is that in which the groups are farthest apart, and hence for which Trace $W^{-1}B$ is largest. The relation between L and Trace $W^{-1}B$ can be appreciated if the two measures are expressed in terms of the latent roots λ_i of $W^{-1}B$. If there are g roots then

$$\text{Trace } W^{-1}B = \sum_{i=1}^{g} \lambda_i \tag{11.5}$$

and

$$L = \frac{|W|}{|T|} = \frac{1}{|W^{-1}B + I|}$$

$$= \frac{1}{\prod_{i=1}^{g} (1 + \lambda_i)}. \tag{11.6}$$

Friedman and Rubin (1967) and Demirmen (1969) examined both measures empirically and found that L performed best. Trace $W^{-1}B$ was somewhat unreliable, and this seems to be because it can be too readily affected by variation in the largest eigenvalue, whereas L, being based on products, reflects changes in the smaller eigenvalues better.

An advantage of L and Trace $W^{-1}B$ is that they remain the same for all linear transformations of the data, whereas SS_w does not. However, if the population is small, so that there are fewer individuals than variates, then neither criterion can be calculated since both T and W will be singular. In fact n, the number of individuals, must be larger than $p + g$, the number of variates plus groups, if the outcome is to be sensible. In these circumstances either SS_w must be used or the number of variates must be reduced, for example by taking principal components.

Finally, we should note that the use of any of these criteria will tend to give groups of roughly equal size.

Example

The only applications of dynamic clustering to soil so far reported have been by Crommelin and de Gruijter (1973), and de Gruijter and Bie (1975) in the Netherlands. In both instances the authors used SS_w as the test criterion. The example given here illustrates the procedures taking account of correlations. It does so using the data for the Kelmscot area again.

We shall suppose that a preliminary reconnaissance has provided a classification, namely that of the 1:63 360 map. We have already seen that this classification contains a good deal of overlap and is by no means the best. Nevertheless it seems a reasonable starting point. We calculate the group centroids, the pooled within-groups variance—covariance matrix, and the test statistics L and Trace $W^{-1}B$. We then calculate for each individual in turn the Mahalanobis distance to each group, and transfer any individual that is nearer to some group centroid other than its own. The relevant information for the first five individuals is given in Table 11.1. All are initially members of group 1. Individuals 1, 2, and 3 are nearer to their own group centroid than they are to any other and so remain members of that group. Individuals 4 and 5 are nearer to the centroid of group 3, and are therefore transferred. As can be seen from Fig. 10.4 quite a number of individuals are in a similar situation, and in fact are transferred in the first stage. When transfer is complete L and Trace $W^{-1}B$ are recalculated, and the procedure

TABLE 11.1

First five sampling sites in the Kelmscot area, their Mahalanobis distances to the three class centroids, and their allocations in the first round of improvement

| Individual | Initial group | Mahalanobis distances to: | | | New Group |
		Group 1	Group 2	Group 3	
1	1	3·24	4·20	3·29	1
2	1	3·38	4·85	3·71	1
3	1	3·31	4·59	3·57	1
4	1	3·17	4·69	3·16	3
5	1	2·82	4·00	2·44	3

TABLE 11.2

Wilks' criterion, L, Trace $W^{-1}B$, within group sum of squares, SS_w, and transfers involved in further improvement of soil classification

Stage	L	Tr $W^{-1}B$	SS_w	Number of transfers
1	0·4697	0·936	1626·0	27
2	0·0564	6·556	1426·0	5
3	0·0337	8·961	1440·4	1
4	0·0296	9·738	1440·4	0

repeated. The classification stabilizes after the third round. Table 11.2 summarizes the process, and Fig. 11.4 shows how the classes become increasingly distinct at each stage.

Table 11.2 shows that Trace $W^{-1}B$ increases as L decreases. The values of SS_w are also given, but SS_w does not decrease monotonically in this instance. A somewhat different result would have been obtained if reallocations had been based on Euclidean distances. Further improvement could be attempted as described above by transferring individuals one at a time or exchanging them. However, we have taken the procedure far enough to demonstrate the principle and something of its power.

Hierarchical and non-hierarchical classification

The choice of a hierarchical analysis (described in Chapter 9) or a non-hierarchical one depends to some extent on the structure of the population. It also depends on whether the investigator's sole interest is in a usable classification, and to what extent he is interested in the infrastructure of groups. The choice also depends on the size of the population. Experience so far shows that the populations of soil with which pedologists work lack hierarchical structure, and few are clustered. In these circumstances a non-hierarchical analysis would seem the best way to create a classification. A hierarchical grouping might be performed, however, to provide the starting point if the investigator has no other clues as to what might be desirable.

A non-hierarchical analysis has advantages for large populations, since it does not require a similarity matrix. The maximum number of individuals that can be classified in this way is more likely to depend on the computer time available to the user than on the size of the core store.

Whether we use a hierarchical method for classification, or an

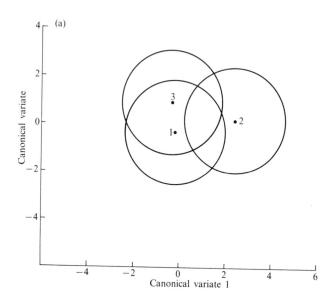

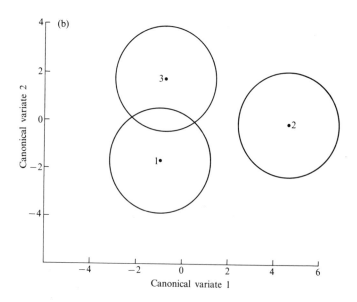

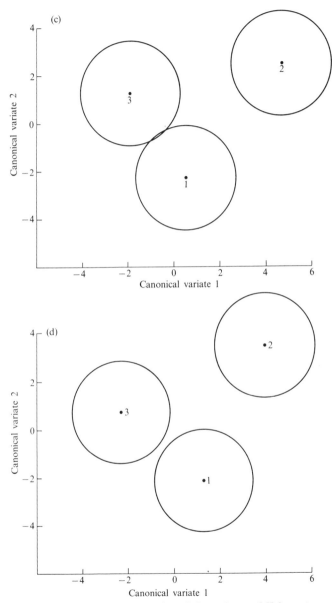

FIG. 11.4. Centres and confidence circles of three classes of Kelmscot sampling sites plotted on canonical variate axes. Figure (a) is for the initial classification, and (b), (c), and (d) show the classification after the first, second, and third rounds of improvement

optimizing non-hierarchical technique as here, the population actually classified is finite. That is, we classify a particular set of individuals on which we have data. This is often all that an investigator requires. When a population is infinite, as it usually is in soil survey, then a sample must be chosen initially for study. Either kind of method can then be used on the sample to create classes to which the remainder of the population can be allocated. In this case the sample must be properly representative if a numerical classification of the soil of an area is to be sensible. But sound sampling will not guarantee satisfaction for a population that lacks clusters. Different samples are likely to produce appreciably different results. Research is needed on the instability of classification resulting from sampling error and how to avoid it by suitable statistical and computing strategies. Surveyors should be aware of these shortcomings, and be prepared to 'steer' the computer with a little intelligent prejudice if necessary. They should also realize that despite immense effort, they can never be sure that they have found the best classification. A sound philosophy is to be satisfied with what seems to be a good classification and use it until it proves to be inadequate.

12. Mapping

To most soil scientists the term *soil map* immediately brings to mind a plan of an area divided by boundary lines into contiguous coloured parcels of different shapes and sizes. Each colour represents a single soil type or some combination of soil types. This is reasonable: most soil maps are like this. However, when we have much sample data from an area there are more informative ways of mapping them. For example, we could print the data values at the points (represented to scale) where they were obtained. All information would then be retained, but the map would be difficult to appreciate for some purposes. Alternatively the values can be portrayed by simple symbols, and this is what is usually meant by mapping when applied to sample data. Some information is lost but this loss can make it easier to see more general patterns. When data are quantitative mapping should be mathematically defined and repeatable. Even so the scientist has many options for displaying his data in map form.

The feasibility of much quantitative mapping depends largely on automation. The calculations and plotting are very tedious using pencil and paper, and constituted a serious obstacle before computers became generally available. Despite the recent advances in automation the choice of mapping procedure is still limited more or less by the equipment and programs available, and by the graphic quality and accuracy desired. These in turn are likely to be determined by financial and policy decisions in which the individual scientist has little say. The field is rapidly developing, however. Bigger and faster machines replace old ones, new methods are devised to improve the use of existing hardware, and whole suites of new software are being written and implemented to handle very large quantities of data, and to produce maps swiftly and with a wide range of graphic type and quality.

It is not possible in one chapter to cover the field in detail. Rather, we shall consider the requirements of a map, the main kinds of quantitative maps, and describe briefly the mathematics underlying some useful mapping procedures. The chapter will emphasize the need to choose techniques appropriate to the data to be mapped, and will indicate the restrictions on that choice imposed by hardware.

Nature of data

In choosing a method of mapping we should first consider the nature of the data to be mapped. We shall assume they are unbiased and properly representative in some sense as discussed in Chapter 4. We shall also assume that the term 'data' in this context may include results from some previous computation.

Data for mapping will derive from a set of sample points P_i, $i = 1$, $2, \ldots, n$, with geographic coordinates x_i, y_i where some property of interest, Z, has been measured to give values z_i. The x, y values might constitute a grid, either square or otherwise, or the points might be scattered randomly or in a more or less haphazard way. In some instances the points are likely to be clustered. Their distribution will to some extent determine the mapping procedure we adopt. More important, however, is the nature of Z, the variable to be mapped, and it will be well to refresh our memory on this. We have the following possibilities for Z:

(i)   a binary variable, usually the presence or absence of some attribute;

(ii)   an unordered multistate variable, like a soil series or the type of stones the soil contains;

(iii) a ranked variable, like stoniness of the soil, or suitability of soil for a particular crop;

(iv)   a continuous variable, like topographic height, pH or clay content of the soil, or principal component scores.

The last allows the widest choice of mapping technique, the first allows the least. A technique that is suitable for any one of these types may be used if desired for all others before it in the list, since it is possible to convert a variable to any of the kinds that precede it, or at least to treat it as though it were one. The reverse does not apply. Finally there is the degree to which the values of Z at neighbouring sampling points are associated. This is especially important when mapping a continuous variable, and we shall consider its implications now.

Spatial dependence

It is common experience that the soil at places near to one another is similar. If our sampling in a survey is dense enough we shall find that data from neighbouring points are likewise often similar, whereas data from distant points more often differ. When this happens we say that the data are *spatially dependent*. Indeed, we might decide to sample sufficiently intensively to ensure spatial dependence. This is vital when land is to be divided for different forms of use on sample evidence alone. On the other hand, when neighbouring sample sites are no more likely to be similar than distant ones there is no spatial dependence in the data. The density at which spatial dependence becomes manifest varies appreciably from one region to another, and also depends on the size of the area surveyed and the soil property of interest. It is difficult to give more than very general guidance. When an area can be seen to consist of several distinct types of land, spatial dependence can be expected in data if several sample points fall in each parcel of each type. If there is on average one or less sample points per parcel then spatial dependence in the data is unlikely.

When a map is intended solely as a display of actual data then spatial dependence or its lack scarcely matters. Symbols can be chosen to represent data values and printed at positions on the map corresponding to the sampling sites. We shall call them *point symbols*. In many instances, however, maps are made with symbolism spread between data points. The intent, either expressed or implied, is that intermediate points have values similar to those recorded at their neighbours, and that interpolation is reasonable. Interpolation is likely to be profitable if the data are spatially dependent. If they are not then this kind of symbolism is quite inappropriate, and only point symbols should used.

We shall consider each kind of data in turn, first for situations in which there is no spatial dependence, and second for those where there is.

Data lacking spatial dependence

Binary data

Binary data are usually mapped by point symbols. Each sampling point is considered separately. In the simplest cases, if the site possesses the attribute in question then a symbol is printed at that position, otherwise the position is left blank. However, a map made in this way is not necessarily satisfactory, because in the absence of other information it does not show where sampled sites lack the attribute. It shows only where the attribute is *known* to be present. It cannot be used to judge proportions, or to compare different parts of an area.

The map can be improved if two kinds of symbol are chosen, one to show where the attribute is present and the other to show where it is absent. Although such a map will faithfully represent the data it might remain difficult for a reader to appreciate the distribution of the attribute in the area if the initial sampling was uneven. So when it is known that survey data will be mapped using point symbols, it is well to plan the survey to give even coverage. Soil surveys with this aim have been developed especially by Rudeforth (1969), Rudeforth and Thomasson (1970), and Rudeforth and Bradley (1972). Even cover is achieved by sampling at intersections of the British National Grid, a square metric grid with principal divisions on British maps at 1 km intervals. Other advantages follow.

First, it is no longer necessary to use a symbol for absence of an attribute. Provided all grid nodes are sampled lack of a symbol at a grid position on a map implies absence of the attribute. The reader must know this in order to appreciate the map, especially if sites possessing the attribute are sparse. Figs. 12.1 illustrates the kind of result obtained from a soil survey of part of Pembrokeshire.

Second, standard hardware can be used for display. A cheap yet elegant method using punched feature-cards is described by Rudeforth and Webster (1973). Although feature-cards are widely used in commerce for indexing information they are not generally familiar to soil scientists. A brief description of their application to soil mapping is given here.

A *feature-card* is a card, or sometimes a sheet of plastic, of a convenient size. Apart from its margins and space for a heading it is ruled with a grid, usually square, and with cells of side 2 to 3 mm. Each cell of the grid can be identified uniquely by its horizontal and vertical coordinates. So provided the grid is continuous (some makes of card have blank columns and rows to divide the card into blocks) the card can be used as a map, representing the sampling grid to scale. Any one card is used to represent one attribute, usually known to indexers as a *feature*. The presence of an attribute at a particular site is recorded on its feature-card, not by printing a symbol, but by punching a hole in the grid cell corresponding to the sampling point. When holes have been punched for all sites possessing the attribute in question the feature-card constitutes a map with holes symbolizing presence of the attribute, while unpunched positions indicate its absence. The map can be seen best against a contrasting background, either a coloured sheet or a light. A separate feature-card can be prepared similarly for each soil attribute recorded in the survey. Fig. 12.1 was originally prepared in this way.

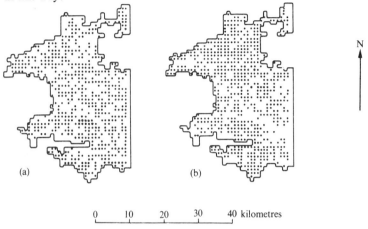

FIG. 12.1. Binary maps on a square grid of (a) soil $\geqslant$ 50 cm thick, A_{50}, and (b) soil that is freely drained, B. This, and Figs. 12.2, 12.3, and 12.4 are from Rudeforth and Webster (1973), and cover west and central Pembrokeshire at 1 km intervals.

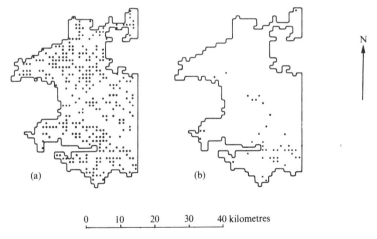

FIG. 12.2. Boolean maps derived by intersection showing (a) soil that is at least 50 cm thick *and* freely drained, i.e. $A_{50} \cap B$ from Fig. 12.1, and (b) soil $\geqslant$ 50 cm thick *and* freely drained *and* $\leqslant$ 30 m above sea level, $A_{50} \cap B \cap C$

Boolean maps

The suitability of land for use rarely depends on a single attribute, so to assess suitability we want to combine information on several attributes. To take a simple example, soil good for tillage in Pembrokeshire is at least 50 cm thick and freely drained. To display the occurrence of such soil we could search the records, note every site where the soil possessed both attributes, and print symbols on the map at those places. However, when maps of the relevant attributes have been prepared already on feature-cards, new maps can be derived from them very swiftly by manipulating the cards themselves. Thus in the above example, we can place the feature-card for soil $\geqslant 50$ cm thick on the one for freely drained. Holes coincide where sites possess both attributes, and the resultant map is readily displayed against its light or coloured background. Fig. 12.2a illustrates the result. Further feature-cards can be added, and Fig. 12.2b shows the result of adding one for land $\leqslant 30$ m above sea level to the map in Fig. 12.2a.

This operation is, in fact, the logical intersection of several sets whose members possess the attributes specified. If, for example, we define A, B, and C as sets of sites possessing respectively a, soil $\geqslant 50$ cm thick, b, soil freely drained, and c, height $\leqslant 30$ m, then we derive Fig. 12.2b by

$$A \cap B \cap C. \tag{12.1}$$

The symbol $\cap$ is the logical or Boolean operator *and*; so the new map shows those sites that possess the attributes *a and b and c*.

Intersection is likely to be the most frequently used logical operation for combining attributes, and it is the easiest to perform with punched feature-cards. However, two other operations are often usual. One is *complementation*, equivalent to applying the Boolean operator *not*. For example, if A is the set of sites where the soil $\geqslant 50$ cm thick then A' consists of the sites where the soil is *not* $\geqslant 50$ cm thick, i.e. is less than 50 cm thick. The set can be displayed as a map by taking the feature-card for set A, superimposing a card punched for all the sampled sites and inserting between them a coloured transparent sheet. The non-transmitting coloured spots give the map required. Fig. 12.3a illustrates the complement of Fig. 12.1a. Subtraction sets can be displayed similarly. If we have cards showing where the soil is $\geqslant 30$ cm thick, set A_{30}, and where the soil is $\geqslant 50$ cm thick, set A_{50}, then we place the card for A_{30}, the more inclusive, on that for A_{50} with the coloured sheet between. The non-transmitting coloured spots show where the soil is

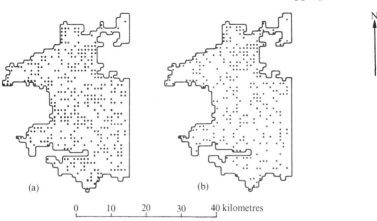

(a)   (b)

0   10   20   30   40 kilometres

FIG. 12.3. Boolean maps showing (a) complement of Fig. 12.1a, A'_{50}, soil < 50 cm thick, and (b) the subtraction set $A_{30} \cap A'_{50}$, soil ≥ 30 cm thick *and* less than 50 cm in the range 30 to 50 cm:

$$A_{30} - A_{50} = A_{33} \cap A'_{50} \tag{12.2}$$

Fig. 12.3b illustrates the result for Pembrokeshire.

The third operation sometimes needed is *union*, equivalent to applying the operator *or*, for which we may use the symbol ∪. We can illustrate it using the sets already defined. Suppose we wish to display as a map sites not prone to drought. Experience suggests that these either have soil ≥ 50 cm thick, set A, *or* are to some extent gleyed (i.e. by implication *not* freely drained), set B', or both. In this case the positions punched on the card representing A are added to those identified for B'. This cannot be done simply by manipulation. But if a card has been punched for B', which is advisable if it is to be used often, then the map can be derived quickly by stencilling first through the card for A and then through that for B' on to a single sheet of paper beneath. Alternatively, if maps of single features have been prepared by printing symbols on transparent sheets then union can be performed very simply by laying one over the other. Fig. 12.4a shows the complement of Fig. 12.1b, and Fig. 12.4b shows the union of this with Fig. 12.1a.

Maps derived in this way from several binary maps can be regarded as 'Boolean' maps, after the nineteenth century mathematician George Boole who developed this form of logic. Of course, they do not have to be prepared using feature-cards. Boolean logic is easily programmed for computers, and the sets required for mapping can be derived quite as quickly automatically when data are held in a computer.

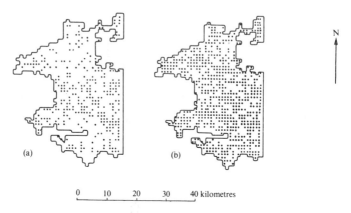

FIG. 12.4. Boolean maps showing (a) complement of Fig. 12.1b, B', soil *not* freely drained, and (b) union $A \cup B'$, soil $\geqslant 50$ cm *or not* freely drained (or both)

Multistate, ranked, and continuous data

The problems of mapping multistate data are similar in most respect to those for binary data. The main difference is that a separate symbol must be chosen for each state of the character to be displayed. Although it is still possible to use punched feature-cards to map such data, it is no longer convenient. Nevertheless display is most satisfactory if the survey is done on a grid, preferably square.

Ranked characters and continuous variables introduce a new feature, namely progression from small to large, rare to abundant, good to bad. Symbols to display this progression are now best chosen as a grey or colour scale. Thus a very light or small symbol might be used for 'small' or 'rare', and a very dark, bold, or large one for 'large' or 'abundant'. When data are continuous the range must be divided into classes, a process we called 'dissection' in Chapter 5. As we saw there, the cutting values may be critical, or just convenient.

Several methods have been developed for mapping data of this kind automatically. An efficient one is embodied in the GRID CAMAP program written by Finch and Hotson (1974) to handle data on square grids. Data are read by computer from cards or card images. A symbol is assigned to each data point according to the data value there. The result is printed on a line-printer modified so that its printing format is $\frac{1}{10}$ inch square; thus the spacing between lines is the same as that between characters within the lines (the spacing between lines is usually $\frac{1}{6}$ inch or $\frac{1}{8}$ inch). A grey scale is obtained by overprinting. Fig. 12.10 is an example.

The symbols on the maps made this way often occupy a large proportion of the available space, so that the maps superficially resemble many that are made on other computing systems. However, it must be stressed that they need be no more than point symbols. Each symbol is centred on the coordinates of the sample point, and its spatial extent has no significance. Users can interpolate between symbols on the map if they wish, but interpolation is not part of the mapping procedure.

Spatially dependent data

When data from neighbouring sample points are related, i.e. are more often similar than are those from more distant points, new possibilities arise for their mapping. Interpolation and the partition of areas into parcels are now reasonable, and may be undertaken in constructing a map. Suitable methods depend on the nature of the variate being mapped, and we shall again consider the various types of data separately. Notice, however, that we could quite properly use point symbolism if we wished.

Binary, multistate, and ranked data

The common aspect of these forms of data is that the values occur as discrete states of the soil. They may be recorded as $0, 1, 2, \ldots$, but their meanings are 'presence' or 'absence'; 'platy', 'prismatic', 'granular'; 'weak', 'moderate', 'strong'; etc. There are no intermediate values. Thus, when we consider what values might reasonably be assigned to places between neighbouring sample points we must think in terms of one or other of the defined states. For binary and multistate data we have no reason to infer intermediate forms, and even with ranked data it would be difficult to decide precisely where to display any intermediate forms. The only safe interpolation rule in this context is to attribute to any place the same state of the soil property as that of the nearest sample point.

Any map made by this rule will consist of a set of contiguous polygons, each polygon containing one sample point and the part of the whole area nearer to that sample point than to any other. The polygons are known as *First-order Boolean regions*, or sometimes *Thiesson polygons* after the climatologist A.H. Thiesson. The polygons can be constructed from the sample points by first joining all pairs of neighbouring sample points by straight lines. (Neighbouring sample points are those in adjacent polygons, though until the polygons have been drawn they cannot be recognized with certainty). These lines are bisected by perpendiculars, each of which is extended until it cuts other perpendicular bisectors, one in each direction. In some instances adjacent polygons will have different character states and be displayed with different symbolism. In others they will have the same state. They will then bear the same symbolism, and the effect will be to remove the line dividing them, so creating a larger polygon.

When data have been collected on a square grid each resulting parcel will be made up of a number of squares. The result could well look similar to some point symbol maps, especially those produced on the line-printer of a computer. Nevertheless it is important to remember that the two are different in principle. The facility is available in the mapping program SYMAP (see below), in which it is known as *proximal* mapping.

Continuous variables

Continuous variables can be mapped by the method just described, or when sampled on a square grid by the even simpler technique employed in CAMAP, provided suitable values are first chosen for class limits. However, more powerful methods are available, and we shall consider these now.

The values z_i of a continuous variable in an area can be represented as a three-dimensional graph whose base is defined by the geographic axes X and Y, and with Z represented vertically. If the data are spatially dependent we can imagine Z, if interpolated, forming a continuous surface of varying shape above the base plane. Our task in mapping, therefore, is to choose and apply a procedure for calculating values of Z between the sampling points, and having done so to display the result. In some procedures interpolation and display are closely integrated, in others they are distinct. We shall consider methods of both kinds, though because the subject is developing so fast this account can be neither comprehensive nor entirely up-to-date.

The surface is displayed, usually automatically, either by drawing lines to represent given levels of Z using a graph plotter, or by layer shading of different symbolism for given ranges of Z on a line printer. The results, especially of the first, look very like topographic contour maps. Indeed they are often called 'contour' maps, and the procedure by which they are made is often referred to as 'contouring'. Perhaps it would be pedantic to say that they are not, in fact, contour maps. Nevertheless the terms need to be used with caution because there is an important difference between topographic contour lines and those we are now considering. The former are drawn to join points of *known* equal value. The lines that we now want to use to represent an interpolated surface, even where that surface passes through the observed values, join points of *inferred* equal value. It would, of course, be impossible to identify actual isometric lines for any property of the soil. And though displaying a soil variable in this way is strictly analogous to contouring the sea bed from a grid of soundings, ambiguity can be avoided if we call the lines *isarithms* or *isolines*.

Interpolation is most straightforward when sampling has been carried out on a regular grid, especially if it is triangular. In several of the methods the more even is the sampling, the more reliable is interpolation likely to be. So other things being equal there is considerable advantage in using a regular grid. When some parts of an area are known beforehand to be more variable than others they are best sampled more intensively than the rest: a regular grid is not then best. However, the principles of interpolation are much the same whether sampling is regular or not. I shall accordingly describe several methods that can be applied to both kinds of sampling.

Polyhedron surfaces

This is a simple method in which display and interpolation proceed together. Sample points are first linked by straight lines to their neighbours to form triangles and none lies inside a triangle (Fig. 12.6a). The whole surface is thus approximated by a polyhedron consisting of small triangular plates. Values of Z are chosen for the isolines. The positions where the sides of the plates possess these elevations are found by linear interpolation and points of equal value joined across each plate. Fig. 12.5 illustrates the process for two points P and Q whose values of Z are known. The height QQ' represents the difference in Z between its value at P and that at Q. An isarithm with value z_c is to pass between the two points, as shown, cutting PQ' at C'. The projection of C' on PQ is C, and must be determined. By similar triangles

$$\frac{PC}{PQ} = \frac{CC'}{QQ'}$$

and therefore

$$PC = \frac{PQ \cdot CC'}{QQ'}. \tag{12.3}$$

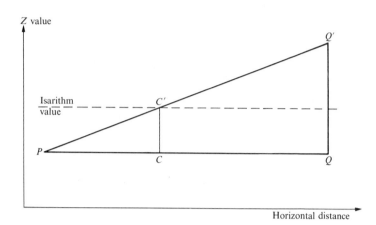

FIG. 12.5. Linear interpolation to find where a contour cuts a line

When contouring by hand, each pair of points that are joined in the network can be treated this way. For automatic contouring the positions of the points must be referred to a constant origin. Suppose the horizontal coordinates and Z values of P and Q are $x_p y_p z_p$, $x_q y_q z_q$. Then the X and Y coordinates of the point where the isarithm z_c cuts the line PQ are

$$\left. \begin{aligned} x_c &= x_p + (x_q - x_p)\frac{z_c - z_p}{z_q - z_p} \\ y_c &= y_p + (y_p - y_p)\frac{z_c - z_p}{z_q - z_p} \end{aligned} \right\} \tag{12.4}$$

The result is a set of contours, each composed of a series of straight segments, as illustrated in Fig. 12.6b.

The main disadvantage of the method is that unless the sample points lie on a regular triangular grid there is no way of specifying uniquely how they are to be joined initially to form a polyhedron. The method is described more fully by IBM (1965) and Bengstsson and Nordbeck (1964) who give algorithms for computing. It is not widely used, and as far as I know has not been used for soil.

Numerical approximation over a grid

Here interpolation and display are carried out in two distinct operations. A uniform fine mesh grid is superimposed on the XY plane. It

(a)

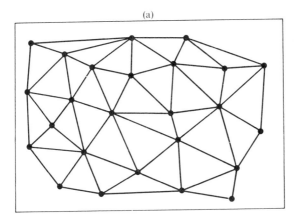

(b)

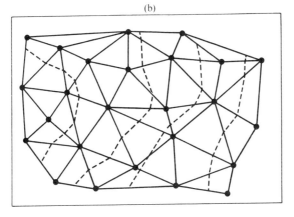

FIG. 12.6. Contouring over a polyhedron surface. (a) Plan of sample points joined to form triangles, and (b) contours (dashed) drawn across triangles

is usually square, and we shall assume that it is, but it can be triangular. Values of Z, say $z_j, j = 1, 2, \ldots, m$, are calculated for the m nodes of the grid from the sample data. When Z is the height of the land surface the result is often known as a *digital terrain model*. More generally it may be called a *figure field*. The surface is displayed by contouring the figure field afterwards.

Several methods have been proposed for interpolating the grid values. A polynomial or trigonometric function in X and Y can be fitted exactly to the sample data if enough terms are included. It can then be used to evaluate Z at all the grid nodes. However, it is likely to be strongly influenced by sampling or observational error, and therefore unstable. It may also be computationally out of reach for large samples. If only few terms are used in the function, then the fitted surface is a regression or *trend* surface. When a single equation is used for the whole of the area sampled, the fitted surface is known as a *global* trend surface. This not only provides interpolated values at grid nodes, it also *smoothes* the surface. The surface is fitted so as to minimize the sum of the squares of the deviations of the measured values from it. The fitted values z_i' differ more or less from the measured ones z_i, and thus detail is lost. This may or may not be desired. Another disadvantage of a global trend surface is that local variation in one part of the area affects the fit everywhere. It seems quite inappropriate that the trend in a soil property displayed across a plane should be affected by fluctuations in the soil in an intricately dissected region at some distance. Or as Gower (1973) colourfully puts it, ' ... when fitting the topography of the North-west Highlands (of Britain) one would not be influenced by what happens in the South Downs'.

Methods have been devised for fitting local polynomial surfaces, either exactly or approximately using the minimum sum of squares of deviations in Z as the criterion of goodness of fit, to the data points around each grid node in turn (see, for example, Batcha and Reese 1974; McIntyre *et al.*, 1968; Cole, 1968). This is probably one of the most satisfactory solutions when data are already on a regular grid, since the interpolated values can be computed swiftly using Newton's difference method, described in Yule and Kendall (1950). However, when the data are irregularly scattered these methods may take too long.

A further refinement of this approach is to use a *spline* function. A spline is a set of polynomials of a given degree, say n, that describe pieces of a line, or in this case a surface. The pieces join in such a way that the spline function is continuous, as also are its first $n - 1$ derivatives. Thus the fitted line or surface varies smoothly everywhere yet remains reasonably faithful to the data. Satisfactory fit is usually obtained with $n = 3$, i.e. a cubic spline. The method seems very attractive for soil variables that are expected to vary continuously across the land, but there are no reports of its use yet. A thorough treatment of spline functions is given in Greville (1969).

One of the most successful solutions to the problem is that embodied in the now widely available SYMAP program (Laboratory for Computer

Graphics 1968; Shepard 1968). This calculates the value of Z at each grid node as a weighted average of the sample values. Weights are inversely related to the square of the distances between the sampling points and the grid node in question. The basic formula for calculating the value of Z, z_j, at the jth grid node is:

$$\left.\begin{array}{l} z_j = \dfrac{\sum\limits_{i=1}^{n} z_i d_{ij}^{-2}}{\sum\limits_{i=1}^{n} d_{ij}^{-2}}, \quad d_{ij} \neq 0 \quad \text{for all } i \\[4mm] z_j = z_i, \quad d_{ij} = 0 \quad \text{for some } i \end{array}\right\} \quad (12.5)$$

where n is the number of sample points and d_{ij} is the distance between the ith sample point and the jth grid node.

The formula generates a continuous surface that passes through all data values that occur at grid nodes. However, in its simple form above it has several disadvantages, and in the SYMAP program it is modified in four respects. Two of these are computational matters, the other two are geometric.

1. The time taken to compute z_j depends directly on n, the sample size. If n is large then the time needed for computing is likely to be unacceptable. However, when d_{ij} is large the contribution of z_i to z_j is small and can safely be ignored. So z_j is computed from near points only. The number of data points used depends to some extent on their distribution. On average the nearest seven are taken, but there may be as few as four or as many as ten. This not only saves computing, it is also good sense to exclude far points from influencing the interpolation, as we have already seen.

2. When any d_{ij} is very small $1/d_{ij}^2$ is very large. The quantity z_j then depends on the ratio of two very large and similar numbers that are likely to be rounded by the computer. This is clearly unacceptable, so some arbitrary small distance is chosen within which d_{ij} is sensibly regarded as zero so that $z_j = z_i$.

3. When two near data points lie in much the same direction from a grid node it seems on intuitive grounds that the nearer of the two should screen or 'shadow' the effect of the further one. Thus, in Fig. 12.7 G is the grid node at which Z is to be evaluated and P_1, P_2, P_3 are sampling points of known Z, z_1, z_2, z_3. P_2 is shadowed by P_3, whereas P_1 is not shadowed. In SYMAP the effect is allowed for by diminishing the weight attributed to P_2 in proportion to the cosine of the angle $P_3 G P_2$.

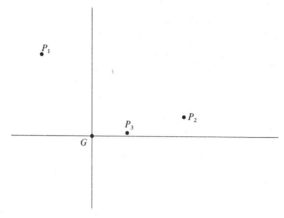

FIG. 12.7. Interpolation at G from sample values at P_1, P_2, and P_3. The point P_2 is 'shadowed' by P_3

4.   As it stands the interpolated surface will have zero gradient at all data points. This is clearly undesirable in principle. An appropriate slope at each sample point is therefore determined from the values of the neighbouring sample points, and used to modify the final interpolated values at the grid nodes. The most obvious result is that, whereas before maxima and minima on the surface could occur only at sampling points, now they can occur anywhere.

The method is described fully by Shepard (1968). It is used by Connelly (1971) in his contouring program, and the proprietary Calcomp program GPCP uses a similar weighting technique that takes into account only neighbouring sample points.

Having interpolated values at all grid nodes, the next part of the task is to display them. SYMAP uses the computer line-printer for this. The initial grid can be matched exactly to that of the line-printer so that a value is interpolated at every printer position. Alternatively, and this is more usual, Z is calculated at every third printer position along the row and every second position in the columns. Values at the intermediate positions are calculated from the initial grid values by double linear interpolation. As in CAMAP, the range of Z is divided into several levels, and symbols chosen to display each level. Again a grey scale is obtained by overprinting. Fig. 12.8 illustrates the kind of result using the contour option in SYMAP.

Other mapping systems use graph-plotters of one kind or another which draw lines at chosen values of Z. Positions on the sides of the

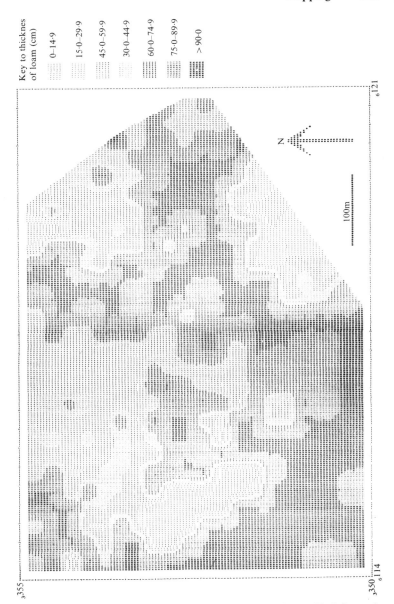

FIG. 12.8. Map of the thickness of cover loam at Hole Farm, Norfolk, made using standard contouring procedure and symbolism of SYMAP. Data were obtained from 452 points on a square grid, and kindly provided by S. Nortcliff and W.M. Corbett

grid squares that possess these values are calculated from the figure field, again by interpolation, and the points joined. They can be joined by straight-line segments across the grid squares. But as curved lines seem more pleasing to the eye the positions are more often joined by curves, and splines are being increasingly used for this purpose.

Contour tracking

Contours can be drawn directly from irregularly scattered sample points using a method devised by Lodwick and Whittle (1970) and modified by Falconer (1971). The procedure has two main aspects. The first is the means by which Z is evaluated at a point J from the data. The problem is the same as in the previous section, and the solutions are similar. To compute a value z_j at a point the nearest fifteen or so sampling points are found and a polynomial surface, preferably quadratic, is fitted to them by least squares. The sampling points are weighted so that those nearest to J carry more weight then those further away. Falconer, for example, assigns weights as

$$w_i = \left\{ \frac{s - d_{ij}}{d_{ij}} \right\}^2 \tag{12.6}$$

where w_i is the weight of the ith sample point, d_{ij} is the distance between the ith sample point and J and s is the distance from J beyond which data are ignored.

The second part of the procedure is to find the positions in the XY plane where Z has values of the chosen isarithm z_c. This is done as follows. Consider a contour that has been drawn by straight-line segments through A and B as far as C in Fig. 12.9. The last segment BC is extended a pre-determined distance d_1 to M, near which the next interpolated point on the contour line is expected to lie. The values of Z are then evaluated, by weighted least squares fit as above, at two

FIG. 12.9. Step-wise contour tracking

points J and K a distance d_2 from M on a line perpendicular to CM. Provided that z_c lies in the range between the values of Z at J and K, then the point on JK where Z has the value z_c is determined by linear interpolation. Let this point be D. Then C is joined to D to form the next segment of the contour. If the values of Z at J and K are both smaller or both larger than z_c then CM is halved and the previous step repeated.

The value chosen for d_1 represents a compromise between smooth contours that are as accurate as the data allow and fast execution in the machine. In Lodwick and Whittle's program d_1 is changed while contouring proceeds according to the local intricacy of the surface.

The technique has a third aspect, namely finding each contour in the first place. This is done by superimposing a coarse grid, interpolating values of Z at its nodes, and then interpolating the positions of z_c on the links of the grid. This seems the least certain part of the whole procedure. Full details and discussion are given in the papers mentioned.

Errors in data

We saw earlier that measurements of some soil properties are subject to large sampling error. If we use one of the interpolation techniques with the intention of contouring them we are likely to create a very bumpy surface. And any map drawn from them would be intricate. Local error of this kind tends to obscure the variation over large areas that we wish to display. It is often regarded as 'noise'. We can eliminate some error by averaging several measurements in the area immediately around each sample point, or by bulking the soil from several positions around it if making laboratory determinations on disturbed material. If neither of these is feasible or if, despite this precaution, we still have local variation that we wish to suppress, then we can choose a procedure that will smooth local irregularities.

Trend surface analysis to fit a low-order polynomial surface to data by standard regression procedures has become popular in geology and geography for displaying regional change free of local variation. When used in this way it smoothes powerfully. Unfortunately there is rarely good reason for choosing any particular order of polynomial, and the occasions for wanting to map a soil property without showing local variation are likely to be very few. And as above, although local variation is suppressed on the map it does affect the result everywhere. Local smoothing of either original data or a figure field seems better.

In the program of McIntyre *et al.* (1968), for example, smoothing is accomplished by fitting a second-degree trend surface to the nearest eight to ten data points around each grid node. The value at the grid node is then evaluated from this surface. The technique therefore interpolates with moderate smoothing. Similar results can be obtained by fitting a splined surface.

Where sampling has been carried out on a grid, a moving average with suitable weights can be used for smoothing. If sampling has been irregular then this method can be applied to the figure field instead. A moving average is a kind of *filter*. It filters out the noise. The size of a filter and the choice of weights are arbitrary. Generally, no great accuracy is necessary. A simple average of the grid value itself plus the surrounding eight values is likely to be adequate.

More formally, to obtain the smoothed value of Z, say z', at a point whose coordinates on the grid are i and j we define a filter with weights:

$$\left\{ \begin{matrix} W_{i-1,j-1} & W_{i-1,j} & W_{i-1,j+1} \\ W_{i,j-1} & W_{i,j} & W_{i,j+1} \\ W_{i+1,j-1} & W_{i+1,j} & W_{i+1,j+1} \end{matrix} \right\} \tag{12.7}$$

The value z'_{ij} is then the sum of the products of Z and the corresponding weights. A simple moving-average filter of nine points can be represented thus:

$$\left\{ \begin{matrix} \frac{1}{9} & \frac{1}{9} & \frac{1}{9} \\ \frac{1}{9} & \frac{1}{9} & \frac{1}{9} \\ \frac{1}{9} & \frac{1}{9} & \frac{1}{9} \end{matrix} \right\} \tag{12.8}$$

It might be desired to give more weight to the central point than to those surrounding it, in which case the following weights given by Tobler (1967) can be used:

$$\left\{ \begin{matrix} \frac{1}{16} & \frac{1}{8} & \frac{1}{16} \\ \frac{1}{8} & \frac{1}{4} & \frac{1}{8} \\ \frac{1}{16} & \frac{1}{8} & \frac{1}{16} \end{matrix} \right\} \tag{12.9}$$

Figs. 12.10 and 12.11 show the effect of applying this filter to soil depth determined by a 2·5 cm diameter auger at points on a 100 m grid.

If it is thought that smoothing should extend over a somewhat larger area, we can operate on 25 grid values. Yule and Kendall (1950) suggest a simple filter which, in two dimensions, has the following weights:

$$\left\{ \begin{array}{ccccc} \frac{1}{81} & \frac{2}{81} & \frac{3}{81} & \frac{2}{81} & \frac{1}{81} \\[6pt] \frac{2}{81} & \frac{4}{81} & \frac{6}{81} & \frac{4}{81} & \frac{2}{81} \\[6pt] \frac{3}{81} & \frac{6}{81} & \frac{9}{81} & \frac{6}{81} & \frac{3}{81} \\[6pt] \frac{2}{81} & \frac{4}{81} & \frac{6}{81} & \frac{4}{81} & \frac{2}{81} \\[6pt] \frac{1}{81} & \frac{2}{81} & \frac{3}{81} & \frac{2}{81} & \frac{1}{81} \end{array} \right\} \qquad (12.10)$$

Other weights can be chosen to accord with prior theory or knowledge of the way a variable is distributed over the ground. Several examples are given by Tobler (1967) and Yule and Kendall (1950), and readers should consult these if they wish to refine their smoothing procedure.

There is little experience of contouring soil survey data. Smoothing seems to have been confined so far to transects, i.e. one dimension only; see, for example, Webster and Cuanalo (1975). Investigators who have noisy data that they wish to map should therefore experiment with filters of different sizes and weights to see what effect each has on the result.

Confidence

We noted earlier that interpolated isarithms differ in principle from surveyed contours. There can be appreciable error in the interpolated values. We should also realize that the actual method by which we interpolate and display a surface has to be feasible in the computing environment in which we work: the program and data must fit into the machine, and jobs must run to completion in an acceptable time. Therefore, the methods used might not be the best from a purely mathematical point of view. None of the methods mentioned provides satisfactory estimates of the error associated with the interpolation. Trend surface analysis should be treated with special caution. The deviations between the measured and fitted values (residuals) might be thought to give unbiased estimates of the error, as they do in normal regression analysis. However, the residuals are usually themselves spatially dependent to some extent, and so confidence limits cannot be gauged. The best we can say of the above methods is that they are intuitively reasonable, that they make good use of the data and resources at our command, and that empirically they work.

With this in mind we may consider the use of the line-printer for display. Many people regard line-printer maps as crude, but when we

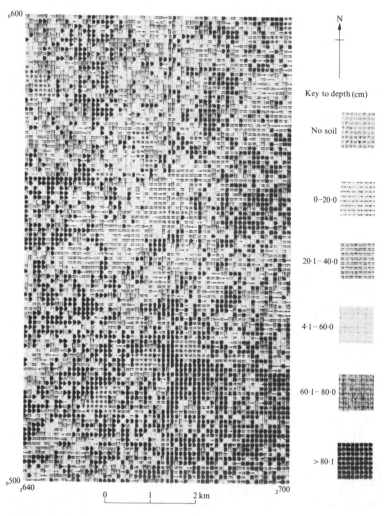

FIG. 12.10. Depth of soil penetrated by auger in the Ivybridge district of Devon. Sampling was carried out at 100 m intervals on a grid, and each printed symbol represents one measured value. This map and Fig. 12.11 were composed using the CAMAP program from survey data provided by T.R. Harrod, S.J. Staines, and D. Hogan

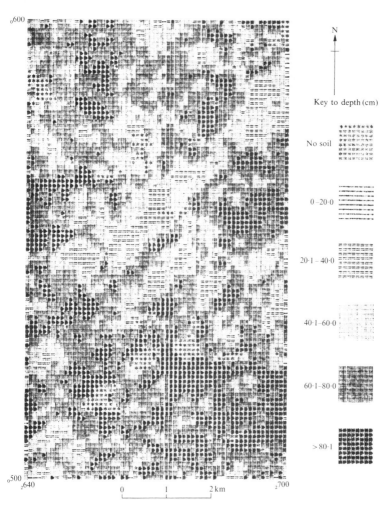

FIG. 12.11. Map of soil depth after smoothing sample data using a weighted nine-point filter, expression (12.9)

cannot be sure that contours are accurate, crude printing is a blessing. The coarse printing grid gives rough edges to contour intervals and avoids any deception that might result from smooth contour lines.

Kriging

A recent advance in statistical theory promises to rectify most of the above deficiencies. It is the theory of *regionalized variables*, or, in the terms we have been using, of spatially-dependent continuous variables. It has its origins in ore evaluation. D.G. Krige, working in the South African gold fields, found that he needed to consider the spatial dependence among sample values in order to estimate the gold content of ore bodies accurately (see Krige 1966). Krige's empirical method was developed by the French mathematician G. Matheron (1965, 1971) into a general theory of sampling and estimation for spatially dependent variables. Matheron called the estimation procedure 'krigeage', translated into English as 'kriging'. In its most general form it is known as 'universal kriging', at least among earth scientists.

When using kriging for interpolation the degree of spatial dependence in the sampled variable is determined first. This information is then used (a) to limit the area over which interpolation takes place, and (b) to assign weight to the sample points lying within such an area for each interpolation point j.

The value at j is then a weighted function of all the data values within a limited area. The result is an interpolated value that is an unbiased estimate of the true value, its variance is a minimum and is in this sense optimal, and the error of the estimate is known. When used to generate a surface from a sample it guarantees an exact fit at the sample points. These are important advantages. Its main disadvantage is that it requires substantially more computing than other methods, and this makes isarithmic mapping very slow.

A detailed treatment of kriging is quite beyond the scope of this book. Matheron's writings cover the subject most fully, but are very tough going. The English-speaking non-mathematician will probably find Olea's (1975) account both readable and sufficiently comprehensive.

The future

So far contouring has been little used in soil survey and kriging not at all. Kriging is being used increasingly in mining: but it has also been applied experimentally in geophysics, meteorology, and submarine mapping. Although we cannot say what impact it will have, its application to intensive soil surveys could be a very significant step forward. It could provide not only the best method of isarithmic mapping, but also affect sampling and estimation procedures. It is a matter that should be investigated seriously in the years to come.

Appendix: Matrix methods and notation

She died because she never knew
These simple little rules and few.
H. BELLOC
The Python

Matrix algebra provides a convenient and succinct notation for expressing large numbers of relationships simultaneously, and the operations
that can be performed on them. The subject is reasonably easy, and
once the conventions are learned most of the ideas of multivariate
statistics and specifications for analysis can be presented in matrix
form. The purpose of this appendix is to describe just sufficient of
matrix algebra to make the material in the main text intelligible.

A matrix is a rectangular array of numbers, or symbols to represent numbers, such as

$$\text{(a)} \begin{bmatrix} 2\cdot 1 & 5\cdot 0 & -6\cdot 1 \\ 3\cdot 7 & 7\cdot 9 & 3\cdot 5 \end{bmatrix} \quad \text{and} \quad \text{(b)} \begin{bmatrix} 3 & 6 & 8 \\ -9 & 5 & 4 \\ 9 & 6 & 5 \end{bmatrix} \tag{A.1}$$

and in general

$$\begin{bmatrix} x_{11} & x_{12} & x_{13} & \cdots & x_{1n} \\ x_{21} & x_{22} & x_{23} & \cdots & x_{2n} \\ \cdots & \cdots & \cdots & \cdots & \cdots \\ \cdots & \cdots & \cdots & \cdots & \cdots \\ \cdots & \cdots & \cdots & \cdots & \cdots \\ x_{m1} & x_{m2} & x_{m3} & \cdots & x_{mn} \end{bmatrix} \tag{A.2}$$

It is usual to enclose the array in square brackets, though sometimes
parentheses, ( ), or double bars, ‖ ‖, are used. A matrix can have any
number of rows and columns, and a matrix with m rows and n columns
is said to be order $m \times n$. However, if a matrix has only one row then it
is known as a *row vector*; if it has only one column it is known as a
column vector. If both m and n are 1 then we have a single number,
which in the language of matrix algebra is a *scalar*.

The numbers in a matrix are called *elements*. They can be referred to individually by two subscripts giving their row and column, in that order. Thus x_{23} in the matrix above is the element in the second row and third column; x_{ij} is the element in the ith row and jth column.

The whole array of numbers contained in a matrix can be conveniently abbreviated to a single symbol, for example

$$A = \begin{bmatrix} 2 \cdot 1 & 5 \cdot 0 & -6 \cdot 1 \\ 3 \cdot 7 & 7 \cdot 9 & 3 \cdot 5 \end{bmatrix} \tag{A.3}$$

It is usual to print symbols for matrices in bold face characters, using capitals for matrices proper and lower case letters for vectors.

Some types of matrix

A matrix that has the same number of rows as columns is called a *square matrix*. If there are m rows and columns then it is of order m. Square matrices are especially important in the analysis of multivariate data. In a square matrix, say X, the elements $x_{11}, x_{22}, x_{33}, \ldots, x_{mm}$ are called *diagonal elements*; their sum is known as the *trace* of X. A square matrix in which the elements $x_{ij} = x_{ji}$ for all i and j is said to be *symmetric*, as for example

$$\begin{bmatrix} 1 & 2 & 6 \\ 2 & 4 & 3 \\ 6 & 3 & 8 \end{bmatrix}$$

It is symmetric about the diagonal.

Two special kinds of symmetric matrix are: a *diagonal matrix*, in which the diagonal elements are non-zero and all off-diagonal are zero, for example

$$\begin{bmatrix} a_{11} & 0 & 0 \\ 0 & a_{22} & 0 \\ 0 & 0 & a_{33} \end{bmatrix} \tag{A.5}$$

and an *identity matrix* or *unit matrix*, which is a diagonal matrix with all diagonal elements equal to 1 and usually denoted by I; thus

$$I = \begin{bmatrix} 1 & 0 & 0 \\ 0 & 1 & 0 \\ 0 & 0 & 1 \end{bmatrix} \tag{A.6}$$

Elementary matrix operations

Transposition

If we have an $m \times n$ matrix and interchange its rows and columns, we obtain a new matrix of order $n \times m$ called its *transpose*. For example, if **A** is the matrix of A.3 above its transpose, denoted **A′**, is

$$\mathbf{A'} = \begin{bmatrix} 2{\cdot}1 & 3{\cdot}7 \\ 5{\cdot}0 & 7{\cdot}9 \\ -6{\cdot}1 & 3{\cdot}5 \end{bmatrix} \tag{A.7}$$

Thus each element a_{ij} occupies the position in the jth row and ith column in the transpose.

If a matrix **X** is symmetric, then $\mathbf{X} = \mathbf{X'}$.

Addition

Two matrices can be summed as in ordinary algebra provided they are of the same size or order, i.e. they have the same numbers of rows and columns. The result is a matrix whose elements are the sums of the corresponding elements in the two original matrices. Thus

$$\mathbf{C} = \mathbf{A} + \mathbf{B} \tag{A.8}$$

means that $c_{ij} = a_{ij} + b_{ij}$ for all values of i and j. Similarly the matrix **B** might be subtracted from matrix **A**, in which case $c_{ij} = a_{ij} - b_{ij}$. Matrices of the same order are said to be *conformable* for addition and subtraction.

Multiplication

Matrices can be multiplied under certain conditions. For example, if we have two matrices

$$\mathbf{A} = \begin{bmatrix} a_{11} & a_{12} \\ a_{21} & a_{22} \\ a_{31} & a_{32} \end{bmatrix} \quad \text{and} \quad \mathbf{B} = \begin{bmatrix} b_{11} & b_{12} \\ b_{21} & b_{22} \end{bmatrix} \tag{A.9}$$

then their product **AB** *in that order* is the 3×2 matrix, say **C**:

$$\mathbf{C} = \begin{bmatrix} a_{11}b_{11} + a_{12}b_{21} & a_{11}b_{12} + a_{12}b_{22} \\ a_{21}b_{11} + a_{22}b_{21} & a_{21}b_{12} + a_{22}b_{22} \\ a_{31}b_{11} + a_{32}b_{21} & a_{31}b_{12} + a_{32}b_{22} \end{bmatrix} \tag{A.10}$$

Thus each element of $\mathbf{C}$ is the sum of the products of the elements in a row of $\mathbf{A}$ and elements in a column of $\mathbf{B}$. The operation is *row by column*. In general if $\mathbf{A}$ is of order $m \times n$ we may multiply it by an $n \times p$ matrix $\mathbf{B}$ to obtain a $m \times p$ matrix $\mathbf{C}$. The elements of $\mathbf{C}$ are then

$$
\begin{aligned}
c_{ij} &= a_{i1}b_{1j} + a_{i2}b_{2j} + \ldots + a_{in}b_{nj} \\
&= \sum_{k=1}^{n} a_{ik}b_{kj}
\end{aligned}
\tag{A.11}
$$

for $i = 1, 2, \ldots, m; j = 1, 2, \ldots, p$.

Note that for multiplication to be possible, there must be the same number of columns in $\mathbf{A}$ as there are rows in $\mathbf{B}$. $\mathbf{A}$ is then *conformable* to $\mathbf{B}$ for multiplication. When $\mathbf{A}$ is conformable to $\mathbf{B}$ for multiplication, $\mathbf{B}$ is not necessarily conformable to $\mathbf{A}$. Even when it is, the product $\mathbf{AB}$ is generally not the same as the product $\mathbf{BA}$.

A matrix can be multiplied by a scalar, which is equivalent to multiplying every element of the matrix by that quantity.

The calculation of variances and covariances is one of the most frequent operations in statistical analysis and is economically represented in matrix form. Suppose we have a set of observations $x_1, x_2, \ldots, x_n$ of some variable and we enter them as deviations from their mean in a column vector $\mathbf{x}$ of order $n \times 1$. We obtain the sum of squares of deviations from the mean by *pre-multiplying* the vector by its transpose:

$$
[x_1 x_2, \ldots, x_n]
\begin{bmatrix}
x_1 \\
x_2 \\
\vdots \\
x_n
\end{bmatrix}
= \sum_{i=1}^{n} x_i^2
\tag{A.12}
$$

This can therefore be represented as $\mathbf{x}'\mathbf{x}$. When there is more than one variate, we also require sums of products. By convention we hold the data for n individuals on which we have measured p variables in an $n \times p$ matrix. The data are *centred* by subtracting their column means to give a matrix, say $\mathbf{X}$, of deviations from variate means. We *pre-multiply* $\mathbf{X}$ by its transpose to obtain $\mathbf{X}'\mathbf{X}$, in which the diagonal elements contain the sums of squares and the off-diagonal elements the sums of products. Multiplying by the scalar $1/(n-1)$ then gives the variances and covariances that we require.

Inversion

One matrix cannot be divided by another in the ordinary sense of algebra. However we can make use of the idea that division by a quantity, say z, is equivalent to multiplication by its reciprocal, $1/z$, and that $z \cdot (1/z) = 1$. In matrix algebra, when we wish to divide by a matrix, say $\mathbf{A}$, which must be square, we first find the matrix $\mathbf{B}$ such that $\mathbf{AB} = \mathbf{I}$, and incidentally $\mathbf{BA} = \mathbf{I}$. $\mathbf{B}$ is called the *inverse* of $\mathbf{A}$ and is usually written $\mathbf{A}^{-1}$. We may then proceed to multiply by $\mathbf{A}^{-1}$.

Not all square matrices can be inverted, for if any of the rows (or columns) of a matrix are linearly dependent there is no unique inverse. The matrix is then said to be *singular*. Sometimes two or more rows or columns of a matrix are almost linearly related. The matrix is thus very nearly singular and is said to be *ill conditioned*. Its inverse is likely to depend heavily on chance variation in the original data and on rounding errors in computing.

Although the inverse of a matrix can easily be defined its calculation is very tedious for order more than about 5. Inversion of larger matrices is almost always done by computer nowadays. The usual method of inversion for hand calculating is known as *pivotal condensation*, and is described in standard texts. It is generally not used, at least without modification, in computer programs because rounding errors can become serious.

Determinants.

Any square matrix $\mathbf{A}$ has associated with it a scalar quantity known as its determinant, denoted by $|\mathbf{A}|$ or sometimes det $\mathbf{A}$. If the order of the matrix is m its determinant is derived from the $m!$ products that can be formed by choosing one and only one element from each row and one and only one element from each column of the matrix. Consider the columns of $\mathbf{A}$; there are $m!$ ways of arranging them, and for each arrangement there is a unique set of diagonal elements which give one of the products required. Each arrangement of the columns can be obtained from the original matrix by interchanging two columns, followed by another two, and so on until the desired arrangement is achieved. The number of interchanges needed to produce the arrangement determines the sign of the product. If the number is even the product has a positive sign; if the number is odd the sign is negative. The determinant is then the sum of these signed products. Thus, if $\mathbf{A}$ is of order 3 then it is easily seen that its determinant $|\mathbf{A}|$ is

$$\begin{vmatrix} a_{11} & a_{12} & a_{13} \\ a_{21} & a_{22} & a_{23} \\ a_{31} & a_{32} & a_{33} \end{vmatrix} = \begin{matrix} + a_{11}a_{22}a_{33} - a_{12}a_{21}a_{33} - a_{11}a_{23}a_{32} \\ + a_{12}a_{23}a_{31} + a_{13}a_{21}a_{32} - a_{13}a_{22}a_{31} \end{matrix} \quad (A.13)$$

It is worth noting that if $\mathbf{A}$ is singular its determinant is zero, but not otherwise.

Quadratic forms

Suppose we have a vector $\mathbf{x}$ and a square matrix $\mathbf{A}$ of the same order. The scalar product

$$\mathbf{x}'\mathbf{A}\mathbf{x} \quad (A.14)$$

is then known as a *quadratic form* since it is a quadratic function of the xs. If, for example, $\mathbf{A}$ is of order 3 then on expansion

$$\mathbf{x}'\mathbf{A}\mathbf{x} = a_{11}x_1^2 + a_{22}x_2^2 + a_{33}x_3^2 + (a_{12} + a_{21})x_1x_2 + (a_{13} + a_{31})x_1x_3$$
$$+ (a_{32} + a_{32})x_2x_3.$$

In general, if $\mathbf{x}$ and $\mathbf{A}$ are of order n then

$$\mathbf{x}'\mathbf{A}\mathbf{x} = \sum_{i=1}^{n} a_{ii}x_i^2 + \sum_{j=2}^{n} \sum_{i=1}^{j-1} (a_{ij} + a_{ji})x_ix_j. \quad (A.15)$$

Note that if $\mathbf{A}$ is symmetric then $a_{ij} = a_{ji}$ for all values of i and j, and expression (A.15) becomes

$$\mathbf{x}'\mathbf{A}\mathbf{x} = \sum_{i=1}^{n} a_{ii}x_i^2 + 2 \sum_{j=2}^{n} \sum_{i=1}^{j-1} a_{ij}x_ix_j. \quad (A.16)$$

Matrix $\mathbf{A}$ is now unique: it is the only symmetric matrix for which the quadratic form can be expressed as $\mathbf{x}'\mathbf{A}\mathbf{x}$.

A quadratic form that is positive for all values of $\mathbf{x}$ other than $\mathbf{x} = \mathbf{0}$, i.e. when all the elements of $\mathbf{x}$ are real numbers and not all zero, is known as a *positive definite* quadratic form. The associated matrix is similarly known as a *positive definite matrix*. If $\mathbf{x}'\mathbf{A}\mathbf{x} \geqslant 0$ the quadratic form and its matrix are called *positive semi-definite*, often abbreviated to psd.

Latent roots and vectors

The derivation of latent roots and vectors involves the following question: given a square matrix $\mathbf{A}$, do there exist a vector $\mathbf{c}$ and a scalar λ that satisfy the equation

$$\mathbf{A}\mathbf{c} = \lambda\mathbf{c}? \quad (A.17)$$

If so, (A.17) is equivalent to

$$Ac - \lambda c = 0 \qquad (A.18)$$

and, alternatively

$$(A - \lambda I)c = 0 \qquad (A.19)$$

where 0 is a null vector and I the identity matrix of the same order as A. It can be shown that these equations have non-zero solutions for c and λ only if the determinant of $(A - \lambda I)$ is zero, thus

$$|A - \lambda I| = 0. \qquad (A.20)$$

Eqn. (A.20) defines the conditions under which (A.17) is true, and is known as the *characteristic equation* of A. If A is of order m the determinant expands to a polynomial of degree m in λ. The characteristic equation therefore has m solutions, $\lambda_1, \lambda_2, \ldots, \lambda_m$, which are known as *latent roots*, *characteristic roots*, or *eigenvalues*. Corresponding to each of the m latent roots λ_i there is a vector c_i that satisfies eqns. (A.17) to (A.19). These m vectors are known as *latent vectors*, *characteristic vectors*, or *eigenvectors*. Unless two or more roots happen to be equal, each vector is unique apart from a scaling factor. In statistical work it is usual to scale a vector so that the sum of the squares of its elements is 1, and this is achieved by dividing each element of the vector by $(c_i'c_i)^{1/2}$.

When two or more roots $\lambda_j, \lambda_{j+1}, \ldots$, are equal there are many possible vectors c_j that will satisfy eqn. (A.17), and any one of these can be chosen arbitrarily.

A simple example in which the latent roots and vectors of a symmetrix matrix are found is given in Chapter 8.

In practice most variance–covariance matrices and correlation matrices are positive definite. As such, all their latent roots are real and positive. Occasionally they are psd, in which case at least one latent root is zero. Many types of similarity or dissimilarity matrix are psd with one zero root and the remainder positive.

Further reading

Be sure that you go to the author
to get *his* meaning, not to find yours.
JOHN RUSKIN
Sesame and lilies

Univariate statistics
There are many textbooks on this topic written from different points of view and assuming different backgrounds and degrees of competence among their readers. The soil scientist should be prepared to look at several before choosing one or two for his own bookshelf. The following four represent something of the spectrum and should be helpful.

MORONEY, M.J. (1956). *Facts from figures.* 3rd edition. Penguin Books, Harmondsworth. An elementary introduction written in an entertaining style.

YULE, G.U., and KENDALL, M.G. (1950) *An introduction to the theory of statistics.* 14th edition. Griffin, London. A classic, covering a broad field in detail but at an introductory level.

SNEDECOR, G.W., and COCHRAN, W.G. (1967). *Statistical methods.* 6th edition. Iowa State University Press, Ames. Another standard text, providing thorough instruction and readily adaptable recipes for research workers. Special emphasis is given to agricultural problems.

KOCH, G.S., and LINK, R.F. (1970). *Statistical analysis of geological data.* In two volumes (volume 2, 1971). New York. A clear presentation of situations and methods for investigating them that have close analogues in soil science.

Multivariate statistics
This topic is inevitably more difficult to grasp than the statistics of single variates. The following texts are roughly in order of increasing difficulty.

HOPE, K. (1968). *Methods of multivariate analysis.* University of London Press.

MORRISON, D.F. (1976). *Multivariate statistical methods.* 2nd edition. McGraw-Hill, New York.

SEAL, H. (1964). *Multivariate statistical analysis for biologists.* Methuen, London. Good, but for mathematicians rather than biologists.

ANDERSON, T.W. (1958). *An introduction to multivariate statistical analysis.* Wiley, New York. Tough going for the non-mathematician. A text that describes applications of multivariate analysis with deep insight is:

BLACKITH, R.E., and REYMENT, R.A. (1971). *Multivariate morphometrics*. Academic Press, London.

Sampling

The standard works by Yates (1960) and Cochran (1963) have already been mentioned in Chapter 4. Two others are:

HANSEN, M.H., HURWITZ, W.N., and MADOW, W.G. (1953). *Sample survey methods and theory*. In two volumes. Wiley, New York. Volume I contains much sound practical advice.

SAMPFORD, M.R. (1962). *An introduction to sampling theory*. Oliver and Boyd, Edinburgh. A sound introduction at a somewhat more elementary level than the others.

Numerical classification

SNEATH, P.H.A., and SOKAL, R.R. (1973). *Numerical taxonomy*. Freeman, San Francisco. Quite the most comprehensive account of the methods available for numerical classification.

SOKAL, R.R., and SNEATH, P.H.A. (1963). *Principles of numerical taxonomy*. Freeman, San Francisco. This earlier work is still worth reading for its detailed analysis and criticism of the conventional wisdom and background to the then newly developing field of numerical classification.

Two journal papers need special mention:

GILMOUR, J.S.L. (1937). A taxonomic problem. *Nature, Lond.* **139**, 1040–42. A classic paper; the first to express classification in a way allowing mathematical examination. Every aspiring taxonomist should read it.

WILLIAMS, W.T., and DALE, M.B. (1965). Fundamental problems in numerical taxonomy. *Advs Bot Res.*, 2, 35–68.

Computing

The last decade has seen a rash of books in this field, many addressed to the businessman rather than the scientist. The first two listed below should help the newcomer to scientific computing find his feet. The remainder describe particular programming languages.

GEAR, C.W. (1973). *Introduction to computer science*. Science Research Associates, Chicago.

NELDER, J.A. (1975). *Computers in biology*. Wykeham Publications, London. Less comprehensive than the first, but emphasizing sound numerical computing.

Algol 60

DIJKSTRA, E.W. (1962). *A primer of Algol 60 programming*. Academic Press, London.

WOOLDRIDGE, R., and RACTLIFFE, J.F. (1963). *An introduction to Algol programming*. English Universities Press, London.

Algol 68

LINDSEY, C.H., and VAN DER MEULEN, S.G. (1971). *Informal introduction to Algol 68.* North-Holland, Amsterdam. A comprehensive description and guide.

WOODWARD, P.M., and BOND, S.G. (1974). *Algol 68-R users guide.* 2nd edition H.M. Stationary Office, London. A simple and clear guide to Algol 68 as implemented by the Royal Radar Establishment, Malvern.

Fortran

McCRACKEN, D.D. (1972). *A guide to Fortran IV programming.* 2nd edition. Wiley, New York.

ORGANICK, E.I., and MEISSNER, L.P. (1974). *Fortran IV.* 2nd edition. Addison Wesley, Reading, Massachusetts.

Basic

KEMENY, J.G., and KURTZ, T.E. (1971). *Basic programming.* 2nd edition. Wiley, New York. Written by the authors of the language.

Mapping

ROBINSON, A.H., and SALE, R.D. (1969). *Elements of cartography.* 3rd edition. Wiley, New York. Chapters 7 and 8 are especially relevant.

DAVIS, J.C., and McCULLAGH, M.J. (eds.) (1973). *Display and analysis of spatial data.* Wiley, London. A collection of somewhat advanced papers.

References

AHMAD, D.S. (1966). *Indian cities: characteristics and correlates.* Research paper No.102, Department of Geography, University of Chicago.

ANDERSON, A.J.B. (1971). A similarity measure for mixed attribute types. *Nature, Lond.* **232**, 416–17.

ARNOLD, R.W. (1964). Cyclic variations and the pedon. *Soil Sci. Soc. Am. Proc.* **28**, 801–04.

AVERY, B.W. (1973). Soil classification in the Soil Survey of England and Wales. *J. Soil Sci.* **24**, 324–38.

BARTLETT, M.S. (1937). Some examples of statistical methods in agriculture and applied biology. *Jl. Ry. statist. Soc., Suppl.* **4**, 137–83.

BARTLETT, M.S. (1947). The use of transformations. *Biometrics,* **3**, 39–52.

BATCHA, J.P. and REESE, J.R. (1964). Surface determination and automatic contouring for mineral exploration, extraction and processing. *Colo. Sch. Mines Q.* **59**, 1–14.

BECKETT, P.H.T. and WEBSTER, R. (1965a). *A classification system for terrain.* Report No.872, Military Engineering Experimental Establishment, Christchurch.

BECKETT, P.H.T. and WEBSTER, R. (1965b). *Field trials of a terrain classification – organisation and methods.* Report No.873, Military Engineering Experimental Establishment, Christchurch.

BECKNER, M. (1959). *The biological way of thought.* Columbia University Press, New York.

BENGTSSON, B-E. and NORDBECK, S. (1964). Construction of isarithms and isarithmic maps by computers. *BIT,* **4**, 87–105.

BENZÉCRI, J.P. (1973). *L'analyse des données.* Vol. 2, *L'analyse des correspondences.* Dunod, Paris.

BERRY, B.J.L. (1962). *Sampling, coding and storing flood plain data.* Agriculture Handbook No.237. U.S. Department of Agriculture.

BERRY, B.J.L. (1966). *Essays on commodity flows and the spatial structure of the Indian economy.* Research paper No.111, Department of Geography, University of Chicago.

BLACKITH, R.E. and REYMENT, R.A. (1971). *Multivariate morphometrics.* Academic Press, London.

BRACEWELL, J.M. and ROBERTSON, G.W. (1973). Humus type discrimination using pattern recognition of the mass spectra of volatile pyrolysis products. *J. Soil Sci.* **24**, 421–8.

BRAY, J.R. and CURTIS, J.T. (1957). An ordination of the upland forest communities of southern Wisconsin. *Ecol. Monogr.* **27**, 325–49.

CAIN, A.J. and HARRISON, G.A. (1958). An analysis of the taxonomist's judgement of affinity. *Proc. zool. Soc. Lond.* **131**, 85–98.

CAMPBELL, N.A., MULCAHY, M.J. and McARTHUR, W.M. (1970). Numerical classification of soil profiles on the basis of field morphological properties. *Aust. J. Soil Res.* **8**, 43–58.

CANARACHE, A. and VINTILÂ, I. (1970). Contribuţii la verificarea normalităţii distribuţiilor de frecvenţă întîlnite în studiul solului. *Analele, Institutului de Cercetări pentru Îmbunătățiri Funciare si Pedologie, Seria Pedologie,* Vol. III (37), 175–191. [In Romanian].

COCHRAN, W.G. (1963). *Sampling techniques.* 2nd edition. Wiley, New York.

COLE, A.J. (1968). Algorithm for the production of contour maps from scattered data. *Nature, Lond.* **220**, 92–4.

CONNELLY, D.S. (1971). An experiment in contour map smoothing on the ECU automated contouring system. *Cartogr. J.* **8**, 59–66.

COOKE, G.W. (1975). *Fertilizing for maximum yield.* 2nd edition. Crosby Lockwood, London.

COOLEY, W.W., and LOHNES, P.R. (1971). *Multivariate data analysis.* Wiley, New York.

CROMMELIN, R.D. and de GRUIJTER, J.J. (1973). *Cluster analysis applied to mineralogical data from the coversand formation in the Netherlands.* Soil Survey Paper No.7, Soil Survey Institute, Wageningen.

CUANALO de la C., H.E., and WEBSTER, R. (1970). A comparative study of numerical classification and ordination of soil profiles in a locality near Oxford. *J. Soil Sci.* **21**, 340–52.

DALE, M.B., MACNAUGHTON-SMITH, P., WILLIAMS, W.T., and LANCE, G.N. (1970). Numerical classification of sequences. *Aust. Comput. J.* **2**, 9–13.

DAS, A.C. (1950). Two-dimensional systematic sampling and the associated stratified and random sampling. *Sankhya* **10**, 95–108.

DAVIS, J.C. and McCULLAGH, M.J. (eds.) (1973). *Display and analysis of spatial data.* Wiley, London.

DE GRUIJTER, J.J., and BIE, S.W. (1975). *A discrete approach to automated mapping of multivariate systems.* Proceedings, International Cartographic Association, Commission III, Enschede.

DEMIRMEN, F. (1969). *Multivariate procedures and Fortran IV program for evaluation and improvement of classifications.* Computer Contribution No.31, State Geological Survey, University of Kansas, Lawrence.

DIJKSTRA, E.W. (1962). *A primer of Algol 60 programming.* Academic Press, London.

DIXON, W.J. (1971). *BMD Biomedical computer programs.* University of California Press, Berkley.

EADES, D.C. (1965). The inappropriateness of the correlation coefficient as a measure of taxonomic resemblance. *Syst. Zool.* **14**, 98–100.

EDWARDS, A.W.F. and CAVALLI-SFORZA, L.L. (1965). A method for cluster analysis. *Biometrics* **21**, 362–75.

FALCONER, K.J. (1971). *A general purpose algorithm for contouring over scattered data points.* Report NAC 6, National Physical Laboratory.

FINCH, A. and HOTSON, J. (1974). *CAMAPG and GRID CAMAP.* Inter-University/Research Councils Research and Development Notes No.13. University of Edinburgh.

FISHER, R.A. (1936). The use of multiple measurements in taxonomic problems. *Ann. Eugen.* **7**, 179—88.

FISHER, R.A., and YATES, F. (1963). *Statistical tables for biological, agricultural and medical research.* 6th edition. Longman (Oliver and Boyd), Edinburgh.

FRIEDMAN, H.P., and RUBIN, J. (1967). On some invariant criteria for grouping data. *J. Am. statist. Ass.* **62**, 1159—78.

GILMOUR, J.S.L. (1937). A taxonomic problem. *Nature, Lond.* **139**, 1040—42.

GOODALL, D.W. (1954). Vegetational classification and vegetational continua. *Angew. PflSoziol.* **1**, 168—82.

GOWER, J.C. (1962). Variance component estimation for unbalanced hierarchical classification. *Biometrics* **18**, 537—42.

GOWER, J.C. (1966). Some distance properties of latent root and vector methods used in multivariate analysis. *Biometrika* **53**, 325—38.

GOWER, J.C. (1967). A comparison of some methods of cluster analysis. *Biometrics* **23**, 623—37.

GOWER, J.C. (1968). Adding a point to vector diagrams in multivariate analysis. *Biometrika* **55**, 582—5.

GOWER, J.C. (1971). A general coefficient of similarity and some of its properties *Biometrics* **27**, 857—71.

GOWER, J.C. (1973). A very old friend revisited again. *Math. Geol.* **5**, 203—05.

GOWER, J.C., and ROSS, G.J.S. (1969). Minimum spanning trees and single linkage cluster analysis. *Appl. Statist.* **18**, 54—64.

GOWER, J.C. and ROSS, G.J.S. (1974). *Multivariate and cluster analysis. Genstat users' guide No.4.* Inter University/Research Council Series Rep. No.18, University of Edinburgh.

GREVILLE, T.N.E. (ed.) (1969). *Theory and applications of spline functions.* Academic Press, New York.

HAMMOND, L.C., PRITCHETT, W.L., and CHEW, V. (1958). Soil sampling in relation to soil heterogeneity. *Soil Sci. Soc. Am. Proc.* **22**, 548—552.

HANSEN, M.H., HURWITZ, W.N., and MADOW, W.G. (1953). *Sample survey methods and theory* (2 volumes). Wiley, New York.

HARMAN, H.H. (1967). *Modern factor analysis.* 2nd edition. University of Chicago Press.

HARVARD COMPUTATION LABORATORY (1955). *Tables of the cumulative binomial probability distribution.* Harvard University Press, Cambridge, Mass.

HILL, M.O. (1973). Reciprocal averaging: an eigenvector method of ordination. *J. Ecol.* **61**, 237—49.

HILL, M.O. (1974). Correspondence analysis: a neglected multivariate method. *Appl. Statist.* **23**, 340–54.

HOLE, F.D. and HIRONAKA, M. (1960). An experiment in ordination of some soil profiles. *Soil Sci. Soc. Am. Proc.* **24**, 309–12.

HOTELLING, H. (1931). The generalization of Student's ratio. *Ann. math. Statist.* **2**, 369–78.

IBM (1965). *Numerical surface techniques and contour map plotting.* IBM Data Processing Application E 20-0117–0.

JACCARD, P. (1908). Nouvelles recherches sur la distribution florale. *Bull. Soc. vaud. Sci. nat.* **44**, 223–70.

JEFFERS, J.N.R. (1959). *Experimental design and analysis in forest research.* Almqvist and Wiksell, Stockholm.

KAISER, H.F. (1958). The Varimax criterion for analytic rotation in factor analysis. *Psychometrika* **23**, 187–200.

KING, S.C. and HENDERSON, C.R. (1954). Variance components analysis in heritability studies. *Poul. Sci.* **33**, 147–54.

KLOOSTERMAN, B. (1975). Input of data to soil information systems. *In Soil information systems* (ed. S.W. Bie). Pudoc. Wageningen, pp. 22–30.

KRIGE, D.G. (1966). Two-dimensional weighted moving average trend surfaces for ore-evaluation. *Jl. S. Afr. Inst. Min. Metall.* **66**, 13–38.

KRUSKAL, J.B. (1964). Nonmetric multidimensional scaling: a numerical method. *Psychometrika* **29**, 115–29.

KYUMA, K. (1973*a*). A method of fertility evaluation for paddy soils. II. Second approximation: evaluation of four independent constituents of soil fertility. *Soil Sci. Plant Nutr.* **19**, 11–18.

KYUMA, K. (1973*b*). A method of fertility evaluation for paddy soils. III. Third approximation: synthesis of fertility constituents for soil fertility evaluation. *Soil Sci. Plant Nutr.* **19**, 19–27.

KYUMA, K. and KAWAGUCHI, K. (1973). A method of fertility evaluation for paddy soils. I. First approximation: chemical potentiality grading. *Soil Sci. Plant Nutr.* **19**, 1–9.

LABORATORY FOR COMPUTER GRAPHICS (1968). *Reference manual for Synagraphic Computer Mapping 'SYMAP' Version V.* Harvard University.

LANCE, G.N. and WILLIAMS, W.T. (1966). A generalized sorting strategy for computer classifications. *Nature, Lond.* **212**, 218.

LANCE, G.N., and WILLIAMS, W.T. (1967*a*). Mixed-data classificatory programs. I. Agglomerative systems. *Aust. Comput. J.* **1**, 15–20.

LANCE, G.N. and WILLIAMS, W.T. (1967*b*). A general theory of classificatory sorting strategies. I. Hierarchical systems. *Comput. J.* **9**, 373–80.

LANCE, G.N. and WILLIAMS, W.T. (1967*c*). Note on the classification of multi-level data. *Comput. J.* **9**, 381–3.

LAWLEY, D.N. and MAXWELL, A.E. (1971). *Factor analysis as a statistical method.* 2nd edition. Butterworths, London.

LINDLEY, D.V. and MILLER, J.C.P. (1953). *Cambridge elementary statistical tables.* Cambridge University Press.

LITTLE, I.P., HORTON, I.F., HAYDOCK, K.P., and PATON, T.R. (1968). The use of canonical analysis of chemical data to distinguish among materials of the valley fill of the Bremer River, south-eastern Queensland. *Aust. J. Sci.* **31**, 86–7.

LODWICK, G.D., and WHITTLE, J. (1970). A technique for automatic contouring field survey data. *Aust. Comput. J.* **2**, 104–9.

MAHALANOBIS, P.C. (1927). Analysis of race mixture in Bengal. *J. Asiat. Soc. Beng.* **23**, 301–33.

MARDIA, K.V. (1972). *Statistics of directional data.* Academic Press, London.

MARRIOTT, F.H.C. (1971). Practical problems in a method of cluster analysis. *Biometrics* **27**, 501–14.

MARRIOTT, F.H.C. (1974). *The interpretation of multiple observations.* Academic Press, London.

MATHERON, G. (1965). *Les variables régionalisées et leur estimation.* Masson, Paris.

MATHERON, G. (1971). *The theory of regionalized variables and its applications.* Cahiers du Centre de Morphologie Mathématique de Fontainebleau. No.5.

McINTYRE, D.B., POLLARD, D.D., and SMITH, R. (1968). *Computer programs for automated contouring.* Computer Contribution 23. State Geological Survey, Lawrence, Kansas.

McKEAGUE, J.A., DAY, J.H., and SHIELDS, J.A. (1971). Evaluating relationships among properties by computer analysis. *Can. J. Soil Sci.* **51**, 105–11.

MOORE, A.W. and RUSSELL, J.S. (1967). Comparison of coefficients and grouping procedures in numerical analysis of soil trace element data. *Geoderma* **1**, 139–58.

MOORE, A.W., RUSSELL, J.S., and WARD, W.T. (1972). Numerical analysis of soils: a comparison of three soil profile models with field classification. *J. Soil Sci.* **23**, 193–209.

MORONEY, M.J. (1956). *Facts from figures.* 3rd edition. Penguin Books, Harmondsworth.

NATIONAL BUREAU OF STANDARDS (1950). *Tables of the binomial probability distribution.* U.S. Government Printing Office, Washington.

NELDER, J.A. (and members of the Rothamsted Statistics Department) (1973). *Genstat.* Inter-University/Research Councils Series Report No.3, Edinburgh Regional Computing Centre.

NELDER, J.A. (1975). *Computers in biology.* Wykeham Publications, London.

NIE, W.H., BENT, D.H., and HULL, C.H. (1970). *SPSS – Statistical Package for the Social Sciences.* McGraw-Hill, New York.

NORRIS, J.M. and DALE, M.B. (1971). Transition matrix approach to numerical classification of soil profiles. *Soil Sci. Am. Proc.* **35**, 487–91.

NORRIS, J.M. and LOVEDAY, J. (1971). The application of multivariate analysis to soil studies. II. The allocation of soil profiles to established groups: a comparison of soil survey and computer method. *J. Soil Sci.* **22**, 395–400.

NORTHCOTE, K.H. (1971). *A factual key for the recognition of Australian Soils.* 3rd edition. Rellim Technical Publications, Glenside, South Australia.

OERTAL, A.C. (1961). Chemical discrimination of terra rossas and rendzinas. *J. Soil Sci.* **12**, 11–118.

OLEA, R.A. (1975). *Optimum mapping techniques using regionalized variable theory.* Series on Spatial Analysis, No.2. Kansas Geological Survey, Lawrence.

OSMOND, D.A., SWARBRICK, T., THOMPSON, C.R., and WALLACE, T. (1949). *A survey of the soils and fruit in the Vale of Evesham 1926–34.* Bulletin No.116 Ministry of Agriculture and Fisheries. H.M. Stationery Office, London.

PEARSON, E.S., and HARTLEY, H.O. (eds.) (1966). *Biometrika tables for statisticians*, Vol. I, 3rd edition. Vol. II, 1972. Cambridge University Press.

QUENOUILLE, M.H. (1949). *Problems in plane sampling. Ann. math. Statist.* **20**, 355–75.

RAND CORPORATION (1955). *A million random digits with 100 000 normal deviates.* Free Press, Glencoe, Illinois.

RAO, C.R. (1948). The utilization of multiple measurements in problems of biological classification. *J. Roy. Statist. Soc.* **B10**, 159–193.

RAO, C.R. (1952). Advanced statistical methods in biometric research. Wiley, New York.

RAYNER, J.H. (1966). Classification of soils by numerical methods. *J. Soil Sci.* **17**, 79–92.

RAYNER, J.H. (1969). The numerical approach to soil systematics. In: *The Soil Ecosystem.* Systematics association Publication No.8. Editor J.G. Sheals, pp. 31–39.

ROMIG, H.G. (1952). 50–100 binomial tables. Wiley, New York.

ROSS, G.J.S. (1969). Algorithms AS 13-15. *Appl. Statist.* **18**, 103–10.

RUBIN, J. (1967). Optimal classification into groups: an approach for solving the taxonomy problem. *J. theoret. Biol.* **15**, 103–44.

RUDEFORTH, C.C. (1969). *Quantitative soil surveying.* Welsh Soils Discussion Group, Report No. 10, 42–7.

RUDEFORTH, C.C. and BRADLEY, R.I. (1972). *Soils, land classification and land use of West and Central Pembrokeshire.* Special Survey No.6. Soil Survey of Great Britain, Harpenden.

RUDEFORTH, C.C. and THOMASSON, A.J. (1970). *Hydrological properties of soils in the River Dee catchment.* Special Survey No.4. Soil Survey of Great Britain. Harpenden.

RUDEFORTH, C.C. and WEBSTER, R. (1973). Indexing and display of soil survey data by means of feature-cards and Boolean maps. *Geoderma* **9**, 229–48.

RUSSELL, J.S. and MOORE, A.W. (1968). Comparison of different depth weightings in the numerical analysis of anisotropic soil profile data. *Proc. 9th Int. Congr. Soil Sci.* **4**, 205–13.

SHEPARD, D. (1968). A two-dimensional interpolation function for irregularly-spaced data. *Proc. Ass. Comput. Mach.* (1968), 517–23.

SNEATH, P.H.A. (1957). The application of computers to taxonomy. *J. gen. Microbiol.* **17**, 201–26.

SNEATH, P.H.A., and SOKAL, R.R. (1973). *Numerical taxonomy.* Freeman, San Francisco.

SNEDECOR, G.W. and COCHRAN, W.G. (1967). *Statistical methods.* 6th edition. Iowa State University Press, Ames.

SOIL SURVEY STAFF (1960). *Soil classification: a comprehensive system. 7th approximation.* U.S. Department of Agriculture, Washington, D.C.

SOKAL, R.R., and MICHENER, C.D. (1958). A statistical method for evaluating systematic relationships. *Kans. Univ. Sci. Bull.* **38**, 1409–38.

SOKAL, R.R., and SNEATH, P.H.A. (1963). *Principles of numerical taxonomy.* Freeman, San Francisco.

SPENCE, N.A. (1968). A multivariate uniform regionalization of British counties on the basis of employment data for 1961. *Reg. Stud.* **2**, 87–104.

THOMASSON, A.J. (1975). editor. *Soils and field drainage.* Soil Survey Technical Monograph No.7. Harpenden.

TOBLER, W. (1967). Of maps and matrices. *J. Regional Sci.* **7**, 275–80.

WARD, J.H. (1963). Hierarchical grouping to optimize an objective function. *J. Am. statist. Ass.* **58**, 236–44.

WEBSTER, R. (1966). The measurement of soil water tension in the field. *New Phytol.* **65**, 249–58.

WEBSTER, R. 1968. Fundamental objections to the 7th Approximation. *J. Soil Sci.* **19**, 354–66.

WEBSTER, R. and BECKETT, P.H.T. (1968). Quality and usefulness of soil maps. *Nature, Lond.* **219**, 680–2.

WEBSTER, R. and BURROUGH, P.A. (1972a). Computer-based soil mapping of small areas from sample data. I. Multivariate classification and ordination. *J. Soil Sci.* **23**, 210–21.

WEBSTER, R. and BURROUGH, P.A. (1972b). Computer-based soil mapping of small areas from sample data. II. Classification smoothing. *J. Soil Sci.* **23**, 222–34.

WEBSTER, R. and BURROUGH, P.A. (1974). Multiple discriminant analysis in soil survey. *J. Soil Sci.* **25**, 120–34.

WEBSTER, R. and BUTLER, B.E. (1976). Soil survey and classification studies at Ginninderra. *Aust. J. Soil Res.* **14**, 1–24.

WEBSTER, R., and CUANALO de la C., H.E. (1975). Soil transect correlograms of north Oxfordshire and their interpretation. *J. Soil Sci.* **26**, 176–94.

WILKS, S.S. (1932). Certain generalizations in the analysis of variance. *Biometrika* **24**, 471–94.

WILLIAMS, C., and RAYNER, J.H. (1977). Variability in three areas of the Denchworth soil map unit III. Soil grouping based on chemical composition. *J. Soil Sci.* **28**, 180–95.

WILLIAMS, W.T., and LAMBERT, J.M. (1959). Multivariate methods in plant ecology. I. Association-analysis in plant communities. *J. Ecol.* **47**, 83–101.

WISHART, D. (1969*a*). Mode analysis: a generalization of nearest neighbour which reduces chaining effects. In *Numerical taxonomy* (ed. A.J. Cole). Academic Press, London, pp. 282–311.

WISHART, D. (1969*b*). *Fortran II programs for 8 methods of cluster analysis (CLUSTAN I)*. Computer Contributions 38, Kansas Geological Survey, Lawrence.

YATES, F. (1935). Some examples of biased sampling. *Ann. Eugen.* **6**, 202–13.

YATES, F. (1948). Systematic sampling. *Phil. Trans. R. Soc.* **A241**, 345–77.

YATES, F. (1960). *Sampling methods for censuses and surveys.* 3rd edition. Griffin, London.

YOUDEN, W.J. and MEHLICH, A. (1937). Selection of efficient methods for soil sampling. *Contr. Boyce Thompson Inst. Pl. Res.* **9**, 59–70.

YULE, G.U., and KENDALL, M.G. (1950). *An introduction to the theory of statistics.* 14th edition. Griffin, London.

Author Index

Subject Index